SICK JUSTICE

ALSO BY IVAN G. GOLDMAN

Nonfiction

L.A. Secret Police: Inside the LAPD Elite Spy Network
(with Mike Rothmiller)

Fiction

The Barfighter

Exit Blue

Isaac: A Modern Fable

Where the Money Is: A Novel of Las Vegas

RELATED TITLES FROM POTOMAC BOOKS

American Poverty: Presidential Failures and a Call to Action
—Woody Klein

*Getting Away with Torture: Secret Government,
War Crimes, and the Rule of Law*
—Christopher H. Pyle

Grave Injustice: Unearthing Wrongful Executions
—Richard A. Stack

*Not a Choice, Not a Job:
Exposing the Myths about Prostitution and the Global Sex Trade*
—Janice G. Raymond

SICK
JUSTICE

INSIDE THE AMERICAN GULAG

IVAN G. GOLDMAN

Potomac Books
Washington, D.C.

Potomac Books is an imprint of the University of Nebraska Press

Library of Congress Cataloging-in-Publication Data
Goldman, Ivan G.
Sick justice : inside the American Gulag / Ivan G. Goldman. — First edition.
  pages cm
  Includes bibliographical references and index.
  ISBN 978-1-61234-487-4 (hardcover : alk. paper)
  ISBN 978-1-61234-488-1 (electronic)
  1. Prisons—United States. 2. Corrections—United States. 3. Criminal justice,
Administration of—United States. I. Title.
  HV9471.G646 2013
  365'.973—dc23

                                                          2013003517

Printed in the United States of America on acid-free paper that meets the American
National Standards Institute Z39-48 Standard.

Potomac Books
22841 Quicksilver Drive
Dulles, Virginia 20166

First Edition

10 9 8 7 6 5 4 3 2 1

Lay then the axe to the root, and teach governments humanity.
It is their sanguinary punishments which corrupt mankind.
—Thomas Paine, *The Rights of Man*

Why all this horror? What is it for?
—Leo Tolstoy, *The Death of Ivan Ilyich*

This book is dedicated to the railroaded, double-crossed, abused victims of sick justice, including those who were, in the words of Tolstoy, "neglected and twisted like uncared-for plants."

CONTENTS

■ PART 4 FAILED EXCESS

■ PART 5 FAILED VISION

PREFACE

the old *Kansas City Times* and later the *Washington Post*. I walked through prison yards, took notes at trials, ate burgers with cops and prosecutors, and even reported a tiny piece of the Watergate stories. Later on I became a boxing writer and wrote about fighters who'd turned pro after doing time in prison and others who were locked up after the sport was through with them. I've paid dues to boxing gyms where a prison record is no more remarkable than an Ivy League degree at a Wall Street bank.

One day someone close to me was scheduled for a hearing on a drug charge, and I showed up to offer moral support. While I waited for that particular hearing, I heard the judge rush though other cases on his roster, one after another, no time to lose. Plea bargains had been settled on most of them. Still, defendants had to confirm in open court that they understood and agreed to the terms, and the court recorder had to get it all down. The judge and the prosecutor shared the chore of reading it all aloud and prompting the defendant to assent from time to time. Defendants were whisked in and out. Few had made bail, so most were in jail jumpsuits, their hands shackled behind them. Relatives looked on with a mixture of concern, resignation, and uncertainty.

One defendant stood out because he was past middle age, much older than the others. A balding black man who looked apologetic for taking up anyone's time. The prosecutor clearly liked this particular defendant, who had a friendly demeanor, like someone who'd take the time to give you good directions. He'd served a prison sentence decades earlier, and the judge asked the prosecutor the nature of the old offense. "Nothing serious," the prosecutor said. He paused and added, "Like this one." This one, whatever it was, had earned the man a two-year sentence.

The judge nodded, and seeing nothing extraordinary about sending a man to prison for nothing serious, banged his gavel on the deal. Wait a minute, I said to myself. Why, if the man's old infraction hadn't been serious, did he go to prison for it? And why, if this new offense was also insignificant, were they sending him back? Maybe there was once a time when this judge and prosecutor had asked such questions, but by this point in their careers, they showed all the cognitive curiosity of chrysanthemums. As defendants in chains paraded past them, they just followed the pattern in place and failed to ask the right questions.

The man's offenses weren't named in open court. Very typical. Contrary to the spirit and letter of the Sixth Amendment, almost everything important in criminal cases is discussed behind closed doors. Observers miss vital facts in the small portion of the process they're allowed to see. The public defender looked on, also undisturbed. She'd finished her work when she made the deal for her client. I began taking notes, and that day I put aside the novel I was writing. This book was born.

Years ago a guard discussing an inmate at the Colorado State Penitentiary told me, "They don't call them cons just because they're convicts." Immediately one of his coworkers snickered in a way that told me the guards repeated this particular mantra regularly, reminding one another that when a convict tells you it's warm out, you better bring a sweater. And yes, most (but not all) prisoners are guilty as charged. Still, that doesn't end the story. Maybe the defendant really did have drug residue under his fingernails. But a prison sentence wasn't necessarily the best way to address his transgression.

As I sorted through the information for this book, I remembered the Colorado guard's adage. What follows is based on facts that can't be refuted or events I saw with my own eyes. In a few rare instances, I couldn't verify a story, but I was careful to identify these cases. There were times, many of them, when I hoped I was being lied to.

It would have been a relief to know the story was untrue. No matter how strict I made the criteria, plenty of material remained. The cases cited in this book are the tip of a monstrous, still expanding iceberg.

I thank everyone who helped bring forth this book. That includes my dear wife, Connie Goldman, a sharp editor who cheerfully pulls no punches; my patient, tenacious agent Sally van Haitsma; nurturing, tireless former Potomac Books senior editor Hilary Claggett; indomitable Melissa Jones; Kathryn Owens; Elizabeth Demers; Laura Briggs; Julie Kimmel; and everyone who took the time to answer my questions, especially those who, in order to shine light on stories that ached to be told, unselfishly recalled events they'd prefer to forget.

PART 1

Failed Fears

1

The Mostly Invisible
Catastrophe

BRENDA VALENCIA, A NINETEEN-YEAR-OLD WITH NO HISTORY OF DRUG USE or criminal behavior, made a terrible mistake in 1991. She gave a ride to her roommate's stepmother, a cocaine dealer. She drove the woman to the West Palm Beach, Florida, home of a man who turned out to be another dealer. Valencia remembers being impressed by the spacious, luxurious house. She watched the World Series on TV with the daughter of the man who lived there, and he and her passenger went outside to talk. The phone rang, and Valencia picked it up. Recalled Valencia, "The guy on the end of the line said, 'Who's this?' I told him and asked if I could take a message. He said, 'Yes, tell him to beep me.' There was nothing said about money or drugs. Just, can I take a message?" But the prosecution would later argue that this phone call helped prove that Brenda Valencia was part of a conspiracy and that her passenger had picked up some money at the home with Valencia's help. Swept up in a raid, Valencia was sentenced to the mandatory minimum. "That's the first thing my lawyer told me," she recalls, "the mandatory minimum, that I couldn't get less than twelve years, seven months. I knew I deserved punishment for being stupid. But twelve years, seven months? I couldn't believe it. I tried to tell them, 'Look at my bank account. I'm not a drug dealer. I'm a student, just a regular person.'"[1]

Although her case was Kafkaesque, it was also terrifyingly routine. In only one respect was it unique: it attracted plenty of attention,

3

probably because U.S. District Court Judge Jose A. Gonzalez Jr., forced to pronounce the zero-tolerance sentence predetermined by law, called that sentence "absurd" and "an insult to justice."[2] Editorials blasted away at the rigidity of the statute that prevented Gonzalez from giving Valencia probation and a stern lecture. But eventually the media moved on. Valencia served the full sentence.

President Bill Clinton, who pardoned 140 people on his last day in office, January 20, 2001, ignored a petition from Valencia, even though it was supported by a letter from Judge Gonzalez. Among those Clinton pardoned was Marc Rich, who had been charged with fifty-one counts of tax fraud and had fled U.S. jurisdiction for a sanctuary in Switzerland before he was indicted. While Rich thumbed his nose at the rules, his wife made substantial donations to the Clinton library and Hillary Clinton's Senate campaign. Now married and the mother of two, Brenda Valencia Aldana works in a counseling program for incarcerated teens. The pardoned Marc Rich, no longer a fugitive, remains a billionaire financier living in a Swiss villa surrounded by his private collection of Monets, Picassos, and Renoirs. The law never touched him.

As for Valencia, her confinement for all those years was no accident. It was part of a deliberate policy pursued by a prison-industrial complex that profits from harsh justice, injustice, and sometimes no justice at all. It was nurtured by intellectual sloth, the war on drugs, and the same gratuitous fear and loathing that Hunter Thompson found dictating so many corners of American society. The economic war waged against the vast majority of Americans by a determined group at the top of the financial scale at last found broad recognition in 2011, when the Occupy movement spread from Wall Street to cities around America. But few Americans have recognized the connection between accelerating economic inequality and the leap in incarceration that accompanied it. Both trends were made possible by the acceptance of the underlying premise that some people's lives have less value than others.

■ FRISBEE SENTENCES

Starting around the time President Ronald Reagan took office in 1981, a combination of economic, social, and political forces hijacked the criminal justice system, tossing punitive sentences around like Frisbees and creating a structure that works contrary to the mission of creating a safer, more humane society. Providing false solutions through political posturing, fear-mongering, and manipulating the twenty-four-hour news cycle has resulted in the incarceration of 2.3 million people, a population about the size of Houston's.[3] Most of these prisoners don't belong behind bars.

A healthy society will always struggle to achieve a balance between freedom and security, but since 9/11 America seems to have abandoned this struggle. Freedom has received short shrift. With fear driving the agenda, we've heaped on additional layers of bureaucratic "security," launched wars of vague purpose, and even surrendered some of our constitutional rights. Obliging courts have allowed government technocrats, hiding behind the little-known Stored Communications Act, to sift at will through our e-mails. The National Security Agency intercepts phone calls without judicial warrants. The National Defense Authorization Act, signed into law in 2012, allows the federal government to arrest American citizens on American soil for suspicion of terrorism and to hold them the rest of their lives without offering them a trial. President Barack Obama added a signing statement to the law, professing that his administration would never allow these abuses of American liberties, but even if he keeps his word, future presidents will retain this ominous power.

Meanwhile, stratification of wealth and income in the United States since 1980 has been well documented. This rising inequality contaminates the criminal justice system. As the government has coddled the top 1 percent, the plight of the 99 percent at its most desperate has been in many cases a life behind bars. The American legal framework has become less dedicated to sifting out the schizophrenics and drug abusers, for example, who have committed no crime against others but who find themselves behind bars because their traditional safety nets have been swallowed up by budget cuts at all levels of government. Their jailing is a crime against humanity. Consider also the petty offenders who, with proper help, could be steered into the mainstream via education and job training, instead of into the career-criminal underclass as a result of their unnecessary incarceration. Because the system holds so many inmates, the truly dangerous offenders more easily fall between the cracks.

The Land of the Free holds more prisoners than any other country in the world and has the highest per capita incarceration rate. Its prisoner ratio of 748 per 100,000 residents is nearly five times that of Spain, which has the highest ratio in Western Europe. With only 5 percent of the world's population, the United States holds 25 percent of its prisoners, exceeding the per capita levels even of dictatorships such as China and Iran. In fact, one of every hundred American adults is behind bars.[4]

Defenders of the American system claim it jails so many people because it does its job more effectively, but any police state might make the same claim. When *Casablanca*'s Captain Renault instructed his subordinates to round up the usual suspects, he wasn't terrribly as concerned about the rights of the innocent.

Obviously there are victims of vicious crimes whose circumstances cry out for justice and dangerous perpetrators who should be locked away for the good of society, but the United States imposes lengthy sentences on the Brenda Valencias, on drug users who can't afford treatment, on low-grade shoplifters, and the mentally ill. In fact, the American Psychiatric Association points out that jails and prisons are the primary mental health care facilities in the United States.[5]

Jurists elsewhere are baffled by America's curious infatuation with keeping so many nonthreatening people behind bars and in such awful conditions. The United States not only imprisons offenders who would not go to jail in other countries; it gives them long sentences. Supreme Court Justice Anthony Kennedy figures American sentences are eight times longer than those meted out in European courts. Justice Kennedy, usually described as a conservative, has noted that California's infamous three-strikes law was sponsored by the prison guards union. "And that," he says indignantly, "is sick."[6] This book's title was derived from Kennedy's searing description of a system that has taken a very wrong turn. In 2010 the prison guards he singled out were averaging more than $100,000 annually and belonged to the most powerful labor union in the state. Their pensions are fatter than those of nurses, teachers, or firefighters, and they continue lobbying for additional prisons, harsher sentencing, and even stiffer parole regulations. The guards make up one small segment of a nationwide prison-industrial complex. Arizona's scheme to lock up suspected undocumented immigrants, for example, was an economic contrivance orchestrated by lobbyists employed by the increasingly powerful private-prison industry.[7] Its corporate chieftains view the jailing of housemaids and busboys as a business opportunity.

Vivien Stern, a research fellow at the Prison Studies Center in London, has said that America's bloated incarceration rate has made it "a rogue state, a country that has made a decision not to follow what is a normal Western approach."[8] James Whitman, a specialist in comparative law at Yale, points out that the United States is the only advanced country that incarcerates people for minor property crimes such as passing bad checks.[9] But such pronouncements and innumerable similar studies have had little to no effect on this shockingly inequitable system.

■ AMERICAN VALJEANS

In the French novel *Les Misérables*, after serving nineteen years in prison for stealing a loaf of bread and for the botched escape attempts that followed, Jean Valjean must carry a yellow passport that identifies him to all as a convict. His life is dogged by a relentless, often irrational judicial system in Victor Hugo's fictional account of corrupted innocence, blind injustice, mercy, and redemption. U.S. prisons coast-to-coast are bursting with Jean Valjeans. The cruel details of "zero tolerance" are largely hidden from view. Jerry DeWayne Williams, for example, attracted fifteen minutes of fame when a judge handed him twenty-five years to life for stealing a slice of pizza in Redondo Beach, California. His sentence was later reduced to six years.[10] Another Valjean, a laid-off construction worker, is serving three and a half years for wheeling a rusty bicycle with two flat tires and no chain out of someone else's garage and then leaving it behind. The defendant, whose case never made the news, was Chris Martinez. He's a friend of our family, and his case was part of the inspiration for this book. The list of Valjeans is endless and depressing. They spend day after day in a system that routinely dumps lesser offenders into a claustrophobic nightmare ruled by gangs and sociopaths.

All three Texas murderers who, in 1998, dragged a hitchhiker to a horrific death behind their truck were ex-cons.[11] Sentenced originally as nonviolent offenders, they were ruined human beings when the justice system spit them out, willing to torture and kill a man because of his race. An intelligent system doesn't make killers out of small-time offenders. But foolish, even indefensible practices have a way of masquerading as reasonable after they've become standard procedure. Still, time has a way of holding up the past to the light of reason and exposing absurdity for what it is. Respected magistrates wearing judicial robes used to sentence people to death for witchcraft. Our Saudi allies still behead "witches." Officials rendering these judgments in the Western world considered themselves sensible people protecting society from danger. Looking back from a more rational perspective, we see that their monstrous proceedings were divorced from truth, justice, wisdom, and decency. But by exercising intellectual honesty and examining solid empirical evidence, we no longer have to wait three hundred years to know when something is terribly wrong.

■ 9/11 EFFECT

In addition to its blanket surveillance of electronic communications, our government confesses to ongoing torture (minus waterboarding), secret jails, vaguely accountable search and seizure, and a macabre list of other extraconstitutional procedures. In fact, our government holds terrorist suspects who, even if freed by the court, will, it assures us, remain jailed anyway. U.S. contractors who have killed unarmed civilians overseas reside in a legal limbo that blesses them with a mysterious immunity from courts. Officers of financial institutions who created absurd derivative securities based on phony collateral weren't prosecuted and even gave themselves fat bonuses. Citigroup, for example, which suffered more than $27 billion worth of losses in 2008, paid an estimated $5.33 billion worth of bonuses for that year, as reported by then New York attorney general Andrew Cuomo in a detailed study he released July 30, 2009. He titled his report "No Rhyme or Reason."

USA Today, after painstakingly assembling records from across America, reported in a major 2010 series that it had uncovered 201 documented cases since 1998 of federal prosecutors (the people's attorneys) falsifying or suppressing evidence, suborning perjury, or committing other serious misconduct, just to boost their convictions. Citing privacy rules, the Justice Department refused to disclose whether any of the guilty prosecutors were subsequently disciplined.

The nation's vast network of penal fortresses, some of them operated by low-bidding private corporations, is a gray, seething petri dish of menace and disease, constituting a cruel and unusual punishment that courts rarely recognize as such. This enormous system has gotten so out of hand that some states, reverting back to earlier eighteenth- and nineteenth-century practices, again jail debtors. Complainants initiating these proceedings are frequently collection agencies owned by the very lawyers who bought the debt for pennies on the dollar.

Psychiatrist Karl Menninger, after taking a good look at America's criminal justice system, speculated that "all the crimes committed by all the jailed criminals do not equal in total social damage that of the crimes committed against them." Society allows this system to steam ahead without knowing whether its practices are effective, "a total waste of time, or worse."[12] Menninger expressed these ideas in 1969, before the war on drugs began.

ROCKEFELLER LAWS

In the 1970s New York governor Nelson Rockefeller, still aspiring to be president, grabbed headlines by championing legislation that sent thousands of drug offenders away for a minimum of fifteen years to life. His "Rockefeller laws," though eventually struck from New York statutes, were a beacon to other ambitious politicians looking for an express elevator to higher office. Michigan passed a bill that mandated life without parole for possessing 1.45 pounds of cocaine or heroin.[13]

From 1980 to 2003 the U.S. prisoner population quadrupled, and the number of imprisoned drug offenders skyrocketed 1,200 percent.[14] In Washington, Congress established stiff mandatory sentences for a wide assortment of federal offenses and abolished parole entirely. The lives of millions of nondangerous lawbreakers were turned into throwaway items. Day after day police and prosecutors squeeze more of these people into America's Gulag, as inmate education and other rehabilitative programs are quietly strangled to reduce the enormous

expense of keeping so many people locked up. Judges not numbed by
the parade of horrors find their hands tied in case after case.

■ WRONG PLACE, WRONG TIME

In 2005 the Supreme Court ruled that federal judges could begin using the Federal Sentencing Guidelines, created as an outgrowth of
the Sentencing Reform Act of 1984, as a guide rather than as a set
of inflexible edicts. Even so, most federal judges continued to mete
out the same stiff penalties anyway, treating them as mandatory. The
thousands of convicts sentenced prior to the 2005 ruling continued to
serve out their mandatory sentences without special appellate privileges. Among them was construction worker Brian Ison, sentenced
in 2001 to eleven years, three months.[15] At age eighteen, Ison was in
the wrong place at the wrong time, buying crystal meth at a mobile
home in rural Kentucky that was raided by Drug Enforcement Administration (DEA) agents. The home had been under surveillance
for months. Under a complex web of drug laws, Ison was convicted
in federal court for manufacturing five hundred grams of meth, even
though only eleven grams were found on the property and he wasn't
a drug manufacturer. Witnesses thought they'd seen him help cook
meth at the mobile home on several occasions. Ison, who'd had a
drug problem since he was sixteen, was engaged to be married with
a child on the way at the time of his trial. His daughter suffers from
muscular dystrophy. His only previous nontraffic offenses were being a minor in possession of alcohol and drinking in public.

Any thinking person who spends much time within the criminal
justice system cannot help but notice how wildly disparate sentences
can be. It's not unusual for federal defendants convicted of down-
loading child porn to get ten years for a first offense (twenty years
if there's been a prior conviction). But in November 2011 a circuit
court judge in Naples, Florida, sentenced Daniel Vilca, twenty-six,
a stockroom worker, to life without possibility of parole for down-
loading hundreds of photos of child pornography. Vilca, who had no
previous criminal record, turned down a plea bargain offer of twenty
years. Had he actually molested a child, he probably would have received a lighter sentence. Former federal judge Paul Cassell reasoned
that Vilca's crime was not victimless; if there were no consumers

of child porn, fewer children would be victimized by it. However, Cassell also added, "a life sentence is what we give to murderers, and possession of child pornography is not the equivalent of first-degree murder."[16]

Because laws are passed by politicians, there is fundamentally no advantage to standing up to extreme sentencing. It's easier for an officeholder to look the other way as thousands of families are ripped apart by years and years of gratuitous incarceration than it is to leave one's self open to just one Willie Horton. After twelve years in the Massachusetts prison system, Horton, a murderer and armed robber, was furloughed under a program that operated during Governor Michael Dukakis's term in office. Once outside the walls, Horton disappeared. He turned up again in Maryland, where he raped a woman and stabbed her fiancée. He was subsequently recaptured. George H. W. Bush seized on the case as he coasted to victory over Dukakis in the 1988 presidential election. He injected it into speeches, and his political action committee gleefully plastered Horton's ugly, sinister mug in TV ads. The story stuck to Dukakis like flypaper. The specter of Horton haunts officeholders to this day.

▪ CONVICT POPULATION AGES

The Pew Center on the States reported in a 2009 study that the average annual incarceration cost for each inmate held by the states is $29,000.[17] When KPBS Radio in San Diego crunched the California numbers in 2010, it figured the state's true per-inmate cost at $50,000. The price triples, KPBS concluded, for geriatric inmates, who have special health needs.[18] The growing population of elderly prisoners is the natural consequence of decades of megasentencing.

"Violent and career criminals need to be locked up, and for a long time," said Adam Gelb, director of the Pew Center's Public Safety Performance Project. "But our research shows that prisons are housing too many people who can be managed safely and held accountable in the community at far lower cost."[19] The number of violent criminals in prison has remained relatively constant for many years. Overcrowding stems from unreasonable sentences handed out to low-level offenders who could be rehabilitated in the community instead.

About a third of the nation's prisoners are in city or county jails, many because they can't post the absurdly high bail amounts with which they're saddled. An addict charged with possessing a small stash of drugs can easily confront bail of a half million dollars. Any attorney who even hints that the bail is excessive risks angering the judge over a fight the defense can almost never win.

Defendants desperate to escape the confinement of tiny county jail cells or horrific dormitories seething with violence and extortion are quicker to plead guilty. As defendants consider their options, their attorneys inform them that if they exercise their constitutional right to demand a trial and then lose that trial, the judge will likely impose a harsher sentence than they would face if they settled out of court. It is standard operating procedure: judges exact a price from a defendant who jams up the docket. If the defendant had a job, he probably lost it after his arrest, and if he was living on his own, he probably lost his apartment. His old life has vanished. But just as a medieval prisoner's confession could result in a grisly execution, the modern plea bargain can land the defendant in an even more dreadful situation than the one that drove him to take the deal.

In the federal system, about 95 percent of criminal defendants plead guilty. Of the remaining few who demand a trial, nearly nine of ten are convicted. "A ninety-plus percent conviction rate isn't something that should be applauded," says Pittsburgh attorney Paul Boas. "I think it's something you should worry about. That's what you see in totalitarian regimes."[20]

Innocent suspects often plead guilty in the face of this pressure and intimidation. Under the right circumstances, almost any innocent person might confess in order to end the nightmare and do less time. Copping a plea to someone else's crime is sometimes a terribly rational choice. Just as the race does not always go to the swift nor the battle to the strong, neither does justice always protect the unjustly accused. The Innocence Project, an arm of the Benjamin N. Cardozo School of Law at Yeshiva University, has helped hundreds of convicts, including seventeen who did time on death row, prove their innocence through DNA testing. The wrongfully convicted inmates served an average of thirteen years before exoneration and release. Approximately 25 percent of them had pleaded guilty.[21] And these weren't offenders who eventually won their freedom through a technical finding. These people were undeniably innocent. Over the last several years other innocence projects aimed at winning release for the wrongfully convicted have sprung up in other states, and their number grows. Each innocent convict released is a badge of both victory and shame.

■ STIFFEST PENALTY

Prosecutors work in a perpetual chess game, always seeking checkmate by routinely pushing for the stiffest penalty. And when a defendant is looking at a possible sentence of ten or fifteen years, a plea bargain offering a three-to-five stint can seem like a gift. Josh Bowers, a professor of law at the University of Virginia, concludes, "Even the innocent defendant may end up taking a plea because it's the rational thing to do."[22]

■ THE HUMAN COST

The hard-liners now running the criminal justice system follow a philosophy akin to the belief system that calls evolution and climate change "unproved theories." They generate fear and disregard the human cost of their policies. Take the case of Joe Haskell.[23] A crystal meth addict with two burglary convictions on his record, Haskell was driving through a Los Angeles alley in 2010 when he spotted some discarded scrap iron and two used doors, which he loaded into the back of his pickup. "It was leaning over the fence. I didn't even enter the yard," he explains. Following his arrest, a hard-nosed prosecutor offered him a fifteen-year burglary sentence, promising twenty-five-to-life if he went to trial. At the last minute the arresting officer, perhaps because of the trivial nature of the offense, came in on his day off and interceded. He helped Haskell cut a deal for seven years for petty theft. When I spoke with Haskell, he was in county jail waiting to enter a state penitentiary. He told me, "I'm doing time for stuff I already did time for. You used to be able to do your time, do something else, and do time for that. Now the time you did before, you do all over again." Haskell has never even been suspected of a violent crime. Inside prison he's known as an easygoing inmate who cools others with his peaceful presence. "I wouldn't harm a bug," he says.

Few of us want someone like Haskell reaching over the fence to take what he pleases, but only the heartless would want him to do twenty-five years for it. When I spoke to him, Haskell was off the meth and spending much of his jail time reading literature from Alcoholics Anonymous. But there are smarter, more effective ways to clean up addicts than sending them to prison. Haskell will be forty-nine when he is released. The odds of landing a good job after a third stretch won't be favorable. Generally in such cases, the ex-con, put back on the street with a small sum of gate money (cash provided to inmates in some states upon parole), quickly goes broke, gets depressed, and starts using again. Maybe he steals something to raise cash. Then he tests dirty for his parole officer or skips the appointment. Or maybe he's nabbed for the theft. Any of these scenarios lands him back inside unless he decides to become an informant. Given the standard deal, he'd need to turn in three offenders on charges that stick. That can be a dangerous choice, but enough people take the snitch route to create an ever-wider network of nabbed, small-time felons. They don't know the kingpins, and even if they did, these small-time offenders probably would be too scared to turn them in. Addicts and their dime-a-dozen suppliers are law enforcement's low-hanging fruit. They leave Day-Glo trails of money, dope, and paraphernalia. Picking these plums off the branches is safer and more lucrative for prosecutors than pursuing dangerous sociopaths, and a lot less work than pursuing white-collar criminals.

Haskell and other sorry souls like him are routinely warehoused behind bars. Their bunks are stacked in gymnasiums, hallways, wherever space can be found. Almost all of them were poor, homeless, drug-addicted, or all three before they went inside, and without constructive, cost-effective intervention, they will almost certainly revert to their preconviction status upon release. They're at the absolute bottom of the socioeconomic pile. No group in America has less political clout. Unlike lobbyists and contributors from the prison-industrial complex, prisoners and their families aren't out there golfing with legislators and inviting them to speak at four-star banquets.

Ironically, when Mario Cuomo governed New York and struggled to find room for all the human detritus from the Rockefeller drug laws, he built dozens of prisons by siphoning billions from the Urban Development Corporation, an agency created to build housing for the poor.[24] The organization ended up performing its mission, only with a special Dickensian twist, building the prisons and workhouses invoked by Ebenezer Scrooge.

Hang around a courthouse long enough and you begin to see that almost everyone in it believes the defendants in their manacles and jail uniforms are guilty. As a case moves from station to station on the legal conveyor belt, evidence—or lack of it—comes into play, but so do attitudes and perceptions. When an Indiana jury convicted ex-boxing champion Mike Tyson of a rape he almost certainly didn't commit, he told himself, well, he'd escaped punishment for other wrongful acts, so he wouldn't let this outcome destroy him.[25]

■ "SERIOUS" OFFENSES

Sentencing got tougher around the time of the Vietnam War as the crime rate went through one of its cyclical climbs. Then along came the eighties and with it the Reagan administration and the nirvana of zero tolerance. Twenty-four-hour news channels began to terrify the public with a never-ending parade of crimes, plagues, and overhyped disasters. British-style sensationalism blasted its way into the basic cable package with the launching of Rupert Murdoch's hard-right, tabloid-inspired Fox News Channel in 1996.

News, journalism textbooks exclaim, is man bites dog, not its inverse. Following this dictum, journalists routinely splash in the blood of exceptional events, the more traumatic and violent the better. Yet this directly contravenes the paradoxical claim that the news conveyed to the public is an accurate reflection of society at large.

During the nineties, as round-the-clock news ramped up the value of whatever was repulsive and objectionable, three-strikes laws, which mandated tougher sentences for each "strike" and an extended or life sentence for a third consecutive felony, became popular. The term "three strikes" had an instantly recognizable, irresistible ring to it. It was lousy law but a brilliant marketing slogan. Twenty-six states and the federal government now have three-strikes statutes covering a smorgasbord of "serious" offenses that in some states, notably California, could include nonviolent or even petty crimes, such as the previously cited bicycle and pizza thefts. Inherent in many of these hard-line statutes is the belief and practice of preventive detention.

That is, even if the defendant didn't inflict much damage on this particular occasion, next time he might, so why not use this opportunity to keep him off the street?

The process became even more grievous after the Great Recession rolled across the country in 2008. To maintain their hard line on criminal justice, states cut funding to social service agencies, thus smothering recreation, drug counseling, and sports programs and axing teaching staffs and classes. At the same time they closed down clinics and libraries and crossed their fingers in hopes that more bridges wouldn't collapse. Parole officers' caseloads rose to impossible heights. They spent so much time keeping track of people who were never a threat in the first place that they paid less attention to dangerous criminals.

To hit the pause button on all this, lawmakers would have to ramp up education, humanize criminal statutes, build aggressive antipoverty programs, and make therapy for drug abuse robust and truly accessible. But that would provide their political opponents with the opportunity to brand them as soft on crime in TV ads financed by the hard-line lobby. The safer political course is to stand back and let sick justice take its course, as it did in the cases of Brenda Valencia, Jerry DeWayne Williams, Joe Haskell, and so many others.

■ AMERICAN JAVERTS

America has a hard time looking beyond its borders for ideas that work. Year after year its health care system puts up relatively awful statistics on longevity, infant mortality, costs, and other key demographic measurements. Yet when reforms were proposed during the early part of the Obama administration, many politicians argued that it was senseless to change what they called the "best health care system in the world," and their argument almost carried the day. In the same vein, few Americans realize how irrational and gratuitously cruel our criminal justice structure is or how it got that way.

The absurdities of the system could never have become so pronounced were they not boosted by the robot logic of Jean Valjean's obsessed nemesis, Inspector Javert, Victor Hugo's humorless peace officer who disdains humanity and compassion. Our system is teeming with Javerts, without whom there could be no Valjeans.

Oddly, the U.S. criminal justice system leans toward victimizing the defendants who deserve a break and awarding prizes to career criminals who don't. When Brenda Valencia was arrested in Florida, she knew no one on whom she could inform to reduce her sentence. Because she wasn't a drug dealer, she had no underworld connections and nothing to trade. "But the guy who originated the deal," she told me, "got fifteen months. His wife served no time at all. The two who did the most got the least time. The two who did the least got the most time."

Tell this story to lawyers who work in criminal courts day after day and they'll look at you quizzically, as though waiting for the punch line. They see these cases all the time. Talking about it just makes it worse. Offenders know it's safer to snitch on people who aren't terribly guilty. Because they're not part of a criminal network, they're less likely to wreak vengeance or spread the word about informants.

If hard-liners took a pragmatic look at the chaos and injustice created by their callousness, they might realize that tossing around harsh sentences has the potential to create crime. It produces a glut of ex-cons who are largely unemployable in a tough job market and, should they return to crime, provides them the incentive to leave no witnesses.

■ THE "OTHER"

Most middle-class people don't know anyone in the penitentiary system and thus tend to think of inmates as the "other," a dangerous, barely human type best kept behind bars. Hapless wretches are routinely shuffled from sad urban rat-scapes into local jails and out to rural penitentiaries without arousing much notice. Swept from the bottom of the socioeconomic strata, their cries are drowned out by the louder voices of dying industries and occupations, unemployment, debts, taxes, underwater mortgages, wars, Monday Night Football, and celebrity dance contests. But there are plenty of neighborhoods with residents who understand how easy it is to get swept into the U.S. Gulag. They know flesh-and-blood human beings—family and friends—who experienced it. One in nine African American men aged twenty to thirty-four is in prison, many because of drug laws that lack a key ingredient—a victim. So even though people residing in high-crime areas are far more likely than other Americans to be harmed by crime, they tend to retain compassion for arrestees.

Seventy percent of children with a parent in prison wind up being incarcerated themselves.[26] It's as though our civilization prescribes jail as a standard solution to all manner of situations, some of which have only a tangential relationship to criminality.

The prison-industrial complex proffering a one-size-fits-all solution to so many societal problems isn't made up of just the guards' union and prison corporations. It also includes service contractors, prosecutors, judges, bailiffs, court secretaries, clerks, police officers, and the politicians passing the draconian laws so diligently sought by their benefactors who maintain the sprawling complex of lockups. Other insider corporations secure contracts for practically free convict labor and sometimes use it to replace nonconvict workers, who then get laid off. Working separately and together, these components of the industry have set our criminal justice system on autopilot and aimed it far beyond the boundaries of the rest of the civilized world. At the same time they've managed to skirt the pragmatic tests for which America has long been celebrated, establishing, bit by bit, an unreasonably cruel system that devours an increasingly larger slice of our citizenry.

2

Fear, Loathing, and Guns

SOCIETIES MORE CONCERNED WITH PUNISHMENT THAN WITH TRUTH CAN appear orderly, but only because the results of their priorities won't be immediately visible. Citizens will know that a potentially disagreeable multitude is safely walled off somewhere, and they won't need to know much more. But that kind of thinking got us where we are, with one in thirty-one U.S. adults in jail, prison, or on parole, according to a 2009 report from the respected Pew Center on the States.[1] The U.S. Bureau of Justice Statistics counted 7,225,800 of these closely monitored or locked-up souls.[2]

When the Supreme Court in 2011 upheld a lower court's order to release thirty thousand prisoners from California's terribly overcrowded penitentiaries, Justice Antonin Scalia issued a dissent that seethed with fear and loathing. Many of the released prisoners, he decided, "will undoubtedly be fine physical specimens who have developed intimidating muscles pumping iron in the prison gym."[3] The plaintiffs in the case had proved that an average of one convict per week was dying because of the awful state of medical care in the state prison system, but if Scalia saw this as a problem, he didn't say so.

In some ways, Scalia's legal opinion echoed the warning from South Carolina's Keziah Goodwyn Hopkins Brevard, an antebellum slaveholder who feared that freed slaves might wreak revenge on their masters. Brevard was willing to liberate the slaves as long as it was to some foreign shore. When she learned of Lincoln's election in November 1860, she wrote in her diary, "God be with us is my prayer and let us all be willing to die rather than free our slaves in their present uncivilized state." She believed that once you wronged someone terribly, if you had that person cornered and under control, the best course of action was to maintain the status quo.[4]

In 2009 Scalia was part of the 5-4 majority that denied inmates the right to postconviction DNA analyses, a remarkable decision that made it far more difficult to sort unjustly convicted inmates out of the prison population.

California's law-and-order governor Jerry Brown, a staunch ally of the prison guards union, reacted to the federal mandate to cut down the number of state prisoners by announcing he would disperse the "released" convicts to county jails around the state, where in most cases conditions would be worse and opportunities for rehabilitation even more circumscribed. There would be no attempt to select the least dangerous among them and place them back in the community. Casey Mullenaux, for example, at age twenty-four was sentenced in Torrance, California, to three years for possessing ten dollars' worth of black tar heroin. Mullenaux couldn't qualify for help from the Innocence Project because he was guilty as charged. He also had a residential burglary on his record, a "strike" in legal parlance, which made him ineligible for drug counseling, probation, "or actually any alternative to prison," as he pointed out to me in a stark letter from his penitentiary cell. Mullenaux is an obviously intelligent, eminently savable person, but at the age of twenty-four, with no violent crimes on his record, his country had already written him off as a total loss. He wrote, "Since I've been here already, it's almost certain that I'll get back here again. And I have."[5]

When low-level offenders like Mullenaux are paroled out of prison, local police monitor their movements. As parolees, they can be stopped and frisked for no reason. Constricted by special rules that strip them of basic rights, they're far more likely to be arrested than the general population. Police tend to assume drug felons like Mullenaux are either behind bars or will be again soon, so getting them jailed again as quickly as possible after they return home may prevent the commission of new offenses. And although parolees may face a bureaucratic nightmare trying to find therapy, drugs themselves are plentiful, and we never run out of jail cells. Parolees can't live where they please or travel where they please, and they're forced to check the box for felony status when they try to improve their situation through work or education. Like the deltas and epsilons in Aldous Huxley's *Brave New World*, they carry a lower rank that's unlikely to change. The Pew Charitable Trusts computed the odds that a previously incarcerated person will make it out of the economic basement (that is, the bottom 20 percent) within twenty years. It's 1 in 50.[6] Advances in computer technology that put the world at our fingertips also stamp our personal histories in indelible ink. The National Employment Law Project found that 90 percent of employers check potential employees for criminal backgrounds.[7] More than two-thirds of the states allow hiring and professional-licensing decisions to be made on the basis of an arrest alone; no conviction is necessary. By age twenty-three, 30 percent of Americans have been arrested; this number was 22 percent in 1967.[8]

In November 2011 the American Bar Association released a database identifying more than thirty-eight thousand punitive provisions that apply to people convicted of crimes, pertaining to everything from public housing to welfare assistance to occupational licenses. There was a time when an American with a criminal past could move to a new place, often out West, and begin life anew, possibly even with a different name. Wide open spaces made reformed lives possible. But now a criminal record is deposited in cyberspace, where it remains beyond death.

In 2010 the Chicago Public Schools declined to hire Darrell Langdon for a job as a boiler-room engineer because he'd been convicted of possessing a half gram of cocaine twenty-five years earlier, a felony for which he received probation. Langdon, a single parent of two sons, had been clean for more than two decades, but only after the *Chicago Tribune* wrote about his case did the school system reverse its decision and give him the job.[9]

■ THE HUMAN FACTOR

In 2011 Michelle Alexander, associate professor of law at Ohio State University, concluded that if we were to "return to the rates of incarceration we had in the 1970s, we would have to release four out of five people behind bars." That's because we "now sentence people to prison for years for types of offenses that once received just probation or days in jail."[10]

Mullenaux's offenses, for example, were opportunities for society to intercede, to set things right, to steer the offender down a different path while it was still relatively simple. Little League coaches will, from time to time, have to deal with a kid who freezes when the ball comes his way. Imagine a coach who blows up, scolds the boy in front of everybody, tells him he'll be a rotten ballplayer for the rest of his life, and instructs him to go sit at the end of the dugout away from his teammates. Now envision a coach who remains cool, boosts the kid's confidence, and picks out little things he can do to help him execute the play properly next time. Which coach do you think will be more effective? Yet the United States operates a criminal justice system that's eager to play its part as a hollering, scolding, ineffective coach. One is reminded of the townspeople in Nathaniel Hawthorne's *The Scarlet Letter*, poised to pounce on any impropriety with both feet.

"There are a certain number of predators out there who need to be locked up," said Neal Griffin, a police lieutenant in San Diego County, California. "But nowadays, especially in the last ten years, I've seen this crazy militarization of law enforcement."[11] It's a by-the-numbers approach, he said, that makes no allowances for extenuating circumstances. Low-level offenders like Mullenaux can't get the kind of break that might alter their course and stitch up rips in the social fabric. It's ridiculous and counterproductive to drop minor offenders into a nest ruled by sociopaths and then brand them as lepers when they are released and try to reenter society.

After Casey Mullenaux gained parole, he took the only bed available to him, in the apartment of his brother Cody, also a recovering addict. Cody tried to keep him straight, but Casey was right back in the same neighborhood of South Los Angeles County, where almost all his connections and relationships were with people inside the drug underworld. He had, of course, other friends from high school days, but those relationships didn't hold up. When ex-addicts are shunned by former acquaintances, they have fewer options and can become depressed. Depressed addicts typically try to end the pain the easy way, completing the cycle by turning back to drugs. I had heard Mullenaux was using again, and about a year after his release, he called me from the Los Angeles Police Department (LAPD) Seventy-Seventh Street Station. This time he was busted for possession of a heroin-tainted syringe. As a one-striker, he was looking at a minimum two-year stay in prison before he'd be considered for parole. "I don't need more prison," he said. "I need help. I don't know why I do this stuff. I don't understand it."[12]

Casey's grandmother, a retired schoolteacher, marveled at how the system worked. "It costs them more to throw him in prison, which makes everything worse, than it would to put him in a program," she said. "It just doesn't make sense."[13] Her shock was typical of middle-class people who brush up against a criminal justice system that mostly deals with the lower end of the socioeconomic spectrum.

I made a few calls on Casey's behalf, but trying to get him residential therapy instead of punishment was like asking to get him into the astronaut program. In chains, he was brought back into Long Beach Superior Court on a Tuesday. The prosecutor had offered him a very typical deal—thirty-two months at 80 percent (twenty-five and a half months of actual prison time). When Casey showed hesitation in court, Judge James D. Otto reminded him from the bench that if he passed up this chance, he could end up serving much more time. Usually the only way to beat a possession charge is by questioning the legality of the search. But cops can search parolees at any time for no reason at all. Mullenaux's court-appointed attorney, who urged him to take the deal, had already told him he was looking at a possible ten years if he went to trial. He did what was rational under irrational circumstances and accepted the "bargain."

■ SUBSIDING VIOLENCE

Violent crime has in fact subsided since the advent of wholesale imprisonment. The Bureau of Justice Statistics tells us that in 1994 there were 51.2 violent victimizations per thousand adults. By 2009 that figure had dropped to 16.9.[14] This represents "a spectacularly dramatic social change," observed University of California–Los Angeles (UCLA) public policy professor Mark Kleiman.[15] But is it the mass jailing that made us safer? No. Although there were far more people behind bars in 1994 than in 1980, the 1980 violence ratio was almost precisely the same, at 51.7 incidents per thousand adults.[16]

Criminologists citing causes for the diminishment of serious crime point to the waning of the crack cocaine epidemic and the greatly increased availability of legal abortion beginning in the 1970s. As far fewer unwanted children were born to poor, teenage mothers, there were smaller waves of underprivileged adolescents practically predestined for crime. Jessica Wolpaw Reyes, an economist at Amherst College, noted the decline of inner-city children's exposure to lead through paint and gasoline, which she said altered brain patterns, vastly decreasing self-control while increasing the propensity to violence.[17]

Still, logic dictates that some of our 2.3 million prisoners might have committed additional crimes had they been running around free. Professor Robert Perkinson of the University of Hawaii estimates that the dramatic rise in imprisonment has been responsible for about 25 percent of the decrease in crime.[18] He may be right, but he doesn't spell out the methodology that brought him to this number. Other academicians look out across the vast American Gulag and like what they see. "The simple truth is that imprisonment works," wrote Kent Scheidegger and Michael Rushford of the Criminal Justice Legal Foundation in the *Stanford Law and Policy Review*. "Locking up criminals for longer periods reduces the level of crime. The benefits of doing so far offset the costs."[19]

But researchers Bert Useem of Purdue and Anne Piehl of Rutgers estimate that increasing the number of prisoners by another 10 percent would cut crime by only one-half of one percent.[20] Raising the incarceration rate essentially means imprisoning more offenders who aren't violence-prone or dangerous. And as legislators struggle to keep prison costs down, inmates are less likely to learn a useful honest trade while incarcerated. They will, however, be exposed to new criminal tricks and a cruel environment in which the strong prey on the weak. By choosing harshness over good sense, society is transforming people who weren't dangerous into thugs whose options to make a legitimate living have been drastically reduced.

"Rises and falls in Canada's crime rate have closely paralleled America's for 40 years," points out Michael Tonry, former director of the Institute of Criminology at Cambridge University. "But its imprisonment rate has remained stable." Tonry, now a criminal law expert at the University of Minnesota Law School, finds the U.S. justice system needlessly harsh and extremely difficult to change.[21]

■ THIRTY-SHOT CLIPS

"The assault rate in New York and London is not that much different," said Marc Mauer, the executive director of the Sentencing

Project, a research and advocacy group. Yet, he notes, the incarceration rate in the United States is approximately five times that in the UK, and "if you look at the murder rate, particularly with firearms, it's much higher"—a whopping four times higher, five people per 100,000 versus 1.28 in the UK.[22] Some of this discrepancy could be attributable to cultural differences, but the firearms factor cited by Mauer is a likelier cause. About 65 million pistols are scattered across the American landscape. Useless for hunting, they're designed to be easily concealed, carried, and used against other humans. They facilitate homicide and suicide on a grand scale. Although they're mostly prohibited to private citizens in the UK, owning them is downright encouraged in many parts of the United States. Places such as Greenleaf, Idaho, and Kennesaw, Georgia, mandate firearm ownership.[23] In those parts of the country where local law makes guns more difficult to purchase, they can and often are easily transported in from elsewhere.

For politicians, taking a hard-line stance on criminal justice is like choosing to accept a free lottery ticket. It can't hurt. Yet some of the same lawmakers who crusade for zero-tolerance criminal statutes also say yes to the sale and ownership of assault weapons, armor-piercing munitions, and the 9-mm Glock semiautomatic pistol that can fire as many as thirty rounds before reloading becomes necessary. A gunman used a Glock in January 2011 to kill six people and wound fourteen at a shopping mall outside Tucson, Arizona. Among the dead was Chief U.S. District Court Judge John Roll. Among the wounded was Representative Gabrielle Giffords (D-AZ).

In 2003, under pressure from the gun lobby, the Republican Congress passed the sinister Tiahrt Amendment, named for Representative Todd Tiahrt (R-KS).[24] The amendment removed from the public record a government database that could trace guns recovered in crimes back to their original dealers. A group of mayors led by New York's Michael R. Bloomberg assailed the amendment for shielding criminals. Other parts of the amendment protect rogue dealers from lawsuits, public scrutiny, and even academic studies. "It was extraordinary, and the most offensive thing you can think of," said Chuck Wexler, director of the Police Executive Research Forum, a nonprofit advocacy group for police chiefs.[25]

3

Informants

tion. This long-standing principle has withered under pressure from the twenty-four-hour news cycle and tabloid players like Rupert Murdoch, but it remains part of the Society of Professional Journalists' Code of Ethics and is still observed by traditional news gatherers. For good reason. When sources are paid cash for their tales, they're tempted to invent some whoppers. Yet prosecutors, who, like journalists, are supposed to investigate the facts of a case, obey no such rules. They routinely reward witnesses with a commodity far more precious than mere cash. They dangle the gift of freedom, a practice that can make unreliable witnesses wildly unreliable—and a tool unavailable to defense lawyers. If a defense lawyer offered a reward to a witness, that would constitute a bribe.

Ex-prizefighter Anthony Fletcher may have been guilty of a crime. It's hard to know his precise innocence or guilt because his defense was botched so badly after he was arrested back in 1992. Fletcher, locked in a tiny death row cell inside State Correctional Institution Greene in Waynesburg, Pennsylvania, grows older one slow day at a time.[1] He was accused of pulling a gun on small-time crook Vaughn Christopher and executing him on a Philadelphia street. Christopher's autopsy report supported Fletcher's statement that the gun was Christopher's, that he had pulled it on Fletcher, and that Christopher was shot while the two wrestled for it. Prosecutors successfully hid the substance of the autopsy report, and Fletcher was sentenced to death largely on the strength of eyewitness testimony from Natalie Renee Grant, a woman wanted for retail theft and pros-titution. Grant's account was disproved by physical evidence that was never presented to jurors. After the court convicted Fletcher of first-degree murder, Grant was granted probation.

This kind of tit-for-tat testimony is one of the most lethal weap-ons in the prosecutors' arsenal. It's difficult to estimate how many convicts are doing time because someone "turned over" on them and was rewarded for it, and it's even more difficult to know how much of that rewarded testimony was true. The *Chicago Tribune* found that of the thirteen Illinois death row inmates found to be wrongfully convicted and released between 1977 and 2000, five, or nearly 40 percent, were prosecuted using jailhouse informants who claimed the defendant had confessed to them.[2]

It gets worse. Perpetrators, when they can find a willing prosecu-tor, sometimes find a way to pin their own crimes on others. That is essentially what happened to Brenda Valencia after she gave a ride to a drug dealer in Florida. A deal with the actual dealer in the case gave authorities both a working snitch and a big-time conviction.

Another irony built into the system: innocent defendants are par-ticularly tempted to go to trial. This means they'll likely serve longer sentences because juries usually convict criminal defendants, who ultimately pay a price for not accepting a plea bargain. Fletcher, then thirty-four, insisted on a trial. He didn't believe an American court would convict him.

■ "TWO GUNS" FLETCHER: A RING MONIKER THAT MISFIRED

Fletcher, at least for a while, escaped the rough streets of South Phil-adelphia by joining the U.S. Army right out of high school. He pol-ished his boxing skills at an army gym in Germany and became a highly successful amateur. After his discharge, he turned pro in the lightweight division. He was already twenty-four, making it a late start, but he fought his way into world-class ranks. Then he suffered a detached retina, an affliction that usually ends a boxing career. It impairs vision and sometimes leads to blindness.

Fletcher's troubles, like the biblical Job's, kept on coming. He was busted for cocaine possession, partially paralyzed by Bell's palsy, and shot four times while sitting in a car watching a playground basketball game in Southwest Philadelphia. A companion sitting behind the wheel was fatally wounded. All the while, Fletcher was still competing as a fighter. He retired at age thirty-four in August 1990. In his ten years as a pro, he'd compiled a record of twenty-four wins and four losses. On retirement he stayed close to the only real home he'd known, South Philly. Few boxers wind up with any money once they retire, so they tend to return to their roots in an environment that's not terribly pleasant or safe.

Christopher, Fletcher said, had earlier stuck up a craps game, taking fifty dollars from him. When Fletcher saw Christopher again after the incident, he punched him, and Christopher pulled out his pistol. It wasn't a shocking tale in that part of the city.

In a standard deal, the prosecutor offered Fletcher the chance to plead guilty to third-degree murder and serve ten to twenty years. When Fletcher refused and opted to roll the dice on a trial, the prosecutor asked for a death sentence. The district attorney at the time was execution devotee Lynne Abraham. "Abraham's office seeks death virtually as often as the law will allow," wrote Tina Rosenberg in the *New York Times Magazine*.[3] Abraham had once posed on the cover of *Philadelphia* magazine cradling a submachine gun.

Had Fletcher accepted the plea bargain offered to him, he'd probably have been freed many years ago and wouldn't be threatened with execution. If you think about it, he's no longer doing time for shooting Christopher. He's on death row for refusing to accept the deal offered back in 1992. It's largely because of such courtroom outcomes that 95 percent of defendants take a deal.[4]

Later it turned out that key facts in Fletcher's case were kept from the jury. Others were manufactured, plain and simple. For example, the prosecutor preposterously claimed that Fletcher was called "Two Guns" because he carried two guns on the street, but any Philadelphia fight fan could have informed the court that the nickname was a boxing alias referring to his ability to land telling shots with both hands. There was a dreadful lack of communication between Fletcher and his court-appointed attorney, Stephen Patrizio, who never corrected the mistake. Patrizio subsequently confessed to a host of other trial errors. Probably the most grievous was his failure to object to the judge's flawed instructions to jurors. The judge was supposed to inform them they could find Fletcher guilty of voluntary manslaughter or involuntary manslaughter instead of murder. An objection at the time might have led to a much lighter sentence or given Fletcher substantive grounds for an appeal. A competent attorney always looks for such gifts, but the defense in this case never tore off the wrapping. In a deposition taken from him later, Patrizio made it clear that his principal strategy was to take the deal. He didn't even challenge hearsay testimony from Grant.

Jurors were also not told that Christopher, shot in his leg and right side, bled to death in the hospital after his mother, a Jehovah's Witness, denied him a crucial transfusion on religious grounds. In addition, vital physical evidence—Christopher's clothes—never made its way from police investigators to the medical examiner's office, leading advocates for Fletcher to believe that they contained powder burns that would have confirmed his account of the shooting.

The eyewitness testimony from Grant allowed the prosecution to argue that it had proved its shaky case beyond a reasonable doubt, even though her version of events didn't square with the facts. She said Fletcher shot Christopher from a distance, but the autopsy showed that the two bullets entered from steep angles, which supported Fletcher's account of a hand-to-hand battle. Hard-nosed detectives who revisited the case later agreed that with or without Grant, circumstances didn't merit a first-degree charge. Looking back after all these years, it's difficult to argue that keeping Fletcher locked up any longer makes sense and even tougher to make a case for lethal injection.

Robert Cassidy, a former associate editor of *Ring* magazine, wrote about Fletcher and holes in the case against him in the August 2000 issue. Ake Sintring, who lives in Sweden, read the article and eventually formed a group to work on Fletcher's behalf. After Sintring brought the case to my attention, I wrote about it in a column for the September 2011 issue of *Ring* and later in a series of articles for BoxingInsider.com. Although Fletcher's history as a prizefighter lifted his case from the pile and got it attention, reversing a conviction is still a steep uphill climb, particularly when the defense attorney fails to lay out grounds for appeal during the trial. Fletcher was caught in a perfect storm. Although Patrizio did an awful job defending his client, somehow his mistakes were deemed not quite grievous enough to win a new trial. So the case has withstood legal challenges even though the charges were never fairly tested. What Fletcher got wasn't imperfect justice, which, though less than desirable, might be understandable. Fletcher's case is an example of sloppy justice, something no one should have to settle for. His attorney never tried to contact Hydow Park, the chief medical examiner who conducted the autopsy. Park later testified during the appeals process that had he been subpoenaed, he'd have supported Fletcher's story, not Grant's, as conforming to the postmortem evidence.[5]

■ COPS, CROOKS, CONFUSION

When informants like Natalie Renee Grant trade favors with authorities, the resulting relationships can sometimes wander into foggy regions where cops and crooks aren't sorted easily. Boss and subordinate might even switch roles. Ex-LAPD detective Mike Rothmiller learned early in his career that drug informants regularly build their own sales and avoid arrest by informing on their enemies, who are generally competing dealers.[6] Their police handlers also win in this deal by padding their arrest statistics. Rothmiller recalls arranging to meet a DEA agent at an informant's home. When he entered the living room, he was startled to find the informant cutting up a mound of cocaine on a glass coffee table and dividing it into sales packages. The agent privately explained to Rothmiller that the dealer claimed to have information on a major marijuana-growing operation. "You gotta do what you gotta do," he told Rothmiller with a shrug.[7]

Barbara Dougan of Families Against Mandatory Minimums (FAMM) pointed out another dubious trick: catch a drug offender and convince the individual to "reel some other poor slob in."[8] Cops pressure the informant to set up bigger purchases to trigger a longer mandatory sentence. They may also instruct informants to set up a buy at an address near a school. That adds another two years. When it works, police can boast of nabbing a kingpin selling drugs around schoolchildren when in fact they've used their authority to create a farce. This happened to Tony Ealy, who in 1994, after being laid off by a failed company in Michigan (he'd also experienced layoffs from two previous employers), was introduced to crack by a former co-worker.[9] Ealy, a workingman his whole life, was quickly hooked. He learned to sell part of his purchases to interested friends to support his habit, but he never bought more than fifty dollars' worth. When police found drugs on a young woman acquaintance, she turned informant. The woman and her handlers set up controlled buys from Ealy. Accompanied by her "boyfriend," an undercover cop, the woman demanded escalating amounts, luring Ealy into larger deals on both ends. In six weeks, thanks to police encouragement, the quantities went from an eighth of a gram to 250 grams. On the fifth and largest sale, police closed in. Ealy pleaded guilty and in 1995, at age thirty-four, was sentenced to 33 to 110 years under the state mandatory minimum laws then in force.

Ealy enrolled in every drug rehab program he could find in the prison system, and finally in December 2010 the state legislature, following the advice of the parole board, commuted his sentence. He was released after spending nearly a third of his life behind bars.

Sometimes when informants experience pangs of conscience, police call upon special tactics. For example, Los Angeles police ran into trouble trying to convince a pimp named John Jones to turn informant and lie for them in a 1994 murder trial. So they lied to Jones, informing him that other witnesses had positively identified Obie Anthony and Reggie Cole as the gunmen who shot down Felipe Gonzalez Angeles outside a whorehouse. They also told Jones that they had additional evidence against Anthony and Cole even though they didn't. Jones never got a good look at the gunmen, but assuming he'd be fingering two guilty men, he went along with the police officers' plan. In exchange for his false testimony, prosecutors promised to give him a lighter sentence on pandering charges. Then they sat mute as Jones, in the witness box, said what he'd been coached to say, which included a declaration that he'd been promised no favors or special treatment for his testimony.

Ironically, the case unraveled after Cole, claiming self-defense, stabbed another inmate to death in Calipatria State Prison in 2000. Because he'd already been convicted of the 1994 murder, he was now at risk for the death penalty. That prompted students interning for the Northern California Innocence Project to look into his case. As they dug into the facts of the inmate slaying, they reviewed the bawdy-house shooting and uncovered a torrent of lies and fabrications, including the dirty deal cops made with Jones. They found that detectives had prompted a second witness by tapping on the photos of Cole and Anthony during an identification session.

Eventually Cole agreed to plead guilty to manslaughter in the prison slaying so that his conviction for the whorehouse killing would be overturned, and he and Anthony were both released after seventeen years in prison. But despite its lies and other extralegal tactics used to secure convictions, the Los Angeles District Attorney's Office still fought to keep them locked up. "When someone gets killed at a brothel, your witnesses aren't going to be priests and nuns," prosecutor Scott Collins said. The judge who released Anthony berated prosecutors for withholding evidence, but apparently the scolding was the extent of their punishment.[10]

The New York Innocence Project found that in more than 15 percent of wrongful convictions overturned by DNA testing, an informant or jailhouse snitch had testified against the defendant. "Often, statements from people with incentives to testify—particularly incentives that are not disclosed to the jury—are the central evidence in convicting an innocent person," said the study. The study found both snitches who had been paid to testify and others who testified in exchange for their release from prison. It also found witnesses who "testified in multiple distinct cases that they have evidence of guilt, through overhearing a confession or witnessing the crime."[11]

■ KILLER INFORMANT

In a notorious case of confused loyalties and nebulous justice, informant James "Whitey" Bulger, a powerful Irish mob boss in the Boston area, worked secretly with the Federal Bureau of Investigation (FBI) to convict his rivals in the Italian Mafia during the 1980s. His handler, John Connolly, who grew up in Bulger's neighborhood, became an agency star as the Italian mob was gradually taken apart thanks to his connection to Bulger. Meanwhile, Bulger, shielded from arrest, prospered while also committing a string of murders plotted with his ally Stephen "the Rifleman" Flemmi. G-men looked the other way while their informant murdered people.[12] When Martin Scorsese made his Oscar-winning film *The Departed*, which was based largely on the Bulger case, many considered the police characters' indifference to the rising body count unrealistic. But their passivity was in fact true to life.

In 2002 a jury convicted Connolly of racketeering, obstruction of justice, and lying to the FBI. Connolly's boss, John Morris, testifying against him under the cloak of immunity, admitted that in exchange for thousands of dollars, he'd also relayed information, including the identity of an informant whom Bulger subsequently murdered, to Bulger and Flemmi. Thanks to his testimony, Morris received dispensation while Connolly got a ten-year prison sentence. Meanwhile, Bulger went underground in 1995, after Connolly warned him an indictment was imminent.

In 2008 another jury convicted Connolly of second-degree murder for telling Bulger that an accountant had agreed to testify against him. The accountant was subsequently murdered. Connolly was sentenced to another forty years. Bulger, among the FBI's ten most wanted, was finally arrested in 2011, at the age of eighty-one, in Santa Monica, California, where he lived quietly with his girlfriend. This scandal that still won't die is among the most embarrassing suffered by the FBI since its impervious oligarch, the late J. Edgar Hoover, was accused of cross-dressing and attending gay orgies.

The Bulger-Connolly connection is unusual in that we know about it at all. Most cop-informant relationships remain under the radar.

PART 2
Failed Laws

4

The War on Drugs
(and Reason)

TWO YEARS BEFORE THE END OF HIS MANDATORY TEN-YEAR TERM FOR CRACK possession, James Allen was transferred from a private prison in Southern California to a federal penitentiary in Oregon so that he could participate in a drug program and knock a few months off his sentence. Clearly no threat to anyone, he was sent unescorted. Authorities handed him a bus ticket, and he traveled approximately a thousand miles on his own so that he could knock on the door of his new prison to be locked up again. Congressional crime busters had terminated parole in the federal system back in the eighties, so it was impossible to do the rational thing and let Allen go home. Absurdities like these transpire every day as various segments of the criminal justice system dutifully follow the path laid out for them by meticulous policies that allow no deviations. And nowhere is irrationality more evident than in the drug statutes.

People don't become addicted to drugs because they're living fine lives. Some drug users may be seeking thrills or just going along with the group, but in most cases they're miserable. "The feeling they're looking for is not to feel anything, which we would all like sometimes," said Peggy Reavey, a drug counselor at an outpatient clinic in Wilmington, a gritty blue-collar neighborhood along the Los Angeles Harbor.[1] Most of Reavey's clients are sent by the court system, and many of them come from jail or prison. Jailing addicts in response to their quest for emotional escape is of questionable value, but under our system, jail is the knee-jerk response to drug use and abuse.

When Reavey worked for another rehabilitation clinic, she met an addict who spent twenty years on the street before she decided she had had enough and sought treatment. "This woman was living under a freeway," recalled Reavey. "She had to get up every morning, bum a quarter, and call. That was the rule. And she did it every day until she got in. She had to wait seventy days."

Although no definitive study has measured the frequency of what psychiatrists call dual-diagnosis behavior, it's no secret that mentally ill folks commonly turn to street drugs to fight off the demons in their minds. These desperate attempts to self-medicate may give sufferers a recess, but eventually the drugs turn on them and inflict pain. And when authorities catch them, these drug users face legal punishment as well.

The cops arrested Allen, an ex-Crip and former heavyweight boxer who's now a sheet-metal worker in Los Angeles, two years after he'd taken a job and gone straight, leaving drugs and gangs behind. He'd been ratted out by an active criminal who wangled himself a better deal from federal prosecutors for giving them a former criminal.[2] Authorities never identified the informant who turned Allen in, but larger fish have long lists of minnows they can trade to police and prosecutors hungry to inflate their numbers. One of the bigger fallacies in the war on drugs is that it focuses on those at the top of the trading chain. Mostly it takes down the small fry, sometimes even reformed small fry like Allen, who was torn away from his job so he could serve time for dealing crack years earlier.[3]

"They [law enforcement] don't really stop to think about what this person is doing now," said ex-convict Brenda Valencia. "So they don't care if one person is dealing drugs and another is living honestly. They just want more bodies to throw in prison." Meanwhile, she said, the hard-core dealers "know how the system works. They cooperate and then they move on somewhere else to do it all over again. They're gaming the system."[4] Sometimes they bargain their way out of a long stretch by agreeing to turn over cash proceeds from sales, a circumstance so common it has a name—cash-register justice. Once again, the bigger the dealers, the more they have to trade.

■ TELL-ALL WARRIORS

In 1993 I was introduced to a retired treasury agent who'd spent most of his career chasing drug offenders and ultimately concluded that it was a waste of time, that a "war" originally intended to prevent drug use only exacerbated it. This was shortly after I'd written a book with ex-LAPD detective Mike Rothmiller that exposed an elaborate police network that spied on politicians and celebrities not suspected of any crimes. The ex-T-man wanted me to help him write a book about the irrational, failed war on drugs from the perspective of a soldier down in the trenches who'd seen its pointlessness from the inside. The retired agent felt used and betrayed. He'd devoted all those working · years to a giant snipe hunt, and he was indignantly angry. When my agent sounded out publishers, they all gave the same answer: The country was teeming with disgusted ex-combatants seeking to expose the war on drugs as a sham and a scam. Several had already produced books, some of them quite good, but to no effect. This was a war without end that proceeds past all barriers, past reason, logic, experience, science, and humanitarian impulse. Publishers told my agent that they were weary of it.

Despite massive, irrefutable evidence that the drug war is counterproductive—that even arresting a kingpin merely creates a job opening for another kingpin—exposing these facts never seems to affect policy. Instead there's a never-ending campaign to choke off the oxygen of the drug trade at every conceivable phase, to seize suppliers, users, and the drugs themselves no matter how quickly they're all replicated. The more this policy fails, the more resources it devours. Over the years it's spawned a vast, powerful industry that thrives on a dysfunctional strategy. Minus the nukes, it works similarly to the military-industrial complex, which remains geared up to fight multiple wars even though it can't name any formidable enemies.

■ "NO HARM TO OTHERS"

In June 2011 the Global Commission on Drug Policy, a high-powered group of former world leaders, including former United Nations (UN) secretary-general Kofi Annan and past presidents of Mexico, Brazil, and Colombia, issued a report that concluded the global war on drugs has been a disastrous failure that foments violence and doesn't curtail drug use. The group urged an end to "criminalization, marginalization and stigmatization of people who use drugs but do no harm to others." The report noted that in the ten years after 1998, despite a massive escalation of the drug war, global consumption of opiates had increased 34.5 percent, cocaine 27 percent, and cannabis 8.5 percent.[5] The Obama administration, knowing the report was in the works, issued a prepared dismissal. "Making drugs more available—as this report suggests—will make it harder to keep our communities healthy and safe," said Rafael Lemaitre, spokesman for the White House Office of National Drug Control Policy.[6] If, as Socrates said at his trial, the unexamined life is not worth living, what are we to conclude about a policy that, despite having been proved a failure after endless examination and reexamination, is doggedly pursued by those in power?

In an op-ed column in the *New York Times*, former president Jimmy Carter hailed the global commission's report as an extraordinary new initiative and pronounced its recommendations "profoundly important." He pointed out that in 1977 he'd advised Congress that penalties leveled "against possession of a drug should not be more damaging to an individual than the use of the drug itself." This simple concept has a wisdom that is immediately apparent. In the seventies, he wrote, the idea was widely accepted.[7] No more. For every defendant who gets a break, there is a Patricia Marilyn Spottedcrow. In 2010, at age twenty-five, Spottedcrow was sentenced to twelve years in prison for selling thirty dollars' worth of pot to an informant.[8] A mother of four, she had no previous convictions. Kingfisher County, Oklahoma, judge Susie Pritchett handed down the sentence about a month before she retired. Her replacement later shaved four years off the sentence. "I'm sleeping next to people who have killed people, and they have less time than me," Spottedcrow said a year after being processed into the Eddie Warrior Correctional Center. Her mother, Delita Starr, was convicted in the same case, but Pritchett suspended her thirty-year sentence so she could raise Spottedcrow's children. Starr, who was earning eight dollars an hour at a truck stop, was also sentenced to five years of drug and alcohol monitoring. On top of it all, Pritchett leveled fines of $2,740 against Spottedcrow and $8,600 against Starr. Both women turned down plea deals of two years in prison because they thought that sentence excessive. After the facts of this bizarre case were picked up by national news media, the parole board and Governor Mary Fallin rushed through Spottedcrow's early parole, and she was released after two years.[9]

POINTLESS PENALTIES

Michelle Collette's father was an addict who bounced in and out of jail during her childhood in Boston. Collette eventually became addicted to Percocet, a prescription painkiller, and she and her boyfriend also sold it. In August 2000 police raided their home and found 607 pills and $901 in cash. They also found more than fourteen grams of oxycodone, an even stronger painkiller, which triggered a five-year mandatory sentence. Collette's boyfriend, who opted for a trial, was sentenced to fifteen years in prison. Collette took a deal for seven years.

At sentencing, Massachusetts Superior Court judge Isaac Borenstein took issue with the sentence that state law forced him to pronounce. "I do what the law requires me to do with not one ounce of pleasure," he told Collette. "I don't think this is fair. I don't think this is what our laws are meant to do. It's going to cost upwards of $50,000 a year to have you in state prison. Had I the authority, I would send you to jail for no more than one year . . . and a program after that."[10] A month into her sentence, Collette discovered she was pregnant, and she subsequently gave birth while chained to a hospital bed.

"TERRIBLE ESCALATION"

Richard Nixon, in 1971, was the first to use the term "war on drugs," but the big shift came at the start of the 1980s, when President Reagan and Congress began directing policy "toward futile efforts to control drug imports from foreign countries." According to Carter, "One result [of this shift] has been a terrible escalation in drug-related violence, corruption, and gross violations of human rights in a growing number of Latin American countries." About 75 percent of new admissions to state prisons are for nonviolent crimes, and "the single greatest cause of prison population growth has been the war on drugs with the number of people incarcerated for nonviolent drug offenses increasing more than twelve-fold since 1980."[11]

There was no easing of the drug war under President Clinton, who raised the director of the Office of National Drug Control Policy (a.k.a. the drug czar) to cabinet-level status. Clinton, whose brother Roger had been addicted to cocaine, understood that drug use wasn't always the harmless pursuit that advocates like the late Hunter Thompson alleged it to be. Clinton ended up signing off on a number of strict bills that treated users and small-time dealers like enemy combatants. At the end of his term, he pardoned his brother, but his hard-line policies persisted. Later, he had a change of heart and appeared with Carter in a 2012 documentary by filmmaker Sam Branson called *Breaking the Taboo*, which called for an end to the ill-conceived war on drugs. The film, narrated by Morgan Freeman, includes pleas from Bill Clinton, Jimmy Carter, former Colombian president Juan Manuel Santos, and other former world leaders, who all call for a halt to the "war" and the creation of a global policy that will confront the drug problem without futile reliance on excessively punitive policies that don't work.[12]

In the summer of 2011 Inimai Chettiar, American Civil Liberties Union (ACLU) policy counsel, noted that the report by the Global Commission on Drug Policy was yet another in a long line of studies condemning U.S. drug policy as nonsensical. "In no other area of criminal law," he said, "do we lock up huge numbers of people because they might pose threats to themselves, but have done nothing to harm another person. . . . Prison neither treats nor trains nor rehabilitates. Instead, prison makes people more likely to commit crimes in the future and makes them effectively unemployable with little hope of a future."[13]

Advocates for generic hard-line punishment argue that perspective comes only from seeing victims in the flesh and hearing their stories. But drug users brought into the courthouse, generally in chains because they can't afford to post bail, are their own victims. They are the human element in the story.

"I was a public defender in the far southeastern corner of Kentucky," said Nathan Miller, who entered private practice after serving more than a year with the state.

> There, if you are caught with drugs, you might as well be caught with a dead body or child porn. The commonwealth attorney's

offers were shocking to the senses in all felony drug-trafficking
cases. For example, when a first-time offender caught selling to
a confidential informant via a controlled buy that involved only
one pill (usually Oxycontin), the standard offer was three years
in state prison. The max is five for such an offense. On two
different occasions, I had a client that wanted their day in court.
The evidence was clear and there was no doubt there would be
a guilty verdict.

In Kentucky jurors can set the sentence, and in both cases the jury
came back with two years after the commonwealth asked for the
max. "This seemed to anger the prosecution," said Miller.[14]

One could argue that Miller's two clients were fortunate to receive a year less than the plea deal they'd been offered. But it could
also be argued that imposing a two-year sentence for selling one prescription painkilling pill is an absurd waste of government resources
and incredible overkill in terms of teaching lessons to the first-time
offender. The two juries, once they examined actual circumstances
and measured them against the standard penalty, clearly concluded
that the standard penalty was excessive. One has to wonder whether
courts that routinely mete out these over-the-top sentences have lost
sight of how long it takes for two or three years to pass—or, for that
matter, how long a week can seem to an individual who is stuck in a
cell. And then, of course, there is the difficulty of spending a lifetime
struggling against the stigma of being an ex-convict.

■ TINY WORLD OF ADDICTS

Addicts tend to choose cocaine, crack cocaine, methamphetamines,
or heroin on a mostly exclusive basis, forming a kind of tribal loy-
alty around their drug of choice. Interviewers find over and over that
each tribe tends to look askance at the others. This is the case even
in homeless encampments. Acquiring drugs becomes the center of
the addicts' universe. They're like greyhounds perennially chasing
a mechanical rabbit. The behavior can manifest itself gradually or
quite quickly. In his autobiography *Life*, recovered heroin addict and
Rolling Stone lead guitarist Keith Richards bragged that thanks to his
worldwide contacts, he was able to obtain high-quality heroin with

little trouble just about everywhere. But elsewhere in the same book he described risking life and limb in various underworld hell-scapes as he desperately chased down another fix.[15]

Declares drug counselor Reavey,

> Your world gets incredibly tiny. When you make it off drugs, you need to fill your world again. So you have to fall in love with being clean, not just with not being an addict, because that's not enough. The ones with jobs and education have a better chance, but drugs, as we say, are cunning, baffling, and powerful. You can be walking down the street and not even feeling bad, and somebody offers you something, and you're right back where you were. Maybe you're a crack addict. But just taking a drink or two can ruin your judgment, and next thing you know you're back to crack. So you have to stay away from triggers. Maybe, for instance, you can't go to weddings anymore.

The great jazz trumpeter Miles Davis recounted locking himself in a room at his father's house in St. Louis and not emerging until he was clean again. The story became part of his legend. But witnesses say that years later, when his health took a wrong turn and it affected his ability to make music, he returned to heroin.[16]

There's no one-size-fits-all approach to the monster problem of drug abuse. In some instances, cutting off the supply of crystal-meth, for example, may be a valid course of action because the physical properties of the drug make it so addictive.[17] Although the final product is easily manufactured from mostly household substances, its base is pseudoephedrine or ephedrine, ingredients that come from sophisticated labs that drug cartels have so far been unable to duplicate. Illicit peddlers must have, somewhere in the supply chain, access to legal manufacturers of these substances. These manufacturers can be monitored and regulated if the government has the will to thwart the pharmaceutical industry (which fights this particular idea along with other regulations).

Researchers now know that crystal meth alters brain structure in a way that impedes the natural creation of dopamine, which stimulates pleasure. Meth addicts thus find themselves in a dismal world that they can't escape without more crystal meth. Explaining all this to an addict is of limited value, even when the explanation comes from a proficient counselor. It's not clear how long it takes to raise the addict's natural dopamine to sufficient levels after he or she gets clean; it could take years. Some users may never respond positively to therapy. Not everyone can summon the ambition, strength, or will that's required. But helping institutions ought to be accessible, not painfully scarce and scattered within a bureaucratic and financial maze, as they are today.

As addicts focus their lives on acquiring prohibited drugs, they typically buy and sell them among themselves and are periodically charged with possessing, transporting, or peddling. The criminalization of these activities makes it more costly to supply and transport the substances, which raises their price. Law Enforcement Against Prohibition (LEAP), an organization of current and former members of the criminal justice system who have turned against national drug policy, points out that marijuana is worth more than gold and heroin more than uranium.[18]

A large number of the arraignments and hearings in today's criminal courts involves drugs, either directly or indirectly. Indirect cases include addicts' acts of theft or violence to obtain the cash to buy drugs at ever-higher prices. The addicts certainly can't claim innocence in these situations, but it's unlikely they'd be committing all these crimes if drugs were, at least to some extent, decriminalized, the way tobacco and alcohol are. Smokers don't hold up gas stations to get cigarette money. The single worst blow the U.S. government could deliver to criminal drug gangs is to decriminalize their product. As things stand, arresting a drug dealer merely creates an opportunity for someone else to sell to his former customers.

■ RAND STUDY

When individuals become addicted to assault, rape, burglary, or murder, it's clear that their compulsions are criminal acts, but it's never been clear why drug users should suffer the same punishments as these other offenders. A RAND Corporation analysis has concluded that a dollar spent on drug treatment is eight times more effective in curtailing the flow of narcotics than a dollar spent to further the practice of mandatory sentencing of drug offenders. And it's much easier and more cost-effective to prevent addiction through education than to cure it later. The RAND study didn't contend that illicit drugs are harmless to the user, and it didn't argue with the mission of curtailing drug use. It merely used empiric means to determine optimum tactics and strategy against drug use.[19]

Likewise, former Seattle police chief Norm Stamper does not claim that it's a fine idea for folks to sit around the house smoking crack. But making drug use a flat-out crime, argues Stamper, a prime mover within LEAP, doesn't work. Criminalizing drugs means they remain unregulated and untaxed. It also means that the criminal networks that take over the distribution of drugs can sell them to children or mix them with rat poison. Further, criminalizing drugs requires police to focus less on fighting real crime and to divert their attention to making drug arrests. Stamper began seriously questioning drug policy when, as an officer on the street, he had to spend several hours processing a low-level marijuana bust.[20]

In May 2009 Obama's drug czar, Gil Kerlikowske, declared an end to the war on drugs, but it soon became clear that all the administration really ended was the use of a nomenclature that had become an embarrassment. Policy remained the same. LEAP, after examining the data, concluded that like the Bush administration, the Obama administration heavily favored spending on punishment over treatment, "even though [Obama] has said drug addiction should be handled as a health issue."[21] The DEA under Obama even stepped up raids against medical marijuana shops, which have been made legal in a growing number of states but are still forbidden under federal law.

Observing what's considered the fortieth anniversary of the drug war in June 2011, LEAP officers tried to deliver a copy of their legalization recommendations to Kerlikowske. The drug czar refused to meet with them. A staffer accepted the document down in the lobby. LEAP executive director Neill Franklin, a former Baltimore narcotics cop, used the occasion to note that in 1971 there were fewer than half a million drug arrests, whereas forty years later there were nearly 2 million annually. According to LEAP, the United States had already spent a trillion dollars on the drug war by the year 2011. Two years earlier *Time* stated the true sum was closer to $2.5 trillion. Whatever the true number, it's clear that the cost has been too high.

The implacable commanders waging the war on drugs have learned to use tools such as the Patriot Act to further their mission.

The original Patriot Act that glided over legislative gates in the wake of 9/11, for example, legalized "sneak-and-peek" searches that allowed authorities to undertake black-bag jobs against suspects without notifying them that their premises had been searched. Naturally, these searches were sold as a way to capture terrorists, but Ryan Grim at the *Huffington Post*, who gained legal access to a July 2009 report from the Administrative Office of the U.S. Courts, reported that of 763 sneak-and-peek search warrants issued the previous year, only three were related to alleged terrorist offenses. That equals less than one-half of 1 percent. Nearly two-thirds (62 percent) were issued to investigate suspected drug offenses.[22] Then-senator Russ Feingold (D-WI) called it "quite extraordinary to grant government agents the statutory authority to secretly break into American homes in criminal cases, and I think some Americans might be concerned it's been used hundreds of times in just a single year in non-terrorism cases."[23]

■ MOST HARMFUL DRUG

A 2010 research project undertaken by Britain's Centre for Crime and Justice Studies ranked the dangers of the most widely used drugs by analyzing a broad range of factors: how addictive the drug is, what harm it causes to the human body, environmental and family damage, and the drain on resources. Crack cocaine, methamphetamine, and heroin were more lethal to individuals, but when wider social effects were also considered, alcohol outranked all other substances.[24]

LEAP calls drug interdiction "prohibition" because America's thirteen years of failed alcohol prohibition are so clearly analogous to the drug war. Prohibition corrupted large swaths of police forces across the United States until it was finally repealed in 1933. Stamper and others who've quit the drug army point out that corruption is one of the many unintended negative consequences of existing policy. J. Edgar Hoover, normally quick to expand his bureaucratic turf, made sure the FBI wasn't responsible for narcotics enforcement. He didn't want his agents contaminated by the bribes that would surely be offered to his agents by drug networks.

So, it shouldn't be any surprise that contemporary criminal syndicates use part of their financial gains, astronomically enhanced by the government's attempts to stem drug flow, to corrupt police. U.S.

Customs and Border Protection (CBP) reported in 2011 that during the previous seven years more than a hundred of its employees had been arrested or indicted for corruption, most in the cases relating to drug smuggling. "We have had recent persons hired within the last few years revealed to have entered on duty with CBP with the intent of engaging in corruption," said James Tomsheck, assistant commissioner for the CBP's Office of Internal Affairs. One-third of the agency's job applicants failed lie-detector tests and it's not known how many of these failed applicants might have been planning to augment their salaries by accepting cash for looking the other way.[25]

■ PLANTING EVIDENCE

Accepting bribes from drug sellers isn't the only form of corruption that police surrender to. Many defendants have accused police officers of planting drugs to secure a conviction. It's impossible to know how frequently evidence planting occurs, but we know it does because sometimes the police are caught. Because the simple possession of a routinely available commodity is enough evidence to secure conviction, police officers have enormous power, and they're not all strong enough to handle it. A much-documented blue veil of secrecy protects indiscretions, great and small, by those who step over the line.[26]

In November 2006 Atlanta police smashed their way into the home of an elderly woman, Kathryn Johnston, after a drug dealer they'd arrested earlier identified her modest house as a narcotics dispensary. In the search warrant, the police falsely claimed that an informant had purchased drugs at the Johnston home and that the drug ring using the house had installed surveillance equipment. These claims allowed them to obtain a no-knock warrant. When the officers began battering down her door, Mrs. Johnston, who lived alone, took out a gun and fired a single shot through the door. Police returned fire, killing her. "She was without question an innocent civilian who was caught in the worst circumstance imaginable," Fulton County district attorney Paul Howard said. "When we learned of her death, all of us imagined our own mothers and our own grandmothers in her place, and the thought made us shudder."[27]

After pouring into the house and finding no drugs, officers planted three bags of marijuana at the scene. They also turned in cocaine they said had been purchased at the house. But the botched raid garnered the attention of federal authorities, and it led them, said U.S. attorney David Nahmias, to discover a "culture of misconduct" in the Atlanta Police Department relating to drug arrests. Previous raids and arrests were also investigated after two officers who accepted plea bargains recounted details of other instances in which police lied to obtain search warrants and fabricated documentation of drug purchases. Officers cut corners, they said in their plea agreements, to "be considered productive officers and to meet [the department's] performance targets."[28]

In 2008 New York Police Department officers in Brooklyn and Queens were caught hanging on to drugs they seized from suspects. At the time, authorities said the officers were using the drugs to reward informants. But the truth was darker. In a case against another officer in 2011, Steve Anderson, a former undercover cop, testified that to boost their arrest statistics, police routinely planted drugs on suspects, including individuals who'd never been arrested before. Anderson said that this practice was called "attaching bodies" to the drugs. In one instance, for which he was later indicted, Anderson himself had bought three bags of cocaine from a waiter and a disc jockey in a nightclub. He gave two of them to another officer, Henry Tavarez, who was having trouble meeting his arrest quota. Tavarez took the drugs back inside the club and used the "evidence" to arrest four people. Both Anderson and Tavarez pleaded guilty to misconduct in their case.[29]

During the 2011 trial of the other officer, a judge asked Anderson what went through his mind as he helped frame innocent people. "Seeing it so much, it's almost like you have no emotion with it," Anderson replied. Prosecutors in Brooklyn and Queens were forced to dismiss about four hundred criminal cases based on these revelations.[30] Lawyers raced around town, vying to find falsely convicted people and file civil cases on their behalf.

■ "SOMETHING I DID NOT DO"

Sheila Devereux, convicted of drug trafficking in Tulsa, Oklahoma, was sentenced to life in prison under the state's three strikes law in 2005. She'd refused to accept a plea deal to serve seven years "because I was not going to plead guilty to something I did not do." She said she had no knowledge of the six-plus grams of cocaine that police said they found in her boyfriend's home, where she'd been staying temporarily while apartment hunting. She was, she said, completely clean of drugs when the Tulsa cops swept through the house. Back then, she said, she still "had faith in the justice system." Her boyfriend ended up taking a deal to serve thirteen years for possessing approximately six hundred dollars' worth of drugs.[31]

Amazingly, Devereux, who was forty-two at the time of her arrest, remained incarcerated even after federal indictments alleged that two of the cops who raided the home, Officer Nick DeBruin and retired officer Harold R. Wells, belonged to a ring of eight Tulsa cops who stole drugs and money, planted drugs, falsified search warrants, tampered with witnesses, and violated civil rights. Tulsa deputy police chief Mark McCrory testified in federal court that at least one of those eight officers was also implicated in a multistate burglary ring that might be linked to several homicides. More than twenty cases were overturned as a result of the alleged ring of dirty cops. Devereux finally gained her freedom in 2011 when a court placed her on probation.[32]

It's worth noting the specifics in the two previous convictions that prosecutors used to secure Devereux's life sentence. In November 1998 she had overdosed on cocaine. After recovering in the hospital, she was taken straight to jail and charged with felony possession. Several years later her truck broke down, and as she waited for help on the side of the road, police pulled up, found a marijuana cigarette in her car, and charged her with her second felony. She'd been sentenced to probation in both cases.

The ex-legislator who had originally introduced the three-strikes life-without-parole bill said later that he was offended by Devereux's life sentence. He claimed the bill was intended as a way to crack down on violent habitual offenders.[33] This intention, however, was apparently not conveyed in the language of the law. Too many legislators never learn that questions of crime and punishment are too complex to be answered by simplistic formulas that simply cannot fit every circumstance. Others learn the lesson too late, after they've inflicted more damage than they can ever repair. Whatever the intent of the legislation that ensnared Devereux, prosecutors were quick to take advantage of its broad language to obtain over-the-top sentences.

On Sept. 30, 2010, when the appellate court denied her appeal, it stated, "We find that [her] sentence does not shock the Court's conscience."[34] The criminal justice system doesn't outrage easily. The statute that put Devereux away for life remains on the books.

■ TWENTY DOLLARS, TWENTY-FIVE YEARS

In 1994 a California judge handed J. K. "Skip" Singh twenty-five years to life for a single rock of methamphetamine that fell out of his boot when he was booked at the jail in Bakersfield.[35] The arresting officer said he pulled Singh over because the light on his license plate was illegally tinted and then arrested him for driving under the influence (DUI) of a drug that turned out to be heroin. But it was the rock that would put him away for good.

No choir boy, Singh was a cast-off child who'd grown up in foster homes. At the time of his arrest in 1994 he was a heroin addict who'd already served sentences for robbery and attempted robbery. He'd also once failed to appear in court. His DUI arrest was on March 4, three days after the state's three-strikes law went into effect.

Heroin and meth habits are mutually exclusive; mixing the two substances in the bloodstream can easily result in death. Singh said that somebody had given him the rock of crystal meth weighing 0.22 gram, or less than 10 percent of a sugar packet, and that he "was planning to give it away." It was worth about twenty dollars on the street.

Singh, a cancer survivor, was in his mid-fifties when we talked in 2011. He pledged to walk a straight line should he ever make it out of prison. This type of talk is not surprising. But when I checked I learned that he actually had a job waiting for him at his brother-in-law's welding business in Missouri. By the time we spoke, he'd already served seventeen years for that twenty-dollar rock. His wife, Linda, still hopeful, visited him regularly. Even hard-core criminals, when they reach middle age, are much less likely to commit crimes, and Singh was unusually forthcoming about his previous offenses, which lent him some degree of credibility. According to younger convicts who served with him, he tenaciously lectured them to straighten out while there was still time. He'd become a father figure to a youthful prison population that was mostly fatherless.

Whatever he was planning to do with that rock those many years ago, the question now was, was it just to put him away for life for that sliver of dope? It's safe to say that no other Western democracy would inflict such a major penalty for a minor incident that involved no victim. But the intractable war on drugs provides a handy tool to put people like Singh away for good when the system tires of them. Twenty-five-to-life inmates rarely make it out of the California prison system. His first parole hearing was set for 2019. Had he beaten the odds and made it out then, he'd have served six years more than Hugo's Jean Valjean.

Singh did not make it to that hearing. Linda called in early 2012 to tell me he died in custody on the last day of 2011. "He developed an aortic dissection," she explained, a very dangerous condition in which there's bleeding into and along the wall of the major artery carrying blood out of the heart. The condition can be repaired with surgery, but Singh was prescribed medication instead. When his medication ran out, he told Linda, he was unable to renew his prescription. "He said he pleaded with the nurse," Linda told me, "but she just said, 'Next.'" Linda made many useless phone calls. People hung up on her, she waited and waited on hold, she was disconnected in transfer, she was sent on round-robins that took her back to the same extension—all the usual telephonic flip-offs that are geometrically expanded when penal authorities are involved.

Finally, after he suffered a series of small strokes, Singh was taken by ambulance from prison in Corcoran to the public hospital in Fresno. "When prisoners come into that hospital their families get one hour with them, one time. That's the rule," Linda said. "I drove up there and sat with him for the hour." He died before doctors could operate. The system didn't exactly kill him, but it didn't move mountains to save him either. It was a death rendered even more anxious and cheerless by his convict status.

■ BLACK GIRLFRIEND

Sergio Ayala was stopped in Pasadena for driving over a painted divider, the arresting officer said in his report.[36] That, recalls Mike Rothmiller, was one of the excuses an instructor at the Police Academy recommended to cadets who might need to fabricate probable cause after they hit the street. "Don't say it was an equipment violation because then you would need physical evidence, such as a broken tail light," the instructor explained. Instead, tell lies that can't be proved. Arresting officers doctor most of their reports in one way or another, Rothmiller maintains. Cops "weave a spell" over them "to make them fit their perceptions."

"Do you know why I stopped you?" the officer asked Ayala. No, he said. According to Ayala, the officer replied, "Well, when I see a black and a Hispanic together I know they're up to no good."

"I remember those words of his though seventeen years have passed," said Ayala, whose passenger, his girlfriend, was black. He was convicted of transporting nine grams of crack under a complicated formula that allowed the prosecution to count seven hundred dollars in cash as though it were part of the drug stash. He's now doing the familiar twenty-five years to life in Salinas Valley State Prison in Soledad, California, and remains tortured by his decision to turn down the six-year plea deal because he knew that under the law, the officer who pulled him over had no right to search him. As years pass it becomes harder and harder to appeal his case. Ayala, born in Mexico, was still struggling with English when he went inside. Other inmates helped him sift through statutes and court records related to his case. But witnesses disappear, cops retire to Idaho, evidence is lost, and what happened so long ago begins to feel trivial somehow, even less worthy of serious scrutiny than it was originally. Ayala's case is like some old cardboard box sitting on a shelf in someone's garage. There may be something inside, but no one is bothering to find out.

■ WRONGFUL SPEECH

Because the drug war is heavily spiced with elements of the irrational, its advocates tend to be more zealous in its defense, even to the point of monitoring its foot soldiers. Ask border patrol agent Bryan Gonzalez, who was fired for wrongful speech.[37] On a slow day in April 2009, as he worked near Deming, New Mexico, Gonzalez and fellow agent Shawn Montoya pulled their vehicles next to each other, rolled down their windows, and shot the breeze. During the course of the conversation, Gonzalez remarked that present policy wasn't working and that legalizing drugs would be the most effective way to curtail violence along the border. He mentioned LEAP and also expressed sympathy for migrants whom agents routinely intercepted crossing from Mexico to seek work. Montoya disagreed, but the conversation remained friendly and, Gonzalez thought, unremarkable. Later, however, Montoya related the discussion to another agent who reported it to Washington. Soon Gonzalez was the subject of an internal affairs investigation.

Gonzalez didn't even know he was being investigated when, obeying what he thought was a routine request from his supervisor, he reported to the El Paso office. In El Paso his interrogators asked questions such as, Do you have plans to overthrow the government? and Are you a socialist? Agents reminded the shocked Gonzalez that he hadn't quite finished his two-year probationary period. They collected his badge and gun that very day. In the termination letter that soon followed, the agency decreed that Gonzalez held "personal views that were contrary to the core characteristics of Border Patrol agents, which are patriotism, dedication, and esprit de corps."[38] Gonzalez later complained that he was fired for using the rights afforded citizens by "the very Constitution I swore to uphold."[39] Aided by both LEAP and the ACLU, he sued for wrongful termination and compensatory and punitive damages.

Terry Nelson, a LEAP board member and former Border Patrol agent, jumped to Gonzalez's defense. "There's no doubt that the so-called war on drugs is a gigantic failure and that it causes violence, hurts our economy and forces dedicated law enforcers to risk their lives in the line of fire for a lost cause," he said. Agents like Gonzalez who put their lives on the line, he added, should have the right "to exercise the First Amendment and share their views on policies that impact them on a daily basis."[40]

Gonzalez's case is reminiscent of Hans Christian Anderson's story "The Emporer's New Clothes," except in the story a child exposes the emperor's nakedness. In this case, Gonzalez was punished for daring to speak the truth, and the emperor continued parading around without any clothes.

During World War II U.S. citizens who'd fought alongside Spanish loyalists against Francisco Franco were harassed by the FBI for being, as the saying went, "prematurely anti-fascist." At some point when drug laws catch up with good sense, victims of absurdity such as Gonzalez may well be seen as having been prematurely reasonable in their assessment of U.S. policy.

◼ MODERN LEPERS

In 1996 then-senator Phil Gramm (D-TX) tacked an amendment onto the Welfare Reform Act that barred drug offenders from receiving food stamps, public housing, or other forms of welfare. During the two minutes of debate allocated to his brainstorm, he said, "If we are serious about our drug laws, we ought not to give people welfare benefits who are violating the nation's drug laws."[41] Why this punishment must last for a lifetime was never explained. Nor was it explained why drug offenses were more serious than murder, rape, arson, or bodily mayhem, none of which were included in the ban.

The bill, with amendment intact, was quickly approved by Congress and signed by President Clinton. The law also enacted collective punishment, meaning if one family member was convicted, all other family members also lost the public housing benefit. It even created a catch-22 provision that made drug offenders ineligible for residential drug treatment because the government would no longer subsidize their room and board.

Two years after the Welfare Reform Act was passed, Congress enacted an equally punitive amendment to the Higher Education Act that denied loans, Pell grants, and even work-study jobs to the tens of thousands of would-be students who every year were convicted of drug offenses. Even those convicted for minor pot offenses were affected.[42] Once again, no other criminal conviction triggered such a ban. It was yet another law demonizing drug offenders for life, making them the modern version of biblical-era lepers.

These laws presume that drug offenders cannot be rehabilitated and that it's pointless to provide them with tools to help them climb out of their situations. Punishment must persist beyond their sentences and even outside the criminal justice system. By barring avenues of escape and rehabilitation, these discriminatory edicts work to perpetuate drug use and trafficking. Many users will consequently see drugs as a way to kill the pain of their statutorily enforced dead-end lives and will sell them to survive when education and employment are blocked.

■ MANDATORY FIVE YEARS

Until recently, statutes treated crack—cocaine cooked in baking powder—as though it were precisely a hundred times more potent than powdered cocaine. Unsupported by science, this equation was nonetheless repeated in an endless series of sensationalist stories that accepted it without checking it out, and these stories ultimately helped to transform hysteria and rumor into law.[43] The penalty ratio for crack was particularly damaging to minorities, especially African Americans, who used crack, a cheaper grade of cocaine, at higher rates than other ethnic groups did. A person convicted of possessing five grams of crack—about the weight of five packets of Sweet'N Low—received a mandatory five-year sentence. Finally, in 2010 President Obama signed legislation that reduced the formula so that it now takes twenty-eight grams to trigger the five-year sentence. The National Association for the Advancement of Colored People (NAACP) calculated that about twelve thousand inmates in custody would be released by retroactive aspects of the new table, which went into effect 2011; ten thousand of those inmates were African American. But Attorney General Eric Holder recommended that the number of early releases be sliced down to fifty-five hundred. The decisions were to rest with the judges who heard the cases. They could grant or deny prisoners' petitions or even initiate them on their own.[44]

Senator Charles E. Grassley (R-IA), the ranking Republican on the Judiciary Committee, called the reform a "bad idea." Representative Lamar Smith (R-TX), chair of the House Judiciary Committee, said he was "disappointed."[45] Crack offenders "knew what they were doing," echoed Jim Pasco, executive director of the Fraternal Order of Police, which represents more than 300,000 law enforcement officers. But drivers who don't come to a complete stop at a stop sign also tend to know what they're doing. It doesn't necessarily follow that they should get extended prison sentences. Without retroactive adjustments, many convicts sentenced under the old formula would remain behind bars, watching recent offenders serving shorter sentences come and go.

"There are still a lot of people out there suffering the ill effects of a horribly unjust law," said Carl Gunn of the Federal Public Defender's Office in Los Angeles. The newer ratio, he said, was only a small step, but at least it was in the right direction.[46]

■ "I'D LIKE TO SEE A CONGRESSMAN"

FAMM tells the tale of DeJarion Echols, a student with a partial football scholarship who had been forced to leave Texas College when he ran out of money and subsequently turned to dealing narcotics to raise enough cash to return to school. In 2006, at age twenty-three, Echols was sentenced to a mandatory ten years for possession of forty-four grams of crack. The $5,700 in cash that police found at his family's home in Waco, Texas, was, under the statutory formula, considered equal to an additional 450 grams. The unloaded rifle under Echols's bed added another ten years to his sentence. Rifles are commonly kept in that part of Texas, and the judge seemed convinced by Echols's contention that the rifle was unrelated to the drugs. But that additional ten years was mandatory because crack was seized at the same address.[47]

The judge, disgusted by the mandatory sentence he was forced to pronounce, declared in court that this was "one of those situations where I'd like to see a Congressman sitting before me."[48] Echols wasn't a career criminal, and his mistake didn't need twenty years to correct, but the zero-tolerance drug law, designed to wage and win a "war," was inflexible. Echols's projected release date is in 2023, and apparently the new sentencing provisions won't apply to his case. He, like so many other inmates, was victimized by panicky statutes passed by legislators in Congress and state capitals. How many of them even remember casting those votes?

For the thousands of drug offenders serving sentences under these laws, time in prison moves slowly. At the federal level, inmates incarcerated for drug offenses comprise half of the prison population.[49] Thanks to the length of their sentences, these numbers keep going up. Few of these inmates are major players in the drug trade, and many, like Echols, have no prior criminal record for a violent offense. They constitute a fraternity of the forgotten, a contemporary version of witches condemned not to burn, but to grow old in the Gulag, where time licks at them like slow fire.

■ PREEXISTING CONDITION

Consider the case of John Ray Wilson.[50] An uninsured multiple sclerosis (MS) patient, he was sentenced in 2010, at age thirty-eight, to five years in prison by a New Jersey judge for manufacturing and possessing seventeen marijuana plants he'd been growing to treat symptoms of his disease. He wasn't accused of transportation or sales and was both the victim and the perpetrator of his crime. "He was in a situation where he had no health insurance and no other way to obtain medical coverage," said his attorney, James Wronko. Jurors weren't allowed to hear the mandatory penalties included in the statutes so that their verdict wouldn't be affected by them. Among the counts against Wilson, one—operating a drug-production facility—was punishable by up to twenty years in prison. The jury acquitted him of that charge.

Ultimately, after much wrangling, Wilson was allowed to make a brief, one-sentence declaration that he had medical reasons for growing the marijuana, but Superior Court Judge Robert Reed wouldn't allow him to explain to the jury that he grew the plants only for personal use. Neither would Reed let Wilson's lawyer call an expert witness to testify about the medicinal effects of marijuana. An appellate court later ruled that the judge had acted correctly and upheld both the trial and sentence, rejecting an argument that five years was too harsh a punishment.

Ironically, Wilson, who'd been suffering from MS for nine years, was convicted one week after Governor Chris Christie approved the establishment of medical marijuana dispensaries in New Jersey. Had they existed earlier, Wilson might have avoided prosecution altogether. He began serving his term in August 2011 and presumably will now be prevented from committing crimes against himself.

At the start of 2013 eighteen states had decriminalized personal possession of marijuana for proved medicinal use. Colorado and Washington had legalized it for recreational use. The herb remains illegal under federal statutes.[51] We reside in a confusing, betwixt-and-between stage of twilight legality. Local authorities in some precincts, hampered by liberalized state law, call in federal authorities to make arrests. The result of all these conflicting statutes is a hodgepodge justice that sends one hapless soul to a lengthy prison sentence while someone else who committed the same act walks off barely inconvenienced.

■ LIFE WITHOUT PAROLE

Marcia G. Shein is a defense lawyer in Decatur, Georgia, who specializes in federal criminal law and takes cases all over the country.

She still loses sleep over the case of a deputy sheriff in Marengo County, Alabama, who at age twenty-five was sentenced to life without parole after being convicted of conspiracy in the sale of crack cocaine and marijuana. "I almost left the practice of law over this case," she told me. "It's just so incredible that they would put someone in jail for the rest of his life on this charge. I have murder cases in which defendants are eligible for release, and this kid gets life without parole. There were no firearms involved; he had no criminal record; there wasn't any violence. It's a tragedy that we've allowed our system to go so far to the right."[52]

The deputy, Wilmer Breckenridge, was convicted based on the testimony of one informant, another deputy who was sentenced to 150 months. There was no corroborating evidence or witnesses, no physical evidence, nothing to tie Breckenridge to the charges except the word of Deputy Robert Pickens, a conniver who sold drugs, took payoffs from dealers, and once even torched his own car to collect insurance money. Pickens testified that Breckenridge had agreed to warn dealers of any impending busts. There were no audiotapes, and not one drug dealer claimed Breckenridge worked with them or took their money. In fact, dealers who'd conspired with Pickens were willing to take the stand and say that they had no such dealings with Breckenridge, but neither side asked for their testimony.

Shein, who didn't come into the case until the appeals stage, said all possible remedies have been exhausted—a motion for a new trial, a commutation of sentence, all of it. She added,

> I did everything I could do for this kid, but I just couldn't break through. The case is so draconian. He's going to have a pine box exit. Unless his health goes bad and he's over sixty-five. Then they might throw him out. He was given, in essence, a prison term death sentence.
>
> All your life something can eat at you. This is the one, the one that breaks my heart. Even the original lawyers admitted they didn't do a good job.

For example, they failed to hire a private investigator who might have proved that Pickens's statements were false. "But the judge just ignored all that," Shein said, "and let him rot in prison. . . . He'd never been in trouble, he's lost his kids, his wife, and he's been transferred eleven different times." Like so many other inmates who once worked in law enforcement, Breckenridge refuses to request protective custody, which is essentially solitary confinement. Prison authorities try to protect his identity, but eventually word leaks out among inmates. According to Shein, "Then they throw him in the hole and transfer him someplace else."

Shein told me that authorities who extract extreme penalties in this and similar cases appear to have lost their reason. "I don't understand how some of these people live with themselves," she said. "I pray every day that one of them would have a child of their own get in trouble before they become prosecutors or judges. Just for a week. That's all it would take."

5

The Death of Rachel Hoffman

NOTHING MORE STARKLY DEMONSTRATES THE DESTRUCTIVENESS OF OUR DRUG laws than the vicious, grievous murder of Rachel Morningstar Hoffman.[1] A psychology major who'd just graduated from Florida State University, Hoffman, age twenty-three, was on track to attend culinary school in Arizona. Friends described her as a free spirit, friendly and open, a post–hippie era hippie. Her family said that Hoffman lived her life according to the Beatles song "All You Need Is Love." She was utterly unprepared for the nightmare world that was thrust upon her.

During a traffic stop and search in February 2007, Hoffman was caught in Tallahassee with less than an ounce of marijuana. In Florida possession of that much pot was a felony punishable by up to five years in prison. In some states her offense would have been treated like a parking ticket. In Tallahassee, however, the law looked upon her as a serious malefactor, and she ended up in drug court. She was told that by allowing this special court to monitor her, she could avoid jail time. In fact, charges would be dropped altogether if she stayed clean for a year. Advocates generally describe drug courts as a tool of reform, a way to steer users away from lives of crime or iniquity by giving them special attention. They may even have started out that way. But because of the way they're administered, drug courts often create a precisely opposite result. Louisville, Kentucky, defense attorney Nathan Miller points to Hoffman's fate as the perfect, tragic example of a heavy-handed "reform" that's another sad component of an out-of-control system.

Hoffman had to surrender many of her constitutional rights to enter the program. And although logic would dictate that authorities could better use their time, fourteen months after her arrest, Tallahassee police conducted a surprise search of her apartment. They needed no warrant because she hadn't been in the drug court diversion program for more than a year. This time they found about five ounces of marijuana and four ecstasy pills. They told her a prison sentence was certain unless she led them to other marijuana and ecstasy users. She refused to betray her friends. But trying to make the best of a bad situation, she eventually agreed to act as a confidential informant and help cops corral people committing what they told her would be serious offenses. She would have to stay in Tallahassee and defer cooking school.

Thus, a totally untrained, slight young woman was drafted as an unpaid undercover agent and charged with the task of inserting herself into the framework of criminal enterprises. The cops handling her had been trained to believe there was no essential difference between a small-time marijuana seller and a dangerous thug, so they assumed that hard-core offenders would also fail to make the distinction and that she'd blend right in. Amazingly, her handlers armed her with $13,000 in marked bills and instructed her to buy 1,500 ecstasy pills, two ounces of cocaine, and a handgun. She'd make this purchase alone and from two men she didn't know. Police knew that at least one of the dealers had a violent criminal history. They also demanded that she wear a wire so that it would be easier for them to get a conviction. The wire, of course, magnified the danger to Hoffman.

The police gave her plenty of assurances and acted as though they knew what they were doing, and she wanted to believe them. They were the experts. She knew nothing about guns, cocaine, hidden taping devices, or undercover work. The cops may as well have pulled a random citizen off the street and parachuted her into a terrorist camp.

Hoffman was naturally excited by the crazy turn her life had taken, but we also know she was frightened and confused by the role police were forcing her to play. The day of the sting she called her father, Irv Hoffman. He had no knowledge that Tallahassee cops had his daughter under their collective thumb and were using her as bait for dangerous felons. "Dad, I'm really thinking about you today," she told him. That was the last conversation they would ever have. She was his only child.

■ "NO IDEA WHERE I AM"

The men targeted by the police changed the location of the transaction at the last minute. Hoffman tried to inform her handlers about the move, but transmission was poor. Amazingly, the police weren't tailing her and didn't have her car in sight. They lost her when she didn't turn into the park where they were waiting. "I have no idea where I am," she said. Those were her last recorded words. Later the police who'd guaranteed her safety claimed that they advised her against going to the new rendezvous; they said that what resulted was her own fault. But given the faulty transmissions over the poor communications setup, it wasn't clear that she even received their last-minute instruction. It all happened fast, there had been no rehearsal.

Two days later Hoffman's body, clad in a Grateful Dead sweat-shirt, was found in a ditch south of the city. She'd been shot five times with the .25-caliber stolen pistol that she'd been instructed to purchase. Police later arrested Deneilo Bradshaw, twenty-three, and Andrea Green, twenty-five, and charged them with murder. As word of the monumental folly seeped out and higher-ups were peppered with questions, a public information officer, David McCranie, was appointed to handle inquiries. Describing Hoffman as "very bright" and "very talented," he took turns blaming her for poor execution of the plan and the shooters for shooting her. He mouthed a series of inapplicable slogans, such as "Safety is paramount," and refused to concede that anyone in the department was at fault. Hoffman's attorney, Johnny Devine, who had not been informed about his client's undercover status, recalled that police tried "to point the arrow in every other direction. They took a defensive step from the start."

Apparently hoping it would buttress their argument that Hoffman herself had a criminal background, authorities publicized her 2003 citation for underage drinking. They also claimed she was a major drug dealer, but as her father later pointed out, she barely had enough money to pay the rent, which doesn't exactly fit the pattern of a major drug dealer. Friends said she and they shared small quantities of weed and sometimes ecstasy. They scoffed at the suggestion that she was a "major dealer."

Well, McCranie said, Hoffman didn't have to accept the confidential-informant deal. Countless other drug offenders have been offered the same deal, he said, and a "lot of people say no." But the whole process was utterly foreign to Hoffman. Her life was hanging by a thread, and no one was watching the thread.

No matter how carefully they are screened, it's inevitable that weak-minded or amoral people will achieve positions of authority. As long as we keep Quixotic, unjust laws on the books, harmless people will suffer. Because the law computed Hoffman's actions as being worthy of prison time, she suspended her life and became an indentured servant in a risky trade.

The day Bradshaw was convicted of killing Hoffman, a reporter found Irv Hoffman beside his daughter's grave. He'd brought a carrot cake, her favorite, and he sat there all day in a lawn chair. It was her birthday. She'd have been twenty-five. "She was full of life and mischief," he said.[2]

After the media spotlight shined on the circumstances of Rachel Hoffman's death, one of the officers involved was fired, but he quickly won reinstatement and was transferred to another job in the department. A year after the murder, Florida passed legislation dubbed "Rachel's Law." Billed as an important edict, it would, the public was told, tighten rules on police use of confidential informants. New rules required police to provide special training for officers handling informants and decreed that such informants be instructed that their sentences wouldn't necessarily be reduced in exchange for their work. The law also spelled out that informants had the right to request a lawyer (a right they already held).[3] Despite the new language, future suspects could still be caught in the same trap that killed Hoffman. Drug-war diehards continued to control the ground.[4]

6

Three Strikes
and You're Out

The law ought to impose no other penalties but such as are absolutely and evidently necessary.
—Thomas Paine, *The Rights of Man*

In November 2012 more than 60 percent of California voters passed Proposition 36, ending eighteen years of a three-strikes experiment gone wrong. The new measure retained the concept of extending sentences for repeat offenders, particularly those facing a third conviction, but it established grounds for people serving time for nonserious and nonviolent crimes to ask for shorter prison sentences.[1] Under the new law's reforms, approximately twenty-eight hundred inmates were eligible to file for sentence review, and judges were obliged to reduce sentences unless doing so would endanger the public.

By early 2013 judges across the state were examining petitions. On February 11, 2013, for example, Los Angeles County judge William C. Ryan reduced sentences for five people convicted of relatively minor crimes. Among them was Richard Packard, eighty-one, who'd already served seventeen years for stealing forty-five packs of cigarettes from a supermarket, and Robert Benavidez, seventy-four, who'd served nearly sixteen years for possessing a balloon containing ten dollars' worth of cocaine and heroin.[2] California's three-strikes rulings—with their catchy, instantly understandable slogan that evoked the all-American pastime, hot dogs, and Babe Ruth—had left a lengthy trail of human detritus.

The tale of Gregory Taylor probably motivated many voters who approved Proposition 36. Modern America's own Jean Valjean, Taylor was locked up for thirteen years after two security guards caught him trying to lift out the screen on the door to a Los Angeles church pantry in 1997. Homeless and hungry, he was a frequent guest at the pantry, but the doors wouldn't open for another hour. Had the guards consulted the priest who operated the facility, the Reverend Allan McCoy—a kindhearted man not unlike Victor Hugo's Bishop Myriel—he'd have informed them that Taylor was a longtime friend who sometimes slept in the church and that he would take care of it. But instead the guards turned Taylor over to local police.[3]

Taylor was one of many thousands of troubled souls trudging up and down Los Angeles's skid row in a journey to nowhere. Like so many of them, he had a history of mental illness and a drug addiction he'd picked up trying to self-medicate out on the street. His public defender argued unsuccessfully that what transpired that morning at the church property involved neither a crime nor a victim, but if a crime existed, it was trespassing, not burglary. Father McCoy spoke on the defendant's behalf, but Taylor was convicted and sentenced under the three-strikes law.

Sentenced to twenty-five years to life, Taylor had at least twelve more years to serve in 2010 when two Stanford law students discovered an error in Superior Court Judge James Dunn's instructions to the jury. Still, trying to free Taylor was tough sledding. The state fought to keep him, but eventually the Los Angeles district attorney stopped contesting the appeal, and Taylor won his freedom.

Taylor was forty-eight when he was freed at last by a judge who declared that his deprived, difficult boyhood; mental health problems; and mild personality placed him "outside the spirit of the three strikes law."[4] Taylor's previous two strikes had been earned more than a decade before the fateful morning he tried to pry open the screen. They were for purse snatching and an unarmed, failed street robbery. While Gregory Taylor was locked up, his brother, Michael Taylor, motivated by Gregory's travails, had become the manager of a food pantry in Pomona, California, and Gregory's plan when he finally gained release was to help feed hungry folks.

After Taylor won his freedom the original prosecutor, Dale Cutler, said he still believed that "the facts strongly suggest that the motivation wasn't for food" and that the defendant had been hoping to steal money or valuables, possibly "icons."[5] He insisted that anyone seeking only food would have waited an hour for the pantry to open, as though the mind of someone like Taylor was functioning with perfect logic and reason. So to Cutler the original sentence was justified. From his retirement perch, he objected to Taylor's case having become what he pejoratively referred to as a cause célèbre.

Taylor won his freedom on a fluke. It was possible only because he had advocates who managed to find the judicial error. But in most cases, even when determined, competent attorneys take up the appeal, no such mistake can be found, so convicted defendants are serving out their terms no matter how great the distance between the sentence and genuine justice.

■ LIFE AND TIME

Most of us understand what it means to lose track of time. Time seems to move quicker when we're thoroughly involved in some activity. But in case after case officials appear to lose their understanding of time's value in relation to human life. That could explain why Assistant District Attorney Cutler and Superior Court Judge James Dunn agreed Taylor should serve a minimum of twenty-five years for his offense. It's as though authorities lost their ability to assess how many days it takes for all those years to pass, how many times a man must rise from his prison bunk each morning to gaze into the mirror and search for signs of the inescapable aging that drained his life of another night. They never seem to wonder how it might affect Taylor to watch killers and child molesters enter the system and gain release while he remains behind.

Three-strikes laws regularly gain and lose force as courts interpret and reinterpret state laws. A federal appeals court in October 2010, for example, reinstated a rule that gave New York State judges the discretion to send nonviolent three-time losers to prison for fifteen to twenty-five years to life.[6] Earlier rulings by lower courts had declared the law unconstitutional.

■ LIFE TERMS FOR MISDEMEANORS

The contemporary three-strikes concept first took hold in Washington State, where voters approved it in a 1993 initiative.[7] Many states quickly followed Washington's lead. Although three-strikes laws are best known for establishing life sentences for third-time offenders, they also create a simple way for courts to extend the sentence for any crime classified as a "strike." In most places three-strikes laws apply to violent crimes only, but in California, which was America's three-strikes capital from 1994 to 2012, the statute applied to "serious," though not necessarily violent, offenses. What's more, a third strike didn't have to be "serious." In some circumstances a misdemeanor could be upgraded to a felony, and the defendant could be imprisoned for life—or at least decades.

Three out of four inmates leaving state prisons were convicted of nonviolent crimes.[8] Most of these former inmates were jailed for drug crimes, and the rest tend to have been convicted of "property" crimes, such as burglary or receiving stolen goods. The law can distinguish between violence and lack of violence in ways that one might not expect. Entering a residence with the intent to steal when residents are home, for example, presents a potential for violence that constitutes first-degree burglary, an offense that remains an automatic strike in California. Darting into an open garage at noon and grabbing a garden hose or a bicycle, is, according to the statute, no different than breaking into an inhabited bedroom at 3:00 a.m. Running into two garages on the same street within a minute of each other can earn an offender two felony counts and two strikes. These interpretations of the law give an ambitious prosecutor a heavy club when the defense looks to strike a deal.[9]

Any burglary below first degree is what lawyers call a "wobbler." It could constitute either a misdemeanor or a felony. Prosecutors filing for first degree can just lean back and wait; unlike an overwhelming majority of defendants, they don't have to sleep in a cell with their head next to a toilet while the case works its way through the court. Meanwhile, defense attorneys often represent clients who may have committed a crime, but that crime is not necessarily the one they are charged with, thanks to loose and varied interpretations of the law.

In 1947, when Vittorio De Sica made his landmark film *The Bicycle Thief*, he'd never have guessed that his American liberators would corral their own underclass in an environment as unforgiving as the one he showed us in desperately poor postwar Italy. Welcome to the nightmare of Chris Martinez, the unemployed construction worker I mentioned in chapter 1.[10] Martinez wheeled a beat-up, rusted bicycle with a broken chain and two flat tires out of an open garage in Manhattan Beach, California, and abandoned it after the owner, standing on a balcony, called out to him. It started out as a stupid prank but ended up as a definable crime. A small-time offender arrested by police later in connection with an unrelated incident sought a better deal for himself by identifying Martinez as a bicycle thief.

The prosecutor offered Martinez, then twenty-four, a sentence of nine years and four months, "and the public defender said it was a good deal I should sign," Martinez recalled. "At that point my maximum amount of time was twenty years." A lawyer friend of the family took over and bargained the deal down to six years, with a minimum of three and a half to be served. Martinez accepted. You might say he got lucky—if you think doing three and a half years in prison for almost stealing a twenty-dollar bicycle is lucky. Did anyone viewing De Sica's movie imagine that his Italian bicycle thief would end up serving such an irrational sentence? Probably not.

Martinez's bicycle sentence came courtesy of the three-strikes law, and with it came a second strike. If he were arrested for a third nonviolent offense today, after the passage of the Proposition 36 reform measure, he could still receive a much harsher-than-ordinary sentence—perhaps life. His first strike was also for a residential burglary. The prosecutor on that case agreed to release him with time served (two months in county jail) if he accepted the strike on his record in exchange. To a defendant in county jail, that can seem like a good deal, but down the road it may start to feel like a payday loan carrying enormous interest. "I have no record of violence," Martinez pointed out. "Matter of fact, I've never been arrested for anything of the sort. Somehow I'm one strike away from a life sentence."

I've known Martinez, a good-natured neighborhood kid, since he was twelve, but like most of his acquaintances, I never took serious notice of his problems, even though I was aware that his father died young and that the death inflicted awful damage on the family's finances and Martinez's upbringing. Shortly before the bicycle incident, Martinez came by the house with my son. I asked if anyone was interested in some leftover pasta we had sitting in the refrigerator. Martinez ended up eating what must have been a half gallon of the stuff. He was half-starved. We need to do something about this, I remember thinking. I knew he'd dropped out of community college to work construction jobs, but by this time the Great Recession was forcing people out of their jobs and homes, and construction contracts were becoming scarce. Although I didn't know it at the time, Martinez was penniless and had no one to fall back on. He shared a small flat with an ex-girlfriend too kindhearted to kick him out. I had plenty on my mind, and although I'm not proud of it, the next time I heard about Martinez, he was in county jail looking at a possible twenty years. Martinez served his three and a half years for almost stealing a bicycle and upon release was admitted as a charity resident into the Beit T'Shuvah substance abuse program in Los Angeles. The last time I talked to him he was employed as a truck driver for the organization's two thrift shops. He finished the 2013 Los Angeles Marathon, and his life had taken a more hopeful, productive turn.

◼ "I COULD GO BACK FOREVER"

I've spoken with a number of two-strikers now out in the world. Their descriptions of their lives are remarkably similar to Martinez's. No matter how determined they might be to mend their ways and stay out of prison, they live in mortal fear of police contact, believing that if they're involved in any sort of fracas, they'll be blamed because of their record. They try to stay away from places—bars, for example—where trouble is more likely to occur. But ex-convicts, usually at the bottom of the socioeconomic ladder, tend to live in neighborhoods that middle-class citizens drive through with windows up and doors locked. For these ex-cons, it's virtually impossible to avoid trouble spots. Trouble spots are right outside their front door.

In addition, an opposite, ugly side of the two-strikers' existence can make some of them extraordinarily dangerous to others. Because they can get a twenty-five-year sentence for a pinch of dope, any confrontation with police is hugely risky. Convicts and ex-convicts know that police officers are sometimes attacked and even killed because the three-strikes decrees make life-and-death situations out of minor infractions. They assume that if an officer of the law has been assaulted and perhaps killed for attempting to make a routine arrest or during an ordinary stop of a pedestrian or vehicle, it's because some desperate ex-felon feared triggering that third strike and decided, why not just point and shoot?

A 2004 study found that in California, 57 percent of inmates serving twenty-five years to life for a third strike triggered the penalty with a nonviolent offense.[11] Once you've done time alongside a convict who will die in prison because he was arrested for possession of a dime bag of heroin or shoplifted a pocket calculator, you've absorbed a lesson you won't soon forget.

Can two-strikers move elsewhere to escape the sword of Damocles? Yes and no. In early 2013, a total of twenty-six states had habitual offender statutes. They practice reciprocity.

■ NINE CASSETTES FOR YOUR LIFE

In 1995 a California court, using the state's 1994 three-strikes law as its foundation, sentenced Leonardo Andrade, a thirty-seven-year-old heroin addict, to fifty years to life for shoplifting nine videocassettes worth $153.53.[12] An army veteran, Andrade had a long string of petty offenses on his record, but none was violent. Opponents of the habitual-offender law saw Andrade's case as an excellent wrench to throw into the three-strikes machinery, and in 2001 they thought they'd won the argument when an appellate court threw out the sentence as excessive. But two years later, in a decision that essentially upheld thousands of life sentences, the U.S. Supreme Court ruled 5-4 that Andrade's trial and sentencing had met every legal test.

Justice Anthony Kennedy, a member of the majority, told the annual meeting of the American Bar Association that same year that it's "a grave mistake to retain a policy just because a court finds it constitutional. Courts may conclude the legislature is permitted to choose long sentences, but that does not mean long sentences are wise or just."[13] So why did Kennedy speak one way and vote another? He'd already freely and frequently expressed his opinion that criminal justice statutes were far too punitive. But though he disapproved of the three-strikes law as written, he decided he couldn't find anything downright illegal about it. Taking a strict constructionist posture, he decided that California bore the responsibility for amending its bad law. As long as an unwise law was written correctly, Kennedy and other jurists like him would uphold it. To do otherwise would be to legislate from the bench. Kennedy's position makes sense in the abstract but looks terribly deficient down on the ground, where people are seeking justice. And if sentencing a man to a life term for shoplifting nine videocassettes isn't the "cruel and unusual punishment" that's expressly forbidden in the Constitution, then what is?

■ FACTORY GIRLS

Harsher penalties for repeat offenders weren't invented with the three-strikes laws. The concept is more than a century old. But previously judges were allowed discretion. It was most unlikely that anyone would be sentenced to life for stealing a pizza slice because that would defy common sense. Aleksandr Solzhenitsyn wrote about impoverished Soviet factory girls who would smuggle out a spool of thread between their breasts. Thousands were caught. The standard sentence was ten years. Many were worked and starved to death before they could complete their terms. The history of humankind teems with forgotten souls like these factory girls. But the United States, founded on higher ideals, was supposed to rise above such barbarities.

When California voters approved the Three Strikes and You're Out initiative with a whopping 72 percent of the vote, they assumed it was the same law as its Washington state predecessor, passed a year earlier. When the idea was originally suggested, backers in California talked only about violent offenses. But the substance of the proposal was changed, and not everyone received the news. California was the place where three strikes met Frankenstein's monster. He came in the form of an ex-con named Joe Davis.[14]

■ THE LAST STRAWS

Davis, a twenty-five-year-old habitual criminal and crystal meth addict, was with his partner, Douglas Walker, on a stolen motorbike in June 1992 when they pulled up to Kimber Reynolds in Fresno. Reynolds, eighteen, was leaving a stylish restaurant with a friend and about to get into her car, which was parked directly in front of the restaurant on a busy street. A student at the Los Angeles Fashion Institute of Design and Merchandising, Reynolds had come back to her hometown for another friend's wedding. Davis, who'd been paroled two months earlier from Wasco State Prison where he'd served time for auto theft, tugged at Reynolds's purse. Reynolds tugged back, and in full view of about twenty witnesses, Davis brought a .357 magnum pistol up to her ear and fired, mortally wounding her. The next day a Fresno special weapons and tactics (SWAT) team cornered Davis in his girlfriend's apartment, and when he tried to shoot his way out, they killed him.

Reynolds's father, Mike Reynolds, a wedding photographer, outraged by this tragedy, began talking about his daughter in the mass media. The loquacious father became a sought-after personality on right-wing talk radio, a burgeoning force at the time. He was a perfect fit for these shows, which liked to keep issues and solutions simple. Reynolds's simple solution: keep criminals locked up. In addition to his media blitz, he pitched his idea in the state capital, Sacramento, where he and his new political friends put together Proposition 184, Three Strikes and You're Out.

Joining forces with Reynolds and his radio hosts was the California prison guards union, which contributed $100,000 to the cause and formed a straw group called Crime Victims United. The National Rifle Association, which seeks to fight crime by making guns and ammo more available, tossed $130,000 into the initiative drive.

The initiative process, often hailed as a great hallmark of democracy, had by this time established itself as a kind of uninformed tyranny in California. Traditionally, legislation is passed through a responsible legislative body that conducted research, held hearings, asked intelligent questions, and picked the brains of experts.

■ SNATCHED FROM A SLUMBER PARTY

In October 1993, sixteen months after Kimber Reynolds was murdered in Fresno, a sociopath and repeat offender named Richard Davis (no relation to Joe) snatched twelve-year-old Polly Klaas from a slumber party in a middle-class section of Petaluma, California.[15] Davis, who had an amazing history of evading arrest and sensible sentencing, drove off with Klaas, almost certainly raped her, then murdered her and dumped her body at an abandoned sawmill. It was a signature evil deed, a parent's worst nightmare.

A couple months later, after much police blundering, Davis was tracked down. He confessed and led police to where he'd stashed Polly Klaas's body. The Klaas murder on top of the Reynolds killing had voters itching to do something, and on Election Day, the three-strikes initiative was there, just waiting for their OK. Voters approved it overwhelmingly, but few noticed that Klaas's father had come out against it. Bereaved and crushed but nevertheless thoughtful, he was shocked by its draconian provisions.

Although California voters ultimately moderated the three-strikes law in 2012, other states continued enforcing harsher provisions. In 2013, Louisiana, for example, was still following a broad three-strikes law passed in 1994 that enabled courts to impose life terms for petty crimes, even if none of the strikes involved violence. Under the provisions of this law, James Belt was sentenced to life without parole in 1999 for selling ten dollars' worth of crack to an undercover cop.[16] He was thirty-seven and had been fighting a crack addiction for six years. His two previous convictions were for stealing a credit card from his college roommate and burglarizing a friend's house for drug money—ugly crimes for sure, but not life-in-prison sorts of crimes. Unfortunately, no one has been able to find any mistakes in Belt's case. Apparently the court followed the letter of the law. So Belt and others like him languish, as forgotten as the Soviet factory girls who'd been banished to the Gulag for stealing spools of thread.

7

Divine Right Prosecutors

HAD YOU CHECKED THE WEBSITE OF THE TULARE COUNTY, CALIFORNIA, DIS-
trict Attorney's Office in November 2012, you'd have seen a studio
portrait of a smiling, middle-aged, balding man with a closely trimmed
white beard. He wore a dark suit and appropriately somber tie. A U.S.
flag dangled on a pole behind his right shoulder. The man was District
Attorney Phillip Cline, a member in good standing of both the local
Rotary Club and Chamber of Commerce. (Cline announced his retirement in October 2012, effective in December, approximately two
years before the end of his term.) Before becoming district attorney,
the site would have told you, Cline "specialized in the prosecution
of homicide cases and won a number of high-profile death penalty
cases." His office's mission was "to represent the people of the State
of California in an efficient, effective and ethical manner."[1]

Nowhere did the site mention that five years earlier, in 2007, a
state appellate court determined that as a deputy prosecutor two decades earlier, Cline had withheld a vital audiotaped statement from a
key witness that pointed to a murder defendant's innocence. But the
discovery was made too late. By that time defendant Mark Sodersten
had died in prison, having served twenty-two years for a crime he
almost certainly didn't commit. Sodersten's death turned the smoth-
ered evidence into what the law calls a moot point. However, the
appellate court was so upset by the finding that it made the ruling
anyway—a highly unusual decision that at least put Cline's deeds on
the record.[2] Cline had sought the death penalty for Sodersten.

75

As it turned out, Cline's luck held. The criminal justice system took no action against him, and the state bar association never expressed so much as mild disapproval. Thanks to Supreme Court decisions that protect prosecutors (but not police), he was immune from civil liability, accorded a legal status that mimics that of medieval monarchs who ruled their kingdoms and principalities by divine right.

The Northern California Innocence Project (NCIP), a legal group dedicated to exonerating wrongfully convicted individuals, is affiliated with the Santa Clara University School of Law. In a study of court records from 1997 to 2009, it reported that in 707 Northern California cases, courts found that prosecutors had committed misconduct. Three percent of these 707 cases went to trial, but in only six was anyone disciplined.[3] There's no reason to believe this phenomenon is peculiar to Northern California. A New York Innocence Project study found that the many cases reversed by Innocence Project offices around the country "exposed official misconduct at every level and stage of a criminal investigation."[4] Common forms of misconduct discovered include employing suggestion when conducting identification procedures; coercing false confessions; failing to turn over exculpatory evidence (although in some cases police fail to turn the evidence over to prosecutors); deliberately mishandling, mistreating, or destroying evidence; allowing witnesses to testify when authorities know or should know they aren't being truthful; pressuring defense witnesses not to testify; relying on fraudulent forensic experts; and making misleading arguments that overstate the conclusiveness of testimony.

In the landmark case of *Brady v. Maryland*, the Supreme Court ruled in 1963 that prosecutors have a duty to share evidence that indicates a defendant is not guilty.[5] But in case after case, prosecutors treat this decision as though it never happened. Even when a prosecutor is caught withholding evidence, nothing much happens. It's a phenomenon that appears to have much in common with on-ice fights in the National Hockey League. If the league really wanted to end them, it clearly could do so.

The Northern California study, conducted by Kathleen Ridolfi, NCIP's executive director, and Maurice Possley, a Pulitzer Prize–winning journalist, examined only those 3 percent of cases that went to trial. The 97 percent of cases resolved without trial nearly all ended in a guilty plea.[6] These cases were no less likely to involve misconduct, but whatever transpired may as well have been on the dark side of the moon. The public sphere saw only the judge banging a gavel to pronounce the negotiated outcome.

◼ ELECTED COURT OFFICERS

In other developed democracies, judges and prosecutors are usually appointed civil servants. But in the United States, state prosecutors are mostly elected. And although federal prosecutors are appointed, they are more likely than their European counterparts to be angling for future political office—and are therefore more inclined to seek a spotlight. Some experts believe that this politicizing of prosecutorial duties has much to do with America's incarceration syndrome.[7] Playing the role of a crusading prosecutor is a traditional political path. Campaigns for prosecutorial office can devolve into a duel decided by which candidate best exploits the voters' fear of victimization.

Cline, after winning a conviction in the Sodersten case, moved up to the elective office of district attorney in 1992 and kept that office for twenty years. He served in California's mostly bleak Central Valley, where the principal industry is agriculture, primarily dairy, grapes, and citrus. Although Hispanics are in the majority in Tulare County, their voter turnout is low. Hard-core conservative Republicans rule, although criminal justice isn't strictly a liberal-conservative issue.

Savvy defense attorney Kevin Donahue, who's practiced almost thirty years in the Democratic stronghold of Los Angeles County, is still puzzled from time to time by the implacable attitudes of prosecutors he faces, and he's not afraid to say so. I asked him to name an instance that particularly bothered him, and he immediately chose the case of a young man who was unquestionably guilty as charged:

> I had this client who was twenty-five years old. He had two years of college. He was a good kid, and he had a clean record. But one night he got drunk and somewhere he got a gun, and he was out there and he was with these people and he was just wobbling drunk, and they were having a good time. They were all friendly. He had his arms around their necks, and at some point he said, "Give me your wallet." And he took their jewelry too.[8]

His offense, Donahue readily concedes, was inexcusable and deserved conviction and punishment. But in California, the minimum for robbery at gunpoint is twelve years. With good behavior, a convict can get 15 percent lopped off the sentence, meaning his client would have to do a minimum of ten years, two months, a far lengthier term, Donahue believed, than was merited. His client needed a lesson, not obliteration. But he was up against another one of those statutes that can often be counterproductive, taking the clay of human beings who still have potential and molding them into broken or bitter ex-convicts whose survival skills aren't taught in any scouting manuals. Donahue, wishing he could do more for the young man, knew the facts of the robbery were clear and made peace with the situation. But when he spoke to the prosecutor, he came away astonished. "She was set on giving him twenty-six years," he recalled. He paused. "Twenty-six years. He'd never been in trouble before, and he didn't hurt anybody. He was just a kid. And twelve years wasn't enough?"

The assistant district attorney was adamant, but Donahue, who knows all the essential names and numbers in the Los Angeles criminal courts, managed to get his client before a judge he thought might show leniency in such a case, someone who would think twice before throwing a life away. Meanwhile the assistant district attorney continued to amaze him: "She told me, 'If he doesn't get at least 22 years I'll never take a case before this judge again.'"

Finally, Donahue negotiated a deal for sixteen years with possibility for parole only after the defendant served 13 years, 6 months. Given the facts of the case, he was convinced that going to trial would have dug a deeper pit for his guilty client. Only after he banged the gavel on the sixteen years did the judge notice that no one had mentioned the other charges. There were several other charges against Donahue's client relating to the one incident, which is typical.

"What you do in these cases," Donahue explained, "is you plead guilty to one charge and drop the others. That's the way it works. But the assistant [district attorney] told the judge, "We're going to trial on the other charges." She was trying to pile on more years. The judge looked at her and said, "I want you to go back to your supervisor and explain what's going on here, that you made an agreement and this is what you're doing about it." Finally they dropped the other charges, and I was supposed to feel like I got a victory because my client got only sixteen years.

Are exceedingly stiff mandatory sentences ever a deterrent to potential lawbreakers? Probably. But the more pertinent questions are, Are they necessary? Are they fair and reasonable? Patrick Russell, a world-renowned boxing referee and retired detective who spent many years as an investigator in the San Diego District Attorney's Office, points out that after carjackings began to surge, Congress passed a new federal statute that made them a federal crime punishable by ten years. "Word got out on the street that what looks like an easy crime isn't so easy after all," Russell recalled. "Just like that, carjacking pretty much disappeared."[9]

The trouble is people like Donahue's client don't hear about these changes. Because they're not hard-core criminals, they're out of the loop. They get the scoop only after it's too late. And the judges, no matter who's in front of them, no matter what the extenuating circumstances, must pronounce at least the minimum statutory sentence. In practice, that means judges no longer have the right to exercise discretion, and that right has been handed to prosecutors who decide whether to file charges and, if they file, the specific nature of those charges. If someone's been killed, for example, the prosecutors might press for first-degree murder, involuntary manslaughter, or any charge in between. They typically seek whatever they think they can get away with in the giant bazaar that operates outside the courtroom. The two sides play a game of chicken, with lawyers testing one another for weakness.

Defendants represented by public defenders or court-appointed attorneys, although they may win the lawyer lottery and end up with a spirited, able defender, are often assigned lawyers who are basically overwhelmed. If you can't afford to hire your own attorney, contends Sergio Ayala, who is doing twenty-five to life in California, "the public defender will only lead you to the slaughterhouse."[10]

Louisville attorney Nathan Miller recalls that when he worked in the public defender's office in southeastern Kentucky, he would routinely carry an impossible caseload of thirty-five to forty felony cases:

At one point I also was responsible for five hundred misdemeanors. People would leave the office and they were supposed
to hire new people to take their places, but often there were no
replacements. The cases would just be turned over to the people
already there. The caseload was such that I couldn't give attention to cases that they deserved. The first time I would see my
clients was the day they would walk into court to plead guilty. I
wanted them to understand they didn't have to take the deal. But
a lot of public defenders are not like that. There's just a lot of
pressure to move cases. It's just the same song and dance every
day. It's heartbreaking, frustrating, and the pay is not very good.

Often, Miller said, cases cried out for the defense attorney to file a
written motion of some kind, but there just wouldn't be time.[11]

■ FEDERAL SENTENCING "REFORM"

The Sentencing Reform Act, part of the Comprehensive Crime Control Act of 1984, was a federal statute that was supposed to increase
consistency in federal sentencing.[12] The act abolished federal parole
and established the U.S. Sentencing Commission, an independent
panel within the judicial branch. Panel members are appointed by the
president and confirmed by the Senate. They serve six-year terms.

The new federal sentencing guidelines went into effect in November 1987. They weren't really guidelines anymore but rather
mandatory decrees requiring longer minimum sentences, even for
first-time offenders. District Court Judge J. Lawrence Irving of San
Diego, a conservative who'd been appointed by President Reagan,
ruled the new guidelines unconstitutional, but he was overruled by
the Supreme Court in January 1989. Complaining that the mandatory
sentences were too harsh, he soon resigned. "If I remain on the bench
I have no choice but to follow the law," he said. "I just can't, in good
conscience, continue to do this. There are rarely two cases that are
identical. Judges should always have discretion."[13] Mandatory sentencing, he said, turns judges into "robots."

Meanwhile, many states retooled their own statutes, using the
harsher federal sentences as a model. Again, the discretionary power
lost by judges flowed mostly to prosecutors.

Jed Stone, a defense lawyer who works in Waukegan, Illinois, noting that prosecutors sometimes seem to exist inside an intellectual enclave, said there's a danger when individuals operate from an insular system in which "there is a failure to see the other side. You begin to view people as others. And when you begin to see people as other than you, they begin to become expendable." Cutting corners to get convictions and piling on additional years can look like a correct course when the mind has fashioned an image of the defendant as a kind of subhuman target. When a person reaches such a mind state, he or she may view evidence that conflicts with a settled conclusion as having no bearing on the case. In Florida, for example, after DNA testing showed that the pubic hairs at the scene of a rape did not belong to the man convicted of the crime, prosecutors arguing against his appeal said that pubic hairs found on the victim's bed could have come from movers who brought furniture to the bedroom a week or so earlier. "They essentially argued that there were naked movers," said Nina Morrison, a senior staff lawyer in the national office of the Innocence Project.[14]

Prosecutors who use such extreme means to attain questionable ends have lost their moral standing. Out on the street, they come to be viewed as just one more criminal gang. That raises the stakes for everyone—police, suspects, and everyday citizens, and society becomes more dangerous, which is precisely opposite to the desired outcome.

8

The Innocent and the Dead

IT'S HARD TO IMAGINE BEING IN THE SHOES OF A CONVICTED INNOCENT. TAKE
the case of Timothy Cole. In 1986 Cole, twenty-six, an ex-soldier
and student at Texas Tech, was positively identified by a student victim of a rape and robbery. After trial and conviction in Lubbock,
Cole was sentenced to twenty-five years. He'd refused a plea bargain
because he said he wouldn't plead guilty to something he didn't do.
After his sentence was read, recalled his mother, Ruby Session, her
son fell to the courtroom floor crying uncontrollably. She got off her
chair and down on the floor with him, hugging and rocking him. She
later said, "My son, a 26-year-old man, lying in his mother's arms.
And that's all I could do. And that's the last time my baby was in my
arms like that."[1]

Performing hard labor surrounded by dust and pollen and sleeping in a poorly ventilated cell, Cole found his childhood asthma kick
in during his sentence. Twice he was found unconscious and rushed
to the emergency room. In 1992 he went before the parole board, but
he refused to be contrite for a crime he didn't commit, and parole was
denied. His letters grew increasingly sorrowful and devoid of hope.
In 1993 he wrote to his mother that his "only dream was to play in
the NBA. That dream won't ever come true. I don't have any more
dreams." In a postscript, he told her, "I get to make phone calls every
60 days now."

Several years after Cole's trial, another Texas convict, lifer Jerry
Wayne Johnson, began writing letters saying he'd committed the

rape for which Cole was convicted, but he wasn't sure who to tell or where to write, and no one with power paid any attention to his confession. In 2007 Cole's mother found one of those letters, but it was too late. On December 2, 1999, Tim Cole had suffered chest pains and collapsed. He died at age thirty-nine. He'd essentially been slowly put to death.

Cole's family found a lawyer with the Innocence Project who agreed to try to clear Tim Cole's name. The group had known about Johnson's confession earlier, but it was wary. Given its resources, the Innocence Project must be terribly selective in the cases it tries to clear. "We've had several of these guys," the lawyer, Jeffrey Blackburn, said, referring to the occasional guilty convict who pleads guilty to someone else's crime. "None of them have checked out." In the Cole case, however, Blackburn discovered that the rapist's semen was still in storage. DNA testing of the semen ruled out Cole as the perpetrator and found a complete match with Johnson.

In 2009 Governor Rick Perry proudly presided over the first posthumous pardon ceremony in Texas history. "Ruby," he told Cole's mother, "it means the world to me to be here today to look you in the eye and tell you that your son is pardoned." A smiling Perry appeared to believe that the state's criminal justice system had been vindicated along with Cole and that all was right with the world. Cole's mother wasn't so sure.

Reporter Beth Schwartzapfel, writing about the case for the online December 12, 2011, edition of *Mother Jones*, said, "The tale of Tim Cole and Jerry Johnson, which I investigated for more than a year, reveals a system in which an innocent man, once convicted, has virtually no chance of redemption—even with the guilty man fighting for it." When convicts say something that conflicts with the official record, authorities generally dismiss it, saying you can't accept a convict's word as truth. But when convicts are testifying for the prosecution, they should most certainly be believed, especially if they reference a private, jailhouse confession that can't be confirmed.

■ THE BLACKSTONE CREDO

Although he didn't invent the idea, British jurist William Blackstone is remembered for declaring that protecting one innocent person from wrongful conviction is more important than jailing ten criminals. That credo, in one form or another, dates back thousands of years and is the foundation of the legal requirement that defendants must be proved guilty beyond reasonable doubt.

But what's now generally known as the Blackstone ratio has been under attack in contemporary America, sometimes by stealth and sometimes with brutal frankness, as when syndicated columnist Jonah Goldberg pronounced it a mindless cliché. "If you want what's right for somebody else simply because you're afraid that you'll be next," Goldberg wrote, "then your motivations are selfish."[2] No matter how many times I read that sentence, it still doesn't make sense. Although Goldberg would surely disagree, his argument stands on the shoulders of Feliks Dzerzhinsky, founder of the Soviet secret police, who famously professed, "Better to execute ten innocent men than to leave one guilty man alive."[3] Dzerzhinsky's argument was straightforward and unadorned: he was insanely fixated on punishing the guilty no matter what the costs—and not afraid to show it. Madness is the only possible outcome for any system that values punishment over decency.

In his column, Goldberg, a leading conservative thinker, blithely made a case for rounding up the usual suspects and keeping them rounded up. "Better ten guilty men go free than one innocent be punished," he contended, is no more than a silly slogan. "*Why* is it better?" he asked, as though he'd stumped us. He closed off the debate with a time-tested technique—fear: "Maybe we will all accept it as the price of liberty when your mother is subsequently raped or your son is shot because, hey, better the rapists and murderers go free than the unlucky go to jail. But, it seems to me, there's an argument to be had here."[4]

University of Michigan law professor Samuel L. Gross has argued that anyone trying to determine a proper innocence ratio against the percentage of rightful convictions is starting with a false premise. "No rate of preventable errors that destroy people's lives and destroy the lives of those close to them is acceptable," he concluded.[5]

Perhaps if Goldberg were doing time for a crime he didn't commit, he'd serve his sentence without a whimper for the greater good and to protect mothers everywhere from rape, but I expect he'd opt instead to yell his head off and lodge "selfish" complaints. In any case, Goldberg performed a service by audaciously spelling out what so many of his political and philosophical brethren believe in their heart of hearts: sending large numbers of suspects to prison, even if some are innocent, realistically means taking lawbreakers off the streets. After all, some of them are no doubt guilty of something, either offenses they've already committed or others they might perpetrate somewhere down the line. So isn't it prudent to lock them up?

Tossing people in jail who don't belong there, however, can eventually transform a free but excessively punitive society into a totalitarian state, which by its very nature is a crime. Barry Scheck, a founder of the Innocence Project, points out that punishing the wrong people is not only morally reprehensible but also counterproductive: "Every time an innocent person is convicted, it means there are more guilty people out there who are still committing crimes."[6]

■ INNOCENCE PROJECTS SPREAD

The first Innocence Project was founded in 1992 at the Cardozo School of Law of Yeshiva University in New York City. Since then other Innocence Projects, all linked to law schools, have sprung up around the country. Students, directed by professors, do most of the heavy lifting. In most cases they focus on reversing convictions through the use of DNA testing. They also conduct research on false convictions in an effort to prevent new ones.

One state, North Carolina, has created its own independent commission to review innocence claims. In addition, some prosecutors' offices have created conviction-integrity units. The one set up in 2010 by Manhattan district attorney Cy Vance Jr., for example, has an advisory panel that includes Innocence Project codirector Barry Scheck. Said Vance, "As prosecutors, it is our duty to bring our best efforts to bear in every case to ensure that only the guilty are convicted."[7]

A study issued in 2004 concluded that thousands of innocent people are in prison at any one time. The study, conducted at the University of Michigan, traced cases that dated back to 1989, the year of the first DNA exoneration. Researchers supervised by Professor Gross found 328 exonerations over the fifteen years, 145 of them involving DNA evidence. They found that the leading causes of wrongful convictions for murder were false confessions and perjury by codefendants, informants, police officers, or forensic scientists.[8]

The authors of the Michigan study speculated that murder exonerations outnumber pardons for other offenses because murder cases attract more attention, especially when a death sentence is imposed. Death row inmates represent a quarter of 1 percent of the prison population but make up 22 percent of those exonerated, which, the authors concluded, suggests that innocent people are often convicted in run-of-the-mill cases. "If we reviewed prison sentences with the same level of care that we devote to death sentences, there would have been over 28,500 non-death-row exonerations in the past 15 years rather than the 255 that have in fact occurred," the study concluded.[9] But it's unlikely that all innocent defendants, even if their cases were seriously reexamined, could jump through every hoop necessary to win exoneration. The average time from conviction to exoneration is about thirteen years, so only those sentenced to lengthy sentences would even bother to try. That said, we should never forget that although two, three, or four years in prison may not look like much stacked against decades-long sentences, time is measured differently inside the walls.

Meanwhile, the number of exonerations increases as DNA appeals wind through the courts. Given the size and complexity of the justice system and all its various federal, state, and local components, deducing the number of wrongful convictions is a guess at best. University of Virginia law professor Brandon Garrett noted that we can't say with any precision how many people are convicted, much less wrongfully convicted, in the United States. "We don't even have a denominator," he said. "But the wrongful convictions we do know about suggest that there's a big problem."[10]

The vast majority of cases end in plea bargains and therefore leave almost no paper trail. They "generate virtually no records that can be retrieved," wrote Michigan's Gross in a 2008 analysis of the statistics available. "No trial transcripts, no appeals, frequently no court hearings of any sort, in many cases no description of the investigation at all beyond a single police report, which (if it could be found) might include little factual information of any value."[11]

Gross estimates that 1 percent of innocent defendants are ultimately exonerated and that from late 1989 through 2003, 850 were exonerated nationwide. If his conservative 1 percent estimate is correct, there are about eighty-five thousand convicted innocents in the prison system, or about two thousand more than could squeeze into our largest National Football League venue, the MetLife Stadium in New Jersey.

■ "JUST HAPPY"

Some people who have been exonerated can be remarkably forgiving, refusing to give in to bitterness. "I just kept waiting," said Scott Fappiano, who spent more than twenty years in prison for the 1983 rape of a New York City woman. He walked free in 2006 after DNA testing ruled him out as the attacker. "I'm just happy that it's over," he added.[12]

Francisco "Frankie" Carrillo was never proved innocent of the Los Angeles drive-by shooting he was convicted for at age sixteen, but he was found guilty on shaky eyewitness testimony that was finally thrown out on appeal in 2011, after he'd done twenty years in prison. "There are some people I'm sure I will never convince of my innocence," he said, "but I'm OK with it." He added, "Only an innocent man can persevere with this kind of experience. There's something that kind of takes you over when you know it wasn't you."[13]

Joshua Marquis, the district attorney for Clatsop County, Oregon, has contended that many of those exonerated may have perpetrated the crimes, though the evidence was too weak to prove them guilty beyond a reasonable doubt.[14] But both science and the behavior of many of those exonerated suggest that a large number of them were truly innocent. In many of the hundreds of DNA exonerations won on appeal, it was proved beyond reasonable doubt that snitches lied in their testimony.

In a space of nineteen years ending in 2011, Texas paid more than $42 million to compensate seventy-four men and women who spent more than seven hundred total years behind bars for crimes they didn't commit. Yet Texas clings to capital punishment, and Texas governor Perry veritably crowed about his state's execution policy during his abbreviated campaign for the 2012 Republican nomination for president. After accumulating 234 executions on his work résumé, Perry said in a September 8, 2011, debate for Republican presidential candidates, "In the state of Texas, if you come into our state and you kill one of our children, you kill a police officer, you're involved with another crime and you kill one of our citizens, you will face the ultimate justice in the state of Texas, and that is you will be executed."[15]

Two months earlier, in July 2011, Texas had executed Humberto Leal Garcia, thirty-eight, a Mexican national convicted of the rape and murder of a sixteen-year-old girl, even though he'd been denied access to the Mexican consulate when he was arrested. Article 36 of the Vienna Convention on Consular Relations, to which 170 nations are party, requires a nation arresting or detaining a foreign national to afford the detainee access to his or her consulate and to notify the foreign national of the right of consular access. The Supreme Court has upheld these particular rights. The U.S. Justice Department, Mexico, and the UN had all urged Perry to stay the execution.[16]

Perry's most controversial death penalty case came in 2004, when Cameron Todd Willingham was executed for the murder of his three daughters in a fire that investigators ruled as arson. But as he sat on death row, scientists compiled a report that posed strong questions about the legitimacy of the evidence. *New Yorker* writer David Grann, whose lengthy September 7, 2009, article described an extraordinary rush to justice, said fire investigators told him that first- and second-degree burns suffered by Willingham were consistent with being in a fire before the moment of "flashover," that is, when everything in a room suddenly ignites.[17]

After the execution, the Texas Forensic Commission ordered a reexamination of the case, and fire scientist Craig Beyler found, as had other scientists before him, that no evidence existed to conclude that arson was committed. Beyler was never able to present his evidence to the commission because Perry abruptly replaced its chairman with someone who cancelled the meeting and disassociated the commission from any further investigation. Once a defendant is executed, the case becomes moot, and authorities no longer have to defend their actions.[18]

■ SIXTEEN YEARS

In 2008, five years after he was cleared of aggravated sexual assault in Texas, Wiley Fountain was discovered sleeping out on the street. He'd done sixteen years for a crime he didn't commit.[19]

It all started in January 1986, when he walked down a Dallas street in a warm-up suit and baseball cap. A man fitting his description had raped and robbed a pregnant woman earlier that evening on a nearby street. Fountain swore he was at home at that time of the crime, and a witness backed him up, but the victim identified him as the perpetrator, and at age thirty, he was convicted and sentenced to forty years. Eventually he was cleared by DNA evidence and issued a full pardon by Perry. The real assailant was never found. Fountain received financial compensation—which is unusual in such cases. The $190,000 he cleared added up to less than $12,000 for each year in prison. But nothing in his life had prepared him to handle such a sum, and it was soon gone. He'd been "living high," he said. Soon he was collecting aluminum cans and sleeping on the street. Then he disappeared.[20]

In 2008 CNN reporter Ed Lavandera interviewed fifteen of the seventeen men who'd been exonerated by DNA evidence in Dallas County, Texas, since 2001. Few had managed to find steady, full-time employment because their convictions routinely popped up in criminal background checks. Lavandera described the men as "scarred" humans. Greg Wallis, who had spent seventeen years in prison, figured he was lucky to make it out alive. Countless fights with other inmates had left him "battered, bloodied and bruised," Lavandera said. "I don't like being around people," Wallis told Lavandera. "If I could do it I'd move into the woods and live off the land."[21]

David Shawn Pope, a self-described "artistic Southern boy," left Dallas and moved in with his mother in Northern California after he was exonerated and released. Seven years out of prison he was still looking for full-time employment. He spent much time playing guitar and writing songs but wrote nothing about his time in prison because "it was so painful," Pope said.[22]

Perry contended that all the Texas exonerations demonstrated that the system works well. "We have a very lengthy and methodical process of appeals," he said a year after Cole's posthumous pardon. "And that is a great and good mark for Texas."[23]

When Georgia executed Troy Davis in 2011, seven of nine witnesses had recanted their testimony against him.[24] Many doubted that authorities had arrested the right man, but not even a mass movement in countries around the world could save him.[25]

■ BOZELLA GETS HIS FIGHT

In 1977 Emma Crapser, ninety-two, was murdered in her Pough-keepsie, New York, home on her return from a bingo game. Six years later, based almost entirely on the testimony of two criminals who repeatedly changed their stories, Dewey Bozella, twenty-four, was convicted of the murder.[26] No physical evidence implicated him. In fact, the fingerprint of another man, Donald Wise, was recovered from the scene. Wise was later convicted of committing a nearly identical murder of another elderly woman in the same neighborhood.

Bozella finally won the right to a new trial in 1990. Prosecutors offered to free him in exchange for an admission that he had committed the crime. The forced confession would have let them off the hook for prosecuting an innocent man. Bozella turned down the deal, but his bad luck held and a jury convicted him again. As years piled on top of each other, he held to his principles. Whenever he came up for parole, he refused to express remorse for the crime he swore he didn't commit, killing his chance for release.

Determined not to surrender to self-pity and hopelessness, Bozella, while serving time in Sing Sing, earned a bachelor's from Mercy College and a master's from the New York Theological Seminary. The Innocence Project persuaded a law firm to work pro bono on an appeal. As his new lawyers delved into the case, they found a retired police lieutenant who'd saved one file from all the cases he'd worked on throughout his career. It was Bozella's. He believed that someone would eventually look into the case again, and he wanted to be ready. The file included all the pieces of evidence favorable to Bozella that, contrary to the rules of the court, had been withheld from his lawyers. Eventually, a court freed him on October 28, 2009. He was fifty-two and had spent half his life in prison.

Bozella, the light heavyweight champion of Sing Sing, made headlines when he fulfilled his long-held dream to be a prizefighter. He won a cruiserweight contest in October 2011 in Los Angeles. HBO reviewed the facts of his conviction and exoneration for viewers and showed highlights from his bittersweet victory.[27] Bozella promptly retired. He received no financial compensation for his lost twenty-six years.

■ "NO RIGHT NOT TO BE FRAMED"

In 1977 eyewitnesses in Council Bluffs, Iowa, identified a white suspect in the fatal shooting of a night watchman at an auto dealership. The suspect consented to a lie-detector test, which he failed. But his case was dropped without explanation. Instead the prosecutors, David Richter and Joseph Hrvol, prosecuted two black out-of-towners, Terry Harrington and Curtis McGhee, plunging them into a Kafkaesque maze. Harrington and McGhee weren't offered the lie-detector test.[28]

Richter, the county attorney, had been appointed to his post and was up for election. He and Hrvol paid a sixteen-year-old car thief $5,000 to testify against the black suspects. The teen kept changing his story about who he saw, what he saw, and even whether the weapon used in the murder was a shotgun or a pistol. Years later, when the case against Harrington and McGhee unraveled, it was in light of "new" evidence—evidence that the prosecutors had suppressed year after year as they went on with their lives. Ultimately, the Iowa Supreme Court ruled that the teenaged witness had been coached by prosecutors and was a "liar and perjurer."[29]

Iowa law prevented Harrington and McGhee, who'd served twenty-five years in prison, from seeking compensation from the county or state, so they sued the prosecuting attorneys. In 2010 the case reached the U.S. Supreme Court. Richter and Hrvol mounted a startling defense. Basically ignoring the facts of the murder itself, they contended there is "no freestanding constitutional right not to be framed." Before justices had a chance to rule, the two sides reached a settlement, making the case moot. But in previous rulings the Roberts court had already granted prosecutors blanket civil immunity. (It would be interesting to see whether immunity would still hold if prosecutors buried a corpse in someone's yard and then prosecuted the resident for murder.) Earlier, ruling against framed ex-convict John Thompson of Louisiana, the five-justice majority asserted that if prosecutors aren't shielded from lawsuits, they'll be targets for a wave of nuisance briefs filed against them by jailhouse lawyers.[30] This supposition almost makes sense until you run into a case like Harrington and McGhee's. Richter and Hrvol continued practicing law after the settlement (although no longer as prosecutors).[31]

■ HIDDEN BLOOD RESULTS

In April 2011 the Roberts court overturned a $14 million civil judgment in favor of John Thompson, who at age twenty-two was set up for armed robbery and murder convictions by prosecutors in the office of New Orleans district attorney Harry Connick Sr., father of the singer and actor.[32] First, prosecutors manipulated evidence to obtain a guilty verdict against Thompson for an armed robbery. Then, they used that conviction to obtain a death sentence when they subsequently prosecuted him for a murder he didn't commit. Thompson served eighteen years in prison, fourteen of them on death row, before an investigator hired by an appellate team of pro bono lawyers found a long-forgotten report sent to the prosecutors on the blood type of the armed robber. It was type B. Thompson was O. Prosecutors had hidden the report. Thompson's lawyers proved that at least four prosecutors knew about the test and its results.[33] In fact, the pro bono team eventually discovered ten separate pieces of evidence that prosecutors had hidden.[34] For example, more than one witness reported seeing a gunman six feet tall with close-cropped hair running away from the murder scene. Thompson was five feet eight with a bushy Afro.[35]

Thompson, now director of the New Orleans–based Resurrection After Exoneration, a support group for exonerated inmates, has painstakingly reconstructed the strategy prosecutors employed to railroad him. In an op-ed piece in the *New York Times*, he wrote that after his arrest in January 1985 they

> took me to the homicide division, and played a cassette tape on which a man I knew named Kevin Freeman accused me of shooting a man. He had also been arrested as a suspect in the murder. A few weeks earlier he had sold me a ring and a gun; it turned out that the ring belonged to the victim and the gun was the murder weapon.
>
> My picture was on the news, and a man called in to report that I looked like someone who had recently tried to rob his children. Suddenly I was accused of that crime, too. I was tried for the robbery first. My lawyers never knew there was blood evidence at the scene, and I was convicted based on the victims' identification.

> After that, my lawyers thought it was best if I didn't testify at the murder trial. So I never defended myself, or got to explain that I got the ring and the gun from Kevin Freeman. And now that I officially had a history of violent crime because of the robbery conviction, the prosecutors used it to get the death penalty.

Locked up in Louisiana's infamous Angola Prison, "I was put in a dead man's cell. His things were still there; he had been executed only a few days before."[36]

Eventually, Thompson wrote, he got "lucky" because the lawyers working on his appeal went to extraordinary lengths. The firm hired an investigator, who discovered the secret blood test. After Thompson's convictions were overturned and he sued the prosecutors and the district attorney's office, jurors in a civil trial awarded him $1 million for every year he spent on death row, but the Roberts court, voting 5-4, made sure he never received it. Justice Clarence Thomas, writing for the majority, concluded that the case was only a "single incident" and didn't prove a pattern of similar violations.[37] Yet Thomas's version of events conflicted with known facts. He disregarded a raft of similar outrages in New Orleans that also consisted of prosecutors concealing key evidence from defense lawyers. One of the prosecutors had worked on six cases that resulted in death sentences. In five of them, courts reversed the convictions for prosecutorial misconduct.[38]

In Louisiana, only convicts sentenced to death have the right to court-appointed appeals lawyers. "But," wrote Thompson, "there are more than four thousand people serving life without parole in Louisiana, almost none of whom have lawyers after their convictions are final. Someone needs to look at those cases to see how many others might be innocent."[39]

■ A DRAMATIC ILLUSTRATION

None of the prosecutors who put Thompson on death row were punished. They weren't even fired. Pace Law School professor Robert Gershman, who has written widely on prosecutors' misconduct, contends, as do other experts, that under Chief Justice John Roberts, the Supreme Court has followed a shocking course, shielding prosecutors with more and more armor to protect their misconduct even as more cases of misconduct are exposed. "The Thompson case," he said, "is a dramatic illustration of how an innocent person was nearly executed. If the [Roberts] court is insensitive to that, it tells you where we are with the criminal justice system."[40]

Two years before the Roberts court pronounced its ruling against Thompson, the same five justices shielded the Los Angeles County District Attorney's Office from being sued for using jailhouse informers who repeatedly lied to juries. The ruling threw out a suit by former marine Thomas Goldstein, who spent twenty-four years in prison for a murder in Long Beach that he didn't commit. The justices barely looked at the facts of the case. They focused their concern not on Goldstein, who was framed, but on prosecutors, who, the court ruled, shouldn't have to live in fear of lawsuits.[41]

In Thompson's suit, a friend-of-the-court brief was filed on his behalf by Paul D. Clement, U.S. solicitor general during the second Bush administration. Clement pointed out that police officers, who receive no immunity for their misconduct, don't seem to suffer from their condition. "Step back and ask yourself the question," he said. "Which of these people should know better? The prosecutor or the police officer?"[42]

Gerald Burge, also framed for murder in Louisiana around the same time as Thompson, served six years in prison. His appeals attorney learned that the investigating officer had hid evidence that established Burge's innocence in the trunk of his car and subsequently dated and eventually married the murder victim's sister. Later it was proved that the officer urged her and her mother to lie on the witness stand. Burge had been sentenced to life without parole. Because he was framed by police and not prosecutors, he managed to win a civil judgment for $4.3 million against the St. Tammany Sheriff's Office and the lead detective, but his case remained tied up on appeal.[43]

Because rogue prosecutors are armed with prodigious, almost otherworldly immunity, they aren't required to provide us with explanations for their bizarre actions. All we can do is speculate, but it appears that in many cases they decide who the perpetrator is and build a case around that conclusion, without considering other possibilities.

Social scientists have repeatedly uncovered a human tendency to see what they expect to see. Once they decide a suspect is guilty, prosecuting authorities seem to look upon the evidence differently—automatically and often unconsciously sorting the data in ways that will conform to their expectations. A closed, limited mind is a major building block of incompetence, but combine it with an abnormal thirst for victory, and results can be deadly. In some cases it is clear that authorities knew the identity of the actual perpetrators and could have assembled cases against them. Yet they chose instead to frame the innocent. Sometimes they appear to be protecting their informants, but this explanation holds for only a fraction of cases.

■ MISSION CORRUPTED

In novelist Pierre Boulle's astute *The Bridge over the River Kwai*, Lieutenant Colonel Nicholson, a prisoner of war, intends to build an outstanding bridge in order to prove his personal skills as well as the case for intrinsic British superiority. Nicholson gradually loses sight of the ultimate objective, which is to win the war, and he becomes a pawn of the very Japanese empire he wishes to prove inferior. Maybe a similar dynamic applies to some prosecuting authorities. No longer recognizing that their own mission is to seek justice, they focus instead on mounting a case against the suspects in their sights. They become servants of injustice, the cause they originally hoped to defeat. Louisville attorney Nathan Miller says that he's repeatedly seen prosecutors "lose sight of what they're charged with doing, which is to seek a just result. Most are just out to win, which is not their job at all."[44]

Various writers have created characters who wrestle with an urge to play God—King Lear, Dr. Frankenstein, Charles Foster Kane. The stories resonate because we recognize the characters, whose stories reflect centuries of human experience. Prosecuting attorneys, conferred with immense powers, can become enamored with the idea of not just playing God, but being God, deciding who lives, who dies, who pays a price, and who is passed over by the dark angels of death and affliction.

It's frequently difficult to determine whether authorities set out to frame someone or whether they are merely incompetent. Take the case of Juan Rivera, who was convicted in 1992 for the rape and murder of Holly Staker, an eleven-year-old babysitter, in Waukegan, Illinois.[45] Rivera, then twenty-one, with a history of psychological problems, confessed to the crime after four days of interrogation, including a twenty-four-hour session that was barely interrupted. At different points during the ordeal, he banged his head on a wall and pulled out a clump of his hair. No physical evidence linked Rivera, a ninth-grade dropout, to the crime.

■ UNINDICTED COEJACULATORS

In 2005 DNA testing proved that the semen taken from Holly's body wasn't Rivera's. But prosecutor Michael Mermel refused to let go of the case. He managed to convict Rivera again in 2009, after suggesting to the jury that Staker was sexually active and that the semen could have come from someone else. Mermel based his preposterous second-ejaculator theory on an incident three years earlier in which Staker had been molested. It wouldn't be the last time that Lake County prosecutors, faced with DNA that didn't belong to the accused, suggested that the source was an unnamed lover. And the theory isn't the property of only that particular office. Prosecutors have used it frequently enough for it to have been given a name by defense attorneys: the unindicted coejaculator theory.

A state appellate court finally reversed Rivera's conviction in December 2011. He was released at age thirty-nine after spending almost half his life in prison, tried and convicted three times for a crime he didn't commit.[46] Mermel, finally feeling pressure, retired the same week after twenty-one years on the job.[47] His annual salary was $137,879. Mermel's boss, State's Attorney Michael Waller, announced he wouldn't run for reelection. Neither was officially disciplined.

Not long before Rivera's release, he was interviewed by Andrew Martin of the *New York Times*. Rivera's arms were decorated with prison tattoos Martin described as "menacing." But Martin also noted, "Rivera smiled easily and became relaxed, almost serene, a fact that he attributes to a religious conversion in prison. 'The only thing that is incarcerated is my body,' he said. 'My mind is free here.'"[48]

Rivera had to serve another six years even after DNA evidence proved him innocent, stark evidence of how firmly authorities can hang on to innocent prisoners when they're determined to do so. The Lake County State's Attorney's Office that wouldn't let go of Rivera is, not surprisingly, the source of an alarming number of wrongful convictions under challenge. "They can never admit a mistake," said Kathleen Zellner, a lawyer suing Lake County on behalf of Jerry Hobbs, who spent five years in jail for killing his daughter Laura and her friend Krystal.[49] In May 2005 he found the girls' bodies near their homes in Zion. Both had been stabbed numerous times. Prosecutors alleged Hobbs killed them because he was angry that his daughter was outside when she was supposed to be home. Both defense attorneys and prosecutors acknowledged that no physical evidence linked Hobbs to the murders.

Two years after Hobbs's arrest, a private laboratory hired by his lawyers discovered that there had been sperm in his daughter's vagina, anus, and mouth. The sperm DNA didn't match Hobbs's. Mermel suggested that Laura could have gotten the sperm on her while playing in the woods, where couples might have sex. Hobbs remained in jail. Ultimately, the DNA was found to match that of a friend of Krystal's older brother named Jorge Torrez, a former Zion resident who was already serving a sentence in a Virginia jail for attacking three women. A judge released Hobbs in 2010, three years after he was proved innocent.

Hobbs, who moved to Texas and was trimming trees for a living, told Martin of the *Times* that he'd confessed to the crime because he hadn't slept in days and figured the truth would come out. "I found my daughter," he said. "She didn't even have eyes in her head. I was already broken. They didn't have to break me."[50]

Mermel said he still suspected that Hobbs was the killer and that the sperm was not related to the crime. Perhaps, he said, Torrez masturbated while visiting Krystal's brother, and then Laura got it on her hands and unknowingly transferred it elsewhere. "They have popcorn-movie night, and the little girl is in the same bed where this guy did it," Mermel said by way of explanation. "How do we get colds? We touch our mouths, we touch our nose. What does a woman do after she urinates?" In the lobby of the prosecutor's office, Mermel demonstrated the theory for Martin by standing and pulling his hand between his legs, as if wiping himself. "Front to back, O.K.?" Waller and Mermel never charged Torrez, but their successors did. He was also charged in federal court for another Virginia murder.[51]

In another case, Mermel opposed a new trial for a man convicted of killing an unidentified woman. When her identity became known years after the initial trial, it turned out that her former husband had once admitted that he had killed her. Mermel dismissed the confession as rants from a "one-armed Cuban feces-covered masturbator." He told the *Chicago Tribune*, "The taxpayers don't pay us for intellectual curiosity. They pay us to get convictions"—a total misreading of a prosecutor's duties.[52]

■ THE WEST MEMPHIS THREE

Solving crimes can generally be broken down into three steps: (1) learn the identity of the perpetrator; (2) make an arrest; and (3) make it stick. When the crime is particularly notorious, authorities feel pressured to pay more attention to a fourth imperative: act fast. No case illustrates this more vividly than that of the West Memphis Three, three innocent teens who were tried and convicted in the hideous 1993 murders of three eight-year-old Cub Scouts.[53] The scouts' bodies were found hog-tied near their homes in West Memphis, Arkansas, a rough-edged town across the river from Memphis, Tennessee. The bodies showed signs of torture, and investigators quickly seized on the theory that the boys were killed as part of a satanic ritual. They targeted people they thought might fit a satanic profile, which quickly led them to nonconformist teen Damien Echols. He cut his jet-black hair in an odd, asymmetrical fashion, listened to heavy metal rock, and wore lots of black. Plus, he'd proclaimed himself a follower of Wicca, a religion based in witchcraft. Police picked up his friend Jessie Misskelley Jr., who had an IQ of 72, and questioned him for hours without his parents or an attorney present. He confessed. Prosecutors, basing much of their case on this confession (which Misskelley quickly recanted), won conviction against Echols, Misskelley, and their friend Jason Baldwin.

That much of Misskelley's confession contradicted evidence did not bother the investigators. He told them the bodies were tied with rope, for example, when in fact the boys' own shoestrings had been used. All three defendants were in classes during the time he said they'd committed the crimes. He also said the other two teens raped the boys, but there was no evidence of rape. Echols drew a death sentence, and the court sentenced Misskelley and Baldwin to life in prison. Fortunately for Echols, his legal team was able to delay execution.

The three would probably still be imprisoned—providing Echols stayed a step ahead of execution—were it not for two documentary filmmakers who journeyed to West Memphis expecting to shoot a film about three teens who were ritual murderers.[54] Instead the filmmakers kept uncovering material that pointed to innocence. DNA testing unearthed no evidence that any of the three defendants had been at the scene or touched the victims. In fact, there was no physical evidence connecting them at all. It turned out that an "expert" witness for the prosecution owned a mail-order doctorate. Another witness was a jailhouse snitch who regularly claimed cellmates confessed to him privately. Bite marks on one of the victims, overlooked by investigators and not mentioned in the trial, didn't match the teeth of any of the defendants. Circumstantial evidence pointed to a man who had his teeth removed years later, after the bite marks were made public. The man told conflicting stories about the circumstances of his dental work.

The case against Echols, Misskelley, and Baldwin was worse than flimsy. Appealing to blind panic and prejudice, it was devoid of substance. Word spread. Books, a fact-filled Internet site, and other films followed. The rock group Metallica took up the cause of freeing the three teens, and lawyers hammered away with a variety of appeals. The original case eventually collapsed, but it took many years.

Ultimately, three men in their thirties, convicted half their lives ago, walked out of prison in 2011. They'd submitted Alford pleas, rarely used pleas through which a defendant can proclaim innocence while acknowledging there is enough evidence for a jury to find him or her guilty. The judge sentenced them to time served—more than eighteen years.

■ FALSE CONFESSIONS

False confessions such as the one used to help convict the Memphis Three are far more prevalent than common sense would dictate. In fact, they've been discovered so often that researchers have published studies explaining the phenomenon. One such study in the March 2004 *North Carolina Law Review* focused on 125 false-confession cases. "There are three groups of people most likely to confess," concluded Steven A. Drizin, a law professor at Northwestern who conducted the study with Richard A. Leo, a criminology professor at the University of California–Irvine. "They are the mentally retarded, the mentally ill and juveniles."[55]

TV and film can't come close to depicting the reality behind the closed doors of the interrogation room for the simple reason that it's not feasible to follow the proceedings minute by minute for four, eight, sixteen, or thirty-two hours. Drizin found false confessions most common in murder cases. "Those are the cases where there is the greatest pressure to obtain confessions," he said, "and confessions are often the only way to solve those crimes."[56] He advocates for videotaping police interrogations to, in effect, allow the public to see the sausage being made.

The ultimate disposition of the Memphis Three case laid bare a prosecution team that perhaps saw its job in a way it's not generally perceived. The perpetrators of the atrocious crime might very well still be residing in the town, but the Alford pleas have allowed authorities to pretend they've solved the murders.

PART 3
Failed Results

9

Walking the "Toughest Beat" in Guccis

DURING THE SAVINGS-AND-LOAN SCANDAL OF THE 1980S, A WARM-UP FOR THE banking and real estate collapse of 2008, a questioner at a congressional hearing asked scheming, silver-tongued financier Charles Keating whether the $1.5 million he'd contributed to politicians could really buy him influence. "I certainly hope so," quipped Keating, who'd eventually do four years for crimes that included swindling thousands of retirees out of their life savings. Keating, who once called a meeting with five senators who had received his contributions (and they all showed up), was a personification of how wrong the system can get when money-hungry public servants exchange legislation for cash.[1]

This leads us to the California prison guards union. It would be tough to find an institution that relies more on political contributions to achieve its ends. Although its membership roll is only about one-tenth the size of the California Teachers Association, its political clout exceeds that of all other labor unions in a state that often leads the way on policy. The California Correctional Peace Officers Association (CCPOA) is a uniquely powerful union that's used to getting what it wants even though it can't call a strike—the ultimate labor weapon—without causing immediate self-immolation. During the reign of Don Novey, who served as president of the union from 1982 to 2002, the state constructed twenty-one new prisons, spiraling the total number of adult institutions to thirty-three. As his union gained might, Novey proved to Democrats and Republicans alike that building prisons and filling them with inmates can gain votes for politicians and simultaneously help their donors. But the state's prison network became a Frankenstein's monster that fed off California's absurdly harsh three-strikes law—the toughest in the nation. The union had a strong hand in creating this legal monster.

To understand how the guards' policies affected the state as a whole, one could measure resources allocated to prisons against resources going to colleges and universities. From 1980 to 2011 the state's higher education spending was reduced by 13 percent in inflation-adjusted dollars, whereas spending on prisons and related correctional programs—boosted by a penal code that the prison guards helped fashion—skyrocketed 436 percent.[2]

As part of Novey's ongoing mission to frighten voters into submission, the union set up straw lobbying groups such as Crime Victims United of California, which was funded 100 percent by the guards. Novey also made sure everyone understood that his union's strength and money could exact punishments as well as rewards. After District Attorney Greg Strickland dared to convene a grand jury to investigate allegations of brutal beatings by prison guards within his Kings County turf, the union opposed his reelection in 1998, spending $30,000 to proclaim that Strickland was soft on crime. He lost.[3]

CCPOA's thirty-three thousand members—prison guards and parole officers—pay monthly dues of about eighty dollars each. That totals approximately $30 million a year, and perhaps a third of this money is spent on lobbying. The last labor contract Novey negotiated (which expired in 2006) earned the average union member around $70,000 a year—and with overtime more than $100,000.[4] Not bad for a high school graduate with no additional education beyond sixteen weeks of training at the Correctional Officer Academy, where trainees earn $3,050 per month to learn their job. More than 120,000 people apply to the academy every year, according to the state Legislative Analyst's Office, but it enrolls only about nine hundred. As the *Wall Street Journal*'s Allysia Finley facetiously noted, its acceptance rate of less than 1 percent makes it far more selective than Harvard, which comes in at 6.2 percent.[5]

■ "OUT ON THE STREET"

After Novey's departure, the guards continued his policy of focusing on politics and showering money on politicians. They had a testy relationship with Governor Arnold Schwarzenegger but still scored plenty of successes during his tenure. In fact, in 2006, three years after Schwarzenegger started his first term as governor, Roderick Hickman resigned as head of the prison system because, he said, the guards were still calling the shots over policy decisions and undermining efforts to divert offenders into nonprison alternatives. When attempts were made to reduce the number of inmates, Hickman said, the union financed scary ads telling voters that powerful forces were plotting to put "felons out on the street."[6] The union's leaders gleefully agree that in no other state do prison guards wield such outsized political control.

Two years before Hickman quit in disgust, polls indicated that voters overwhelmingly favored Proposition 66, a measure to reform the three-strikes law by requiring that a third charge be violent or "serious" to trigger a third-strike sentence. But the guards spent $1 million to beat back the measure, and in the last days of the November campaign, the union teamed up with Governor Schwarzenegger and former governors Jerry Brown, Pete Wilson, Gray Davis, and George Deukmejian to launch a burst of radio and TV ads warning that the measure "would release 26,000 dangerous criminals and rapists." The claim was preposterous, but the coalition rolled right over 66.[7]

In 2008 came Proposition 5, the Nonviolent Offender Rehabilitation Act, to build a firmer foundation under an underfunded drug reform initiative that had passed overwhelmingly in 2000. Proposition 5 sought to reduce prison overcrowding by letting courts provide treatment rather than prison for nonviolent drug users. A key provision would have stopped sending parolees back to prison for one failed drug test. This aimed at the cornerstone of the guards' penal strategy, which was to level lengthy sentences against drug users. The union funneled $1.8 million into the campaign to defeat Proposition 5, more than half the funds raised for the effort.[8] The guards and their allies in the prison-industrial complex, realizing they'd made a terrible mistake by not blocking the 2000 reform initiative, labeled Proposition 5 the "Drug Dealers' Bill of Rights." Their slick ad campaign was fronted by Martin Sheen, who had a reputation as a political liberal. Further blurring fantasy and reality, Sheen was best known to the public for portraying President Jed Bartlet on *The West Wing*. The actor's smooth, baritone delivery of ad scripts outweighed stiff objections from experts. The guards once again prevailed at a cost of fifty-five dollars each—a bargain.

In 2008 Brown, whose first two terms as governor ended in 1983, was already gearing up his 2010 comeback campaign. The CCPOA contributed $2 million to his campaign.[9] Union officers went through the motions of grilling Brown's gubernatorial opponent, Republican candidate Meg Whitman, but came away revolted by her hints that someone ought to take another look at the guards' pension deal, which awarded lifetime retirement payments at age fifty-five for up to 85 percent of salary.[10]

After Brown's decisive win, the union, the largest single contributor to his campaign, won the guards their sweetest contract yet. Some of its provisions were startlingly brazen. They stipulated, for example, that ten guards at each of the fifty-four penal institutions could attend their annual union convention at taxpayers' expense. The new deal gave members eighteen more days off over the life of the two-year contract, bringing the typical guard's time off to more than eight weeks. Under the old contract, guards could earn up to $130 a month for remaining physically fit. Now they could earn it by simply going to the doctor for an annual physical, a unique provision that may not exist anywhere else in the western world. And buried inside the legalese was a complicated but lucrative giveaway that allowed them to save an unlimited number of vacation days and exchange them for cash at a higher pay rate upon retirement. Brown signed off on all this while the state faced a $25 billion deficit and was sending out pink slips to thousands of teachers, social workers, and health-care professionals. (Guards suffered no layoffs or days off without pay. Who would watch the inmates while they stayed home?)[11]

While the guards prospered, state health and social welfare programs were eviscerated, some state roads crumbled into imitations of third world goat paths, and resident tuition at the University of California for the 2011–12 academic year rose 18 percent to $12,150. The University of California had 234,000 students; its sister system, California State University, more than 400,000; and the California Community Colleges more than 2.9 million. Their faculty and staff members numbered in the hundreds of thousands. Yet they lacked the political clout of thirty-three thousand prison guards and parole officers, whose prison system ate up a larger portion of the budget than all three systems of higher education combined.

■ SUPREME COURT ORDER

Brown named as his labor secretary Marty Morgenstern, who'd negotiated earlier lucrative compensation packages for CCPOA while working for Governor Gray Davis. Brown's personnel director Ronald Yank had served as the union's attorney. Still, calls for a more reasonable way of handling criminal justice were starting to be heard. For example, a July 7, 2008, NPR report on San Quentin State Prison exposed 360 men whose bunks were stacked in a gymnasium like warehouse merchandise.[12] Only a day earlier four prisoners had been injured seriously when a riot broke out in San Quentin's dining hall.

In February 2010 the *San Francisco Chronicle* learned that prison officials were planning to shave $250 million from rehabilitation spending in prisons over the next several months.[13] They had also dismissed about 850 prison workers who were running programs on substance abuse, anger management, high school equivalency, and marketable skills such as plumbing, horticulture, and graphic arts. News of the cutbacks came from teachers on their way out the door, not the Corrections Department, though it maintained a still-thriving Public Relations Department. At San Quentin State alone, thirteen of nineteen programs were eliminated, reported teachers there, including the high school program. The cuts dramatically demonstrated prison officials' priorities. The system was disabling programs that could help inmates quit their incarceration cycle.

When Brown took over in January 2011, the prisons were so crammed with humanity that a federal judge in San Francisco found that an average of one inmate per week was dying as a result of medical neglect or malfeasance.[14] This, the court ruled, was a cruel and unusual punishment forbidden by the Bill of Rights. Finally, in May 2011 the Supreme Court, in a 5-4 ruling, agreed that the inmate total of approximately 143,000 must be cut by around 33,000 within two years.[15] The ruling noted that California prisons were built to hold 80,000. An over-the-top legal code guided by prison guards and executed fondly by out-of-control district attorneys had brought the kettle to a boil.

Yet nineteen states, including Louisiana, Colorado, Illinois, Pennsylvania, and Texas, had filed a friend-of-the-court brief supporting the California status quo. The states sought "flexibility" in the face of tight budgets and growing prison populations, and as their brief freely admitted, they feared similar suits might be filed against them.

Justice Anthony Kennedy, a Sacramento native, joined with the four liberal justices to side against conservatives in this decision. Speaking from the bench, he cited examples of suicidal prisoners being held in "telephone booth-sized cages without toilets." Others, ill from cancer or in severe pain, died without being examined by a doctor. Sometimes, he said, as many as fifty-four convicts shared a single toilet. He quoted a former Texas prison director who, after touring California lockups, called conditions "appalling," "inhumane," and unlike any he'd seen in more than thirty-five years of prison work.[16]

Yet then–Los Angeles County district attorney Steve Cooley was one of many around the state who predicted a crime wave if minor offenders were let out of prison. Many, he said, "will commit crimes which would never have occurred had they remained in custody."[17]

The leader of the California State Senate's Republican minority, Bob Dutton, argued that California should construct new prisons fast.[18] He didn't say how to pay for these facilities though, and Dutton opposed virtually every effort to close the already immense budget deficit with new taxes. He also suggested that the state pressure the federal government to take custody of thousands of illegal immigrant felons housed in the state system.

Brown, rather than paroling or releasing low-level offenders or reestablishing the rehabilitative programs that had gradually been shed, answered the directive by sending many newly sentenced prisoners to serve their time in county jails not designed for lengthy stays. "Our goal," said the state's Secretary of the Department of Corrections and Rehabilitation, Matthew Cate, apparently without a trace of irony, "is not to release inmates at all."[19] Yet county jails around the state were already packed, and their finances were a mess.

"California is a victim of its retributive sentencing policies—tough on crime," said Heidi Rummel, a University of Southern California law professor and former prosecutor. Incarcerating nonviolent offenders into old age "is extraordinarily expensive and probably doesn't have a significant impact on public safety."[20]

Lois Davis, a senior policy researcher at the Rand Corporation, said that when the state shifts inmates to counties, it should also shift enough money "to fund the treatment needs of this population."[21] But Brown proposed no additional funding. He and his disciples were like defeated generals planning to mount more attacks with divisions that had been annihilated by the enemy. Someone had to pay the piper for three decades of zero tolerance, but the state government and its fifty-eight counties all sat there waiting for the other guy to pick up the tab.

"What we found," wrote Rand's Davis, "is that ex-offenders tend to return to California communities with the least amount of healthcare, mental health and substance abuse resources. So where does that leave us? The state has been unable to meet the medical needs of prisoners, a disproportionate number of whom are afflicted by chronic ailments, so we are going to transfer them to county jails, from which they will eventually be released into the communities that are least able to help them."[22]

Even as Brown issued his irrational directives, some sheriffs, like Rod Hoops in San Bernardino County, began releasing low-level offenders and parole violators. The parole offenders hadn't necessarily committed new crimes. In most cases they'd broken rules, which meant they were supposed to do more time, usually about four months, tacked on in a simple administrative proceeding. In some cases they lost hard-won jobs to do the additional time, and in almost all cases they had no educational or rehabilitation programs open to them while they sat in their cells. The state had been routinely sending seven of ten parolees on a well-worn path to nowhere—back to prison—within three years. It's not coincidental that the state's parole officers also belong to the guards union.

Backed into a corner by the Supreme Court ruling, some elements of the state government began experimenting with more reasonable policies. Under the rules of a trial program for thirty-five parolees in Sacramento, parole violators were sent back to county jail for a few days instead of to state prison for months.[23] Angela Hawken, an associate professor of public policy at Pepperdine University who was charged with evaluating the program, called preliminary results "remarkable," especially in terms of deterring drug use.[24] Similar programs were in Hawaii and Washington State.

■ "NO CHANGED CIRCUMSTANCES"

Roughly two-thirds of California's ex-cons were reading below a ninth-grade level, in 2006, according to corrections department figures.[25] More than half were reading below a seventh-grade level, making them functionally illiterate, unable to read and follow complex written directions.[26] A total of 21 percent were reading below a third-grade level.[27] If the prison guards were truly interested in dealing seriously with public safety, they'd have advocated programs to improve these statistics. During that same year only 6 percent of California inmates managed to get into academic classes, and 5 percent attended vocational classes.[28] In February 2010, Kamala Harris, the Oakland prosecutor who in November 2010 was elected state attorney general, noted, "We know that when you go to prison and come out with no changed circumstances, you are prime to re-offend."[29]

■ LIFE FOR MINOR CRIMES

The Supreme Court order did nothing to change the ways of district attorneys who, using penalties still on the books, maintained the flow of inmates into the state system. "I think . . . eventually we will have the same [prison overpopulation] problem," said Michael Bien, whose law firm in 1990 launched a case addressing the poor mental health care in California prisons.[30] Bien's 1990 suit ultimately led to the 2011 Supreme Court ruling that the state must shrink its prison population by 33,000.[31] In one of the many ironies resulting from California's steroidal Gulag growth, the state cut $587 million in state-funded mental health services in 2009–11, according to the National Alliance on Mental Illness, a patient advocacy group.

Said Laurie Levenson, a criminal law scholar and former federal prosecutor on the faculty at Loyola University in Los Angeles, "We have to stop the insanity of sending nonviolent drug offenders and low-level theft offenders to prison for life. Nobody is saying we should let murderers out." Michael Romano, head of the Stanford Innocence Project, noted that California inmates were still serving life sentences for stealing a two-dollar pair of socks or twenty-dollar work gloves.[32]

Still, there were signs that the guards union might be losing its stranglehold on the state's criminal justice system. The union lost a $12.3 million defamation and breach of contract case after it elbowed out officials in Corrections USA, a national organization of prison guards. A bold bid to spread the union's power beyond the California border brought its net worth down from $16.5 million in 2006 to $4.7 million in 2010, according to testimony. At the same time, Chief Financial Officer Jeff Nicolaysen testified that the union had still budgeted $6 million the next year for lobbying, political campaign contributions, and advertising.[33]

The Supreme Court order, quickly followed by the passage of Proposition 36, didn't right all the wrongs, but a new course may have been set. And like California fashions, the new policies could spread to other states. In 2013 the National Conference of State Legislatures reported that as states strapped for cash began looking for ways to chip away at their oversized prison budgets, thirty-five adult correctional facilities in fifteen states had closed in the previous two years. Texas, Florida, Michigan, and New York each cut their prisoner rosters by more than a thousand prisoners. All had closed prisons in the previous two years.[34] It was still too early to tell whether the policy of zero tolerance had reached its peak or, like a bear market on Wall Street, would rise again while tracing a zigzag course toward new highs.

10

Mongo and Squeaky

SEVERAL YEARS BEFORE I THOUGHT ABOUT WRITING THIS BOOK, I DROVE 130 miles from Los Angeles to visit James Allen, the ex-fighter who was then doing time at a no-name private prison holding two thousand inmates in the high desert town of Taft, California. With me was Allen's trainer, Charlie Gergen. The prison sat along the edge of a dreary town set among scattered oil wells, many sucked dry and no longer cranking. This was a minimum-security institution—no concrete walls, just cyclone fences and razor wire. We passed some guards who had Wackenhut tags sewn onto their gray, wrinkled, mostly ill-fitting uniforms and entered a mournful lobby. A lanky woman in her forties stood at the counter. Let's call her Squeaky. She was in a guard uniform and had a lined, woebegone face befitting a town where jobs promising wildcatting adventures had been replaced by low-wage employment that required spending days and nights keeping men inside a cage. Squeaky ignored us as we fished blank visitor forms from a basket on the counter and filled them out.

Eventually she approached us and glanced at the forms in a half-interested manner. A flicker of satisfaction crossed the dead mask of her nondescript face. "You can't go in," she announced. It turned out that my khaki trousers were forbidden because inmates could also wear khakis, although all the inmates we'd seen from outside the fences wore white pants and shirts. Normally penitentiaries have visitation rules that include, for example, lists of acceptable clothing and what you can have in your pockets, and generally these rules are relatively easy to obtain. But this, the first private prison I'd ever dealt with, treated these rules as though they were top secret. I'd called ahead more than once for the rules, and each time I had been passed from one uninformed, not terribly nice person to another. Some contradicted each other. Others sounded like they were making up answers on the fly. Eventually the line or the thread of the conversation would go dead.

I apologized to Squeaky for my khaki offense and said I had shorts in the car. No, she said, shorts aren't allowed either. OK, I said, Gergen would go in alone while I tried to scare up other pants in town. She told us to wait, so I scratched the shopping trip and waited. Meanwhile she let other people come and go across the swinging door at the end of her counter. More time passed. We'd been in the lobby practically an hour when she finally walked over to us smiling. I hadn't seen her smile before and thought it might be a good sign. She pointed to the institutional clock on the wall and said, "Too late." It was one minute after the hour, so we weren't eligible to enter, she explained. We hadn't been told about any admittance deadline, only what time visitors had to leave, which wasn't for another two hours. Now we realized she'd been toying with us just to reach the sweet spot on the clock.

A word about Wackenhut: Wackenhut is a private security firm that was renamed the GEO Group in 2003. As the GEO Group, it currently runs lockups in fourteen states and is a component of British-based G4S, the world's largest security company. G4S, a corporate monument to the global bull market in both security and privatization, employs more than 580,000 employees in 110 countries and is the second-largest private-sector employer on the planet, exceeded only by Walmart. Its GEO subsidiary advertises itself as "a world leader in the delivery of private correctional and detention management, community residential re-entry services as well as behavioral and mental health services to federal, state and local government agencies."[1] GEO operates in the United States, Australia, South Africa, and Britain, apparently willing to go anywhere there's a market for English speakers in wrinkled gray uniforms to maintain penal order. I didn't know any of this when I visited the prison in Taft.

Back to Squeaky. We'd been nothing but polite to this woman. Gergen and I were showered, neatly attired, well-behaved, and completely sober, and we carried no weapons, narcotics, or other contraband. But for reasons known only to her, she'd selected us for harassment. I tried to appeal to her better nature: "Look, it's a five-hour round trip. We're not criminals. We just want to visit our friend." She could at least let Gergen in to visit him, I pleaded. It might help Allen's path to rehabilitation. Wasn't that her goal too?

Nothing doing. So, as many of us do when we're being dismissed by some clerical creature, I asked to speak with her supervisor. I had to ask her twice. "All right," she said, drawing out the last syllable, pronouncing it as though we'd asked to be sheared and castrated. Squeaky picked up the phone and moved away from us so that we couldn't hear the conversation. Throughout all this, Gergen said not one word. He was a glib, loquacious Aussie who could tell funny stories all night about fights and trysts he'd experienced during a lifetime at the boxing trade, but he preferred to let me do the talking on this one.

We waited several more minutes and then heard something I recall quite distinctly—a voice from far away, booming, angry, as though somebody were shouting insults at a referee across a football field: "Who's been giving one of my people trouble?" It felt vaguely familiar, almost like déjà vu, and then it was repeated, closer this time: "Awright, where are they? Who's been giving one of my people trouble?" Later I would make the connection to a fairy tale I'd first heard as a toddler: "Fee-fi-fo-fum, I smell the blood of an Englishman." After climbing the beanstalk, Jack heard the giant before he could see him.

The shouter turned a corner and came into full view. He was a water buffalo, white, coming at us fast. I was waking to a bad dream with everything reversed because reality was suddenly bizarre. The illusion had been the belief that we were operating in a world of reason and sanity. No wonder Squeaky looked so delighted. She knew all along she had this wrathful ringer on the bench.

The bellowing was in the form of a question, so I volunteered an answer. "I'm the one giving her trouble." But that wasn't correct. "What I mean is, she's giving us trouble." The shouter, now shifting his course a mite so it was aimed straight at me, was also in uniform, but not the wrinkled regulation gray. He wore a white, pressed shirt with military-type patches and captain's bars on the shoulders and dark trousers. He had a mustache, a balding crew-cut, a bull neck, weighed about 240 pounds, and was in his early forties. What to do? Here he comes. I stood my ground, forcing him to barrel into me or stop. He pulled up nose to nose, playground style.

I'd been training at a boxing gym for years, and although I considered ballooned-out weight lifters a threat, I knew the ones to watch out for were the wiry Tommy Hearns–type guys who could paralyze you with a four-punch combination you wouldn't see coming. And I knew something more important. If this ape managed to hurt me, I had Gergen in my corner. And Gergen was one of those Tommy Hearns–type guys who could paralyze him with a four-punch combination he'd never see coming.

But then what? Guards armed with mace and clubs were moving in and out of the lobby all the time. Even if we were able to fight our way out of this place, we were, as Gergen would recount later, city slickers in *Deliverance* country. And of course prison officials had our names and addresses. We'd filled them out on the visitor forms. This was a variation on the typical prison dynamic, which involves mostly urban prisoners and rural guards. Each group looks on the other as a bunch of aboriginal aliens who don't belong, except the guards are more obsessed with the inmates than the inmates are with their guards. To convicts, guards are usually the lesser of far worse evils. As a minimum security prison, this place was supposed to exude less tension than a typical penitentiary, but apparently no one had told this to Mongo and Squeaky, who generated hostility and strife for no apparent reason. They seemed to have categorized us as uppity inmates, and their mistake was so vivid that against my will, I too was infected. I felt a terrible powerlessness, a dreadful inability to exert control over my situation. What hell it must be to be a prisoner.

At this point, the only reasonable response was to move on, if that was still possible. I saw no way to turn this situation around, and if Gergen had a solution, he'd have tried it. No matter how legitimate your grievance might be, it's against the law to break into a prison. It was Mongo's move. Each moment he did nothing eroded his position. This allowed a saner dynamic to creep into the room. They sensed we weren't actually the typical inner-city targets that they normally tormented and that there might be an awful stink if they called in the cavalry. They'd have to settle for the satisfaction of knowing they'd done a good day's work: we ended up driving five hours for nothing.

■ THE STANFORD EXPERIMENT

Clearly the Mongo and Squeaky farce had wider implications. After all, these prison workers had authority over people's lives. Although their jobs called for an even temperament, the woman was vicious and the captain was a standard bully bereft of diplomatic skills. Almost certainly their behavior had caused problems for others before us and would do so again. When I was a newspaper reporter, I visited numerous lockups—local, state, and federal. Never had I run into guards or administrators anything like Mongo and Squeaky. Prison and jail staff might not always be particularly kind, but in my experience they were always polite enough and never clearly crazy. Nor had inmates ever told me stories resembling what we'd witnessed in Taft. But I hadn't dealt with a for-profit prison before. Had this made the difference? In a word, yes.

In 1971 Stanford psychologists hired male students to play roles in a mock prison for two weeks, twenty-four as inmates, twelve as guards. It all seemed harmless enough, an intriguing experience for everybody. The idea was to study the psychological effects of their roles on the volunteers, both guards and prisoners. But in almost no time at all the guards turned abusive, and although instructed not to harm prisoners, they resorted to torture to secure obedience. Prisoners reacted in various degrees of shock, distress, anger, and depression. Five showed such acute symptoms that the researchers let them out early. Others staged a rebellion. There was madness in the air, a sinister, almost supernatural force akin to whatever seized Stephen King's Jack Torrance in *The Shining*. The project director, also feeling the lure of sadistic authoritarianism, shoved the malevolent genie back in its bottle by shutting down the experiment after six days.[2]

The events at Stanford provide disturbing clues about the darkness that, under absolute conditions, can overwhelm our humanistic tendencies. The experiment, no doubt still providing thesis material for grad students, appeared to be pretty strong evidence in favor of careful selection when staffing jails and prisons. But if you pay only nine or ten bucks an hour, you can't always find perfection. The presence of Mongo and Squeaky and their bullying behavior was a logical result of the inefficiency and indifference that are part of the for-profit prison dynamic. Like them, the "guards" at Stanford were trained in a hurry and not paid handsome wages.

Hiring mercenaries to keep prisoners locked up, obedient, and dependent on profit-making companies is a giant step away from morality and good sense. Bear in mind that private prison firms can boost profits by cutting corners or even filing new charges against inmates. It's one thing to hire rent-a-cops to protect property, but quite another to substitute them for sworn officers and place them in charge of captive humans. The American Friends Service Committee isn't alone in its view that private prisons are "inherently unethical." These prisons are part of the same outsourcing mania that seized Chicago when it leased all its parking meters to a private firm. The firm made many promises and then proceeded to raise meter prices exponentially and screw everybody.[3]

GEO/Wackenhut all by itself has enough penal atrocities on its rap sheet to rival the Hell's Angels. The offenses include racial bigotry, cheating, lying, fraud, gratuitous strip searches, sexual assault, and inmate death. Yet the company's contracts keep coming. It's the American Gulag's own Halliburton, whose KBR subsidiary built showers on U.S. bases in Iraq that electrocuted military personnel and then won new Pentagon contracts anyway. The following are a few examples of GEO/Wackenhut's known transgressions:

- June 2010: GEO Group signs a consent decree with U.S. Department of Labor for discriminating against African-American job seekers at a Colorado detention facility; it distributes $290,000 to 446 applicants.
- May 2010: GEO Group pays out $3 million in a class-action suit for strip searches of as many as ten thousand arrestees without cause at six jails in Pennsylvania, Illinois, New Mexico, and Texas.
- February 2010: GEO Group settles for $7.5 million with a whistle-blower and Miami/Dade County, Florida, for fraudulent billing practices.
- March 2007: GEO Group settles with the family of a female inmate for an unknown amount after the inmate was assaulted and raped in a Texas county lockup and died in the jail.

- August 1999: Wackenhut loses a $12 million contract with a jail in Travis County, Texas, after several guards are charged with sexually assaulting female inmates; it pays $625,000 in fines for related mismanagement.[4]

Clearly Gergen and I got off lucky. But we'd left Allen behind, and we worried he'd have to answer to Mongo and Squeaky for our transgressions. I decided the best way to protect him was to put the incident on the record. I did not trust Wackenhut, so I contacted the Federal Bureau of Prisons, which had awarded the contract, to see if anyone there would care. Eventually, I was passed along to a public affairs officer who, learning that I wrote a column for a boxing magazine, actually did show concern of a sort. He asked me not to make the bureau look bad in my column.

Later I described our brush with Mongo and Squeaky to Allen. He wasn't surprised in the least. "I live with that every day," he said simply.

11

Prison Privateers and Jailing for Cash

PRISON CORPORATIONS ARE ENTREPRENEURIAL KIN TO THE THÉNARDIERS IN Hugo's *Les Misérables*. Paid to care for Cosette by her struggling, tragically deceived mother, they saw her as a commodity to exploit for labor and income. Modern Thénadiers hire hordes of lobbyists and propagandists to induce us to ignore the conflict of interest that's built into the very concept of a private prison, to disregard the plain truth that the mission of incarcerating humans is incongruent with the profit motive.

These privateers most obviously cross the line when they subtly advocate jailing people even though they either know or at least strongly suspect that it serves no social purpose. Those who lack the gene for rapacious greed might have a hard time believing that corporate chieftains, politicians, and other members of the Gulag industry would actually seek to unjustly imprison their fellow citizens merely to make extra dollars. Jailing the wrong people for cash sounds like an exaggerated cliché, the kind of evil that might be conceived by villainous buffoons in a Batman comic. But it's a multibillion-dollar industry that, unlike the Joker and the Penguin, has no caped heroes to oppose it.

Alan Greenspan, no leftist crank, famously observed that the U.S. invasion of Iraq in 2003 was "largely about oil"[1]—that is, it was a war fought for booty. Conducted under the cloak of government, it was the modern equivalent of releasing privateers on the high seas to scare up loot. In the scheme of things, locking up loads of people to make a fast buck is at least less lethal than bombarding them with the shock and awe of a modern death storm in order to harvest their resources. And those who can convince themselves that gratuitous incarceration somehow benefits society might fail to view it as the atrocity that it is.

Only a small segment of the global corporate structure makes a direct profit from expanding the Gulag. The rest of it probably doesn't much care one way or the other, although theorists, such as Frances Fox Piven at the City University of New York, make the case that the establishment sees wholesale incarceration as a useful method to preventively marginalize the oppressed masses before they can take their grievances into the street.[2] In any case, while a trip to the cooler may constitute a black hole of grief, danger, boredom, and towering unpleasantness to inmates, to a small army of beneficiaries it is an opportunity to extract some of the $70 billion a year generated from the care and feeding of the American prison-industrial complex. Maintaining these institutions is one of those chores, like processing sewage, that most folks prefer to leave to someone else. The distastefulness of the job makes it more lucrative for private companies willing to handle it. County jails, for instance, are generally run by deputies within the sheriff's departments. Working in the jail is often considered either a punishment or a form of hazing, so deputies assigned there tend to be rookies and rejects.

"The guards are in prison too," observed Patrick Russell, a retired investigator for the San Diego District Attorney's Office whose penitentiary trips generally left him vaguely disquieted. His is a common reaction to the impenetrable grimness. He continued, "Can you imagine what kind of person would work in one of those places day after day? Now imagine doing two shifts back to back so you can pull in overtime."[3] Custodial duty sits at the bottom of the police pecking order, even beneath the vice squad chore of hanging around men's rooms to monitor them for gay sex.

■ GLOBAL TEL LINK

Another element that makes the confinement business profitable is that no one with any political or financial clout is terribly finicky about what kind of job you do. An Alabama-based outfit by the name of Global Tel Link, for example, buys exclusive rights to connect calls made from the temperamental phones they install for inmates in jails and prisons around the country. The phones process only outgoing calls, which must be made collect, and calling charges are exorbitantly priced. When a firm serves customers who are a captive audience, it doesn't need to run spring sales to attract their business. A poll of users would find that malfunctions are common. Sometimes the other party seems to be speaking from deep inside a mine. Other times the call goes dead altogether. Although the average American knows little or nothing about these irksome connections and the steep bills that accompany them, a multitude of poor and powerless folks struggle with them every day.[4]

Prisoners and their families endure shoddy service and high prices in one jail transaction after another, whether they're making a call, arranging for a package, or purchasing toothpaste. Service can range from lousy to impossible. It's a natural consequence when the people awarding the monopoly contracts do not consult actual customers about what they experience.

▪ THE *MUSIC MAN* PRISONS

With a market capitalization of $3.8 billion,[5] Corrections Corporation of America (CCA) is the nation's largest private prison operator, running more than sixty correctional and detention facilities, owning most of them and leasing the rest. As of March 2013, it employed nearly seventeen thousand full-timers to watch over its inmates, who are spread out over institutions with a total capacity of ninety thousand.[6] Of course that's only a tiny sliver of the U.S. inmate population, which is why stock analysts figure the company has awesome growth potential. Citing "the long-term trend toward harsher incarceration in the United States," *Forbes* concluded that "the future looks bright" for CCA. The magazine pointed out that from 1980 to 2008, the prison population gained 375 percent and added, "That figure exceeds the growth in the general population—+32.4%—by more than a factor of 10."[7]

Forbes predicted that California, the biggest state with the biggest prison population, will at some point have to turn to private prisons to staunch some of its red ink (*Forbes* wrongly assumed private jailers would deliver on their promises to lower costs), and gushed without a trace of irony, "Fully 9.5% of the California state budget is allocated toward prisons. Only 5.7%, by comparison, goes to universities. Twenty-five years ago, prisons were 4% of the budget. Higher education represented 11% of the state budget." Actually, current state prison expenditures are higher than that—more like 11.5 percent. Still, it makes you wonder about the mind set of financial reporters who seem to think these malevolent priorities are something to celebrate: "The bottom line is that Corrections Corp. can't build prisons fast enough, and it will never run out of demand for its product. . . . Low costs, strong margins and an endless supply of 'customers' make this business model as good as they get."[8] In 1985 CCA gained attention when it boldly and publicly offered to take over the entire state prison system of Tennessee for $200 million. The bid was ultimately defeated by strong opposition from public employees and many skeptics within the legislature.

When Brenda Valencia finally finished her sentence for drug charges, she hoped to help stem the mandatory-sentencing currents that had put her away for so many birthdays and Christmases. "It's very difficult, getting the system to change," she said. "It's actually a money-making industry, and it's really strong." Trying to alert the public to tragic stories about imprisoning hapless souls for no good reason wasn't working, she said. So instead of trying to change the system she settled for counseling young girls. She tries to change lives one at a time.

Like the fast-talking Harold Hill in *The Music Man*, CCA is particularly adept at selling its spiel to rural communities. In some cases it's actually convinced town fathers to issue bonds to build a private prison on speculation, with no guarantee that a governmental entity will make use of the facility. Without owning horses, they bought horse carts, the theory being "build it and they will come." Once such a project is launched, local citizens and their political appendages become a lobbying branch of the company, working to get somebody's prisoners inside the spanking new, purposely sterile, sorrowful structures, which, of course, are then operated by CCA. One might think that these little towns would try juicing the local economy by establishing something with a little more pizzazz, perhaps a music camp or a solar power institute, but they're particularly vulnerable to the siren song of watchtowers and razor wire. A big selling point is that no special knowledge is demanded of guard recruits. CCA gives them four weeks of training, and bam—they're surrounded by bars, inmates, and tedium.

Once the place begins employing people and operating as an actual prison, it becomes a special interest in the same league with all the bridges to nowhere, superfluous military installations, and other budget boondoggles. The Gulag industry can always justify putting more people in prison and imposing longer sentences, no matter what's going on outside the walls: if crime rises, we must need more people behind bars. If crime goes down, wholesale imprisonment must be succeeding.

CCA unabashedly concedes that anything softer than a hard line is the enemy of its profits. In a 2010 annual report filed with the Securities and Exchange Commission, the company stated, "The demand for our facilities and services could be adversely affected by . . . leniency in conviction or parole standards and sentencing practices."[9]

■ "GET TOUGH"

Frank Keating, who during his campaign promised to "get tough" on crime, was elected Oklahoma governor in 1994. Not long after he assumed office, he directed a CCA executive to evaluate the state's prison system, which was like asking a life insurance company whether you should buy life insurance. Not surprisingly, the CCA man concluded that the parole system was too lenient, that Oklahoma needed to hold convicts longer, and that private prisons should be employed to lock up the expected overflow. Keating, a Republican, began contracting with prison companies, CCA among them. "It is high time Democratic legislators demonstrate the leadership and concern for our citizenry in providing the necessary funding to contract with private prisons for high security bed space," he declared, calling the situation an "emergency."[10]

The state allocated millions of dollars to private prison corporations that promised they could do the job cheaper, and the state's prisoner population climbed as toughened statutes stiffened sentences and the courts relied less and less on probationary programs.

From 1995 to 2010 the state's prison population grew 48 percent from 17,983 inmates to 26,720. State appropriations increased 145 percent to more than $461 million.[11] As tax income shrank with the 2008 global economic spiral, the state drastically cut prison treatment and training programs and per diem rates paid to the prison privateers. By the end of 2010 it was appropriating only $2.22 a day to feed each inmate, down about 25 percent from previous budgets. (By comparison, the Salvation Army figures its Golden Meals for seniors cost it $5.50 apiece. That's per meal, not per day.)

When conditions inside deteriorate this much, it's past time to ask how many of these prisoners actually need to be there. The state legislature commissioned a study of the female inmate population and concluded 68 percent of them posed no threat to public safety.[12]

■ AMERICAN LEGISLATIVE EXCHANGE COUNCIL

The American Legislative Exchange Council (ALEC) is a secretive, right-wing lobbying group of corporations and legislators that works to privatize most of the known universe, including the penal system. ALEC, one of those vital junctions where hard-right politics meets corporate revenues, is particularly keen on mandatory sentencing, a practice that basically transfers social welfare dollars from communities to prison corporations and private servicing companies.[13]

One of the most powerful lobbying arms in the country, ALEC seeks to expand the role of private enterprise in the criminal justice system by taking on additional duties, such as monitoring parolees.[14] This expansion would give significant power to people who aren't sworn officers and presents a particularly sticky situation when employees monitoring released inmates work for a firm that also runs prisons. The firms would clearly have a powerful incentive to cast released prisoners back inside their prisons-for-profit, where every empty bed is a slap in the face to net income. But because ALEC treats all forms of government regulation like infectious diseases, nothing in its model legislation prevents this clear conflict of interest.

In addition to the corporations that fund it, ALEC members include hundreds of conservative legislators from all fifty states and about eighty members of Congress. It's a lobbying group that writes a lot of "model" legislation, which often seeps its way into law with few people aware of its origin. Beginning around 2010, however, more journalists began looking into what had been a barely known organization. ALEC tries to keep a low profile so legislator members can take full credit for dropping prefabricated ALEC bills into the hopper. These bills are designed to generate profits for corporate members who share the bounty by legally compensating member politicians through campaign donations or business activities.

ALEC doesn't believe in coddling convicts. "Additional economic burdens should not be placed on taxpayers," it says. "To the greatest extent possible, the program's costs should be borne by criminals."[15] Courts and lawmakers often agree, stacking fees and surcharges upon offenders' backs like bags of rocks. There are fees for incarceration, probation supervision, drug tests, "reparations," and other items and services. In many cases the legislatures and local governments that levy the charges aren't even aware of the others already in place. Typically when inmates' families deposit money for commissary items such as deodorant or candy bars, the institution deducts as much as 50 percent to pay fees that most folks outside the criminal justice system have never heard of. Uncollected amounts can follow the ex-offender and cause him to be jailed for nonpayment. Ex-convicts already face terrible odds against finding a job. Coming out the gate with debts chains them to additional dead weight. These postprison punishments resemble the old Soviet practice of forcing released prisoners to remain in Siberian exile, further distancing them from the goal of resuming normal life.

If ALEC policymakers spent a little time outside the visitors area of any jail in America, they'd see a lot of beat-up vehicles with mismatched fenders and oil leaks. Young women pour out of Greyhound buses tugging small children. They wear clothing by Walmart or Target. Families of inmates are mostly nonwhite, but the real common denominator is poverty, not race. The New York Bar Association estimated in 2006 that 80 percent of U.S. defendants charged with a felony are indigent.[16] The ALEC notion that we can tithe them and their families to subsidize the criminal-industrial complex rests upon the crackpot fantasy that these people are sitting on mountains of dope and hidden cash.

One ALEC idea is to allow convicts to secure early release by posting a bond, which is much like selling pardons. A related money-buys-privilege concept is the trend to add toll lanes rather than carpool lanes to clogged roads. Mississippi enacted a clone of the ALEC early release bill in 2007, and Michigan and South Dakota passed their own versions later. It works very much like the bail system set up for non-convicted defendants, which also allows money to buy extra privileges. Bonding companies charge a fee to the inmate's family—most often 10 percent of the bail amount—to post bond. The ALEC bill gives the company the right to place early parolees back in custody if they fall out of compliance by, for example, being unemployed.[17]

Wafting up from beneath the prison privateer's sales pitch is the same musky promise that pervades so many outsourcing bids: We can do it cheaper because we'll cut corners you wouldn't dare cut yourselves. The private employees receive the kind of wages and benefits (or lack of them) that your average public institution wouldn't want to be a part of, at least not directly. *Forbes*, noting that wages represent 70 percent of a prison's budget, reports, "Private prison operators pay security guard wages rather than correctional officer wages, giving a significant advantage."[18]

■ SALARIES AND PERKS

But even when companies pay their guards wages that are a third or less of state employees' wages, much of the savings goes toward executive salaries and perks and stockholders' dividends. What the taxpayers get is rent-a-cops like Mongo and Squeaky in charge of their inmates. And if they can avoid it, the firms don't mention to townsfolk that employees from other locations around the company can bid on the new jobs opening up, leaving locals fewer spots than the Music Man promised.

Certainly marketing brochures issued by private prison companies don't mention the February 2001 study released by the U.S. Justice Department titled *Emerging Issues on Privatized Prisons*.[19] It concluded that private prisons saved the government at best 1 percent of costs. Worse, the authors found that on a per-inmate basis, there were 40 percent more assaults on inmates in private facilities and 49 percent more assaults on staff, and in two statistics that stand out like skunks at a picnic, there were 11.3 times as many riots and nine times as many AIDS cases. Private institutions also experienced significant problems with staff turnover. According to the last self-reported industry statistics from 2000, the average private prison staff turnover rate was 53 percent, whereas the public prison turnover rate was 16 percent. "Nevertheless," concluded the federal study, "there were indications that the mere prospect of privatization had a positive effect on prison administration, making it more responsive to reform."[20] In other words, it may be a good idea to threaten to turn your prisons over to corporations, but it's a bad idea to actually do it.

An exhaustive 2005 study by Professor Thomas J. Bernard of Penn State also found that private lockups might save approximately 1 percent, but that's only after 70 percent of them obtain tax subsidies. Bernard said that prison corporations routinely claimed they operate for 20 percent less than public institutions, but he found no evidence to back this assertion.[21]

Undaunted, in early 2012 CCA sent letters to forty-eight states offering to buy up their prisons as a remedy for "challenging corrections budgets." In exchange, the company sought twenty-year management contracts, plus an assurance that the prison would remain at least 90 percent full. If crime were to decline, the state would still have to go out and find bodies for CCA. The proposed contract therefore kept the concept of justice conveniently out of the equation. "We believe this comes at a timely and helpful juncture and hope you will share our belief in the benefits of the purchase-and-manage model," read the letter from Harley Lappin, CCA's chief corrections officer, a former director of the Federal Bureau of Prisons.[22]

The ACLU found that the number of inmates in private prisons increased by roughly 1,600 percent between 1990 and 2009 and that in 2010, the two largest private prison companies alone took in nearly $3 billion in revenue while their top executives each received annual compensation packages worth well over $3 million.[23] Ohio officials, accepting CCA's math, continued this trend in 2011, when they sold off one of the state's largest prisons to CCA as a way to make some quick cash and slim down its budget.[24] Around the same time Louisiana's Republican governor, Bobby Jindal, proposed accepting private bids for three of his state's prisons, but he couldn't convince the legislature to go along.

■ 40 PERCENT MORE ASSAULTS

A 2003 joint study by the Florida Department of Corrections, Florida State University, and the Correctional Privatization Commission found that in "only one of thirty-six comparisons was there evidence that private prisons were more effective than public prisons in terms of reducing recidivism." The same study also found that two private prisons spent only about half as much on health care per inmate as comparable state prisons did.[25] A 2008 study published in *Crime and Delinquency*, which tracked more than twenty-three thousand released convicts, found that "private prison inmates had a greater hazard of recidivism in all eight models tested, six of which were statistically significant."[26] Increased recidivism significantly negates financial benefits, if they exist at all. Also, because private prison companies are private entities, they're not covered by the Freedom of Information Act or most public records statutes; this allows them to sweep dirty outcomes under their private rugs. They're accountable to their shareholders, not the public, and therefore citizens interested in learning about their methods and results have to contend with a layer of secrecy. In 2008 CCA general counsel Gus Puryear admitted that the company did not disclose detailed audit reports to contracting government agencies. In response to a question from U.S. Senator Dianne Feinstein, he confirmed that the company "did not make customers aware of these documents."[27]

Undaunted, former academic Richard P. Seiter, executive vice president and chief corrections officer of CCA, proclaimed in March 2008 that the "private corrections industry has established itself as a viable and dependable partner to government. . . . Not only can private operators provide flexibility and cost efficiency to government agencies, they do so without sacrificing quality or safety."[28]

■ PHONY DEBATE

The issue of private prisons and their relative effectiveness is similar to the debates over cigarette smoking and climate change.

Corporations inconvenienced by the facts pay a bounty to "experts" who find a way to ignore them. It's not difficult to find polemicists to tell you that the privatization glass is always half-full, that Mongo and Squeaky spell progress, and that governing through actual government institutions is sloppy and unsound. Seiter is a PhD who used to be an associate professor in the Department of Sociology and Criminal Justice at Saint Louis University. As an expert advocate for CCA, he earned $1,138,550 in 2009. That year his former university employer paid an average of $72,000 to its associate professors, less than a fifteenth of Seiter's corporate compensation.

The Arizona Department of Corrections, after studying the issue, found private prisons often house only relatively healthy inmates and disguise this shortcut to lower costs. "It's cherry-picking," said State Representative Chad Campbell, leader of the Arizona House Democrats. "They leave the most expensive prisoners with taxpayers and take the easy prisoners."[29]

Five of eight private prisons serving Arizona didn't accept inmates with "limited physical capacity and stamina," severe physical illness, or chronic conditions, according to the state's analysis, issued in April 2011. None took inmates with "high-need" mental health conditions. Some inmates who became sick were "returned to state prisons due to an increase of their medical scores that exceeds contractual exclusions."[30]

Russ Van Vleet, a former codirector of the University of Utah Criminal Justice Center, after reviewing years of research, said, "There's a perception that the private sector is always going to do it more efficiently and less costly. But there really isn't much out there that says that's correct." Savings from privatizing prisons, he said, "are not guaranteed and appear minimal." Confronted with the emptiness of the corporate claims, Steve Owen, spokesman for CCA, contended, "There is a mixed bag of research out there. It's not as black and white and cut and dried as we would like."[31]

■ CORPORATE THÉNARDIERS

One referee that sees an eternally bright sun shining on the concept of corporate prisons is the conservative Reason Foundation. David H. Koch, billionaire oligarch and tireless champion of privatization, serves on its board. CCA touts an "independent" joint study by the Reason Foundation and Howard Jarvis Taxpayers Foundation. This study concluded that California's soaring prison costs ($47,000 per year per inmate, the study said) could be easily curbed by contracting with private prisons. The state's savings would be $120 million a year for each batch of five thousand inmates transferred from state lockups to private prisons, the evidence-defying study contended. "Public-private partnerships (PPPs) offer a powerful policy option as part of a comprehensive strategy to address California's corrections crisis," the report concludes.[32] Naturally, this study, released in April 2010 and revised a year later, ignores all the bona fide independent research that reaches the opposite conclusion.

Private prisons are "a big business here in Kentucky," pointed out Louisville defense attorney Nathan Miller. Two of the state's fourteen prisons are operated by CCA. "This entails construction contracts," said Miller, "and after the prison is built, there are providers of phone services, food services, and all that. And they can pretty much charge whatever they want. It's a big moneymaker for a lot of people. They keep it stocked with drug offenders, mostly."[33]

The Federal Bureau of Prisons says that approximately 15 percent of its 210,000 inmates "are confined in secure facilities operated primarily by private corrections companies and to a lesser extent by state and local governments, and in privately operated community corrections centers."[34] This is in spite of the bureau's own research showing the many serious problems posed by jailing people for cash.

12

Captive Employees

SOFIA COSMA, ONE OF GREATEST PIANISTS OF HER TIME, WAS AN AUSTRIAN
Jew who managed to flee into Soviet territory one step ahead of her
Nazi pursuers. But after crossing the border, she was arrested and
transported to Siberia to dig potatoes for seven years. Her crime? She
possessed an Austrian passport. Austria, which had been absorbed
into the Third Reich and no longer existed as a separate country, was
nevertheless a ghost enemy of the Soviet Union, and so, Cosma was
a Soviet enemy too.[1] Stalin's security functionaries made this and
other grievous arrests based on bureaucratic bungling, institutional
paranoia, and a propensity to punish first and ask questions later. But
a fourth cause may have been more powerful than the others—an addiction to free labor. Why let a woman play the piano when you can
force her to bring in your potato crop?

The use of forced convict labor provided convenience and savings to the Stalinist regime, whose mission to build an economic
foundation for the empire naturally trampled petty anachronisms,
such as manifesting equal justice under the law. The Gulag where so
many inmates suffered and died wasn't a new concept. Slavery had
been around thousands of years.

There is "not an increase in crime," contends the Center for Interdisciplinary Studies in Philosophy, Interpretation, and Culture at
State University of New York–Binghamton, "rather an increase in
people being used to work for free in the factories, fields, telemar-
keting and lingerie production behind the walls of the existing prison

135

system. The privatization of prisons exposes rehabilitation inside the walls of prisons to be a myth. Such companies as TWA, Victoria's Secret and many others enjoy the benefits of free labor without the threat of unions, the need for heath care or employee benefits of any kind."[2]

Depending on the task and the pay, convicts do in fact compete for jobs behind bars. They have nowhere else to go and generally figure that even poor wages are better than no wage at all. Providing inmates with valuable work habits and skills does have merit, but at what point is the prison-employer partnership an economic model aimed more at exploiting cheap, captive labor than at benefitting society? Further, there is clearly a danger of corruption when businesses approach the government for the purpose of finding cheap labor. Hiring convicts can in fact be a method to replace free workers with people who accept less than minimum wage and don't ask for benefits. Some of these companies hiring convicts compete with rival businesses that remain tethered to the normal employer-employee relationship.

Brenda Valencia had the distinct feeling while she was toiling in prison industries that she'd been converted into an economic chit. "So many of these people answering phones? They don't tell you, but they're inmates. We took a lot of those 411 calls. They're taking away a lot of jobs so they can pay inmates 48 cents an hour," she said. Unicor, a public corporation that operates under a Department of Justice mandate to employ inmates, boasts that its inmate call centers are the "best kept secret in outsourcing."[3] In one ironic use of convict call centers, a contractor for GOP congressional hopeful Jack Metcalf hired Washington State prisoners in 1994 to call and remind voters that he was pro-death penalty. Metcalf won the election.[4]

Renting inmates to corporations as laborers is a recycled idea that state governments had tried before. After the Civil War the South used convict labor as a legal device to reconstitute backdoor slavery.[5] With little or no evidence that they were guilty of crimes, poor African Americans were sentenced to forced labor and rented out to private contractors. Tens of thousands were arbitrarily arrested and leased to coal mines, lumber camps, brickyards, railroads, quarries, and plantations. Chained together and treated with cruel abandon, the prisoners lacked the rights of farm animals. They were pawns in a system that reeked of brutality, ruthlessness, and corruption. In states where slavery had only recently been made illegal, institutions didn't blanch at reconstituting its base elements, and finer questions about conflict of interest were barely considered—nor was the concept of liberty for all.

In the early twentieth century, Texas leased its entire prison system to private interests. Around the same time, Florida leased most of its convicts to companies that used them to mine raw materials and kept them in brutal work camps. Tennessee Coal and Iron Company actually rented out the Tennessee State Penitentiary and its inmates for its own purposes. Upon entry, convicts were turned over to the company, which kept most of them to perform grueling work and rented out the remainder to other slave industries.

Ultimately, the rent-a-convict system did not survive the ceaseless attacks from labor unions and civil libertarians. Other opposition came from corporations, which complained that they shouldn't have to compete against unpaid labor. Perhaps the most significant factor was the cruel death of a white youth named Martin Tabert, who succumbed to the torture and neglect of his Florida captors. Tabert's terrible fate received national attention, thanks to intense coverage by Joseph Pulitzer's *New York World*.[6] The tragedy put the entire rent-a-convict system, and Florida governor Cary Hardee in particular, under siege.

At age twenty-two, Tabert left his parents' North Dakota ranch to see the world. A few months later, in December 1921, he was arrested in Leon County in Northern Florida for riding a freight train and sentenced to twenty-five dollars or ninety days in prison. Tabert managed to wire home for money, and his parents promptly sent him seventy-five dollars, but the local sheriff, J. R. Jones, had already leased him to the Putnam Lumber Company in Clara. Stamped "unclaimed . . . party gone," the letter with the money was returned. Tabert's parents assumed their son had been released, but in fact he was cutting and clearing lumber in a swamp. He became terribly ill and unable to fulfill his quota. An overseer wielding a "black auntie"—a leather strap four inches wide, five feet long, and often smeared with oil and soaked in sand—flogged him mercilessly, and he died a few days later without receiving medical care. All because he'd hopped on a freight car.

The *World*, which found a host of credible witnesses to the chain of atrocities perpetrated against Tabert, won the 1924 Pulitzer Prize for Public Service for its coverage of a system that intertwined financial advantage with criminal court administration. Governor Hardee, who at first defended the leasing system as humane, ultimately signed an order abolishing it. The last state to do away with the post–Civil War convict leases was Alabama in 1927. Yet today, the lessons of Tabert's awful fate, a fate shared by countless others, many of them African American, have been largely forgotten.

■ OUTSOURCED BEHIND WALLS

Americans are less than thrilled with the outsourcing of jobs to cheap-labor hotspots in the underdeveloped world. They rarely consider that many go not to India, Guatemala, or rural China, but to American penitentiaries. Honda, for example, was paying prisoners two dollars an hour to perform jobs that used to earn United Auto Workers members ten times that.[7]

Private use of prison labor, once established so it's profitable for both the company and the government, is quite clearly an additional incentive to lock people behind bars and keep them there. U.S. law bans the importation of goods produced by convict labor, but these products are not always easy to trace. Convict industries in China have grown adept at muddling the true history of their merchandise. Meanwhile, nothing in U.S. law prevents American convict-manufactured goods from being exported.

Senator John Ensign (R-NV) introduced a bill in January 2011 to require all low-security prisoners to work not forty, but fifty hours a week. This detail demonstrates how quickly convict labor can devolve into a form of slavery. According to Ensign, creating a national prison labor force makes even more sense in a tough economy.[8] In some minds, killing union jobs by filling them with convicts is a double victory.

State Representative Kevin Mannix of Oregon urged Nike to cut its production in Indonesia and bring the jobs to his state's prisons. He promised, "There won't be any transportation costs; we're offering you competitive prison labor."[9] The Montreal-based Centre for Research on Globalization concluded that thanks to prison labor, "the United States is once again an attractive location for investment in work that was designed for Third World labor markets." It found a company that shut down its *maquiladora* (an assembly plant in Mexico near the border) "and relocated [its operations] to San Quentin State Prison in California." It also found a firm that fired 150 Texas factory workers and contracted the services of prisoner-workers from the GEO Group's Lockhart, Texas, prison, "where circuit boards are assembled for companies like IBM and Compaq."[10] No dependable source has totaled the costs and savings involved in America's various prisoner-contracting programs. Although inmates are no longer flogged to death for failing to make work quotas, their cheap labor provides another incentive to grow the prison system beyond reasonable necessity.

PART 4
Failed Excess

13

Deporting for Cash

WHEN PRIVATE PRISONS RENT OUT JAIL SPACE TO THE GOVERNMENT, THEY'RE paid whether the inmates are innocent or guilty. It's another one of their perks. The process works the same way when jails hold Americans accused of being non-Americans. Administrative or judicial errors translate into profits in this business, and the longer it takes to sort out a mistake, the more profitable it is. U.S. Immigration and Customs Enforcement (ICE) detains approximately thirty-three thousand immigrants at any one time.[1] Many are held in private, for-profit facilities; but precisely what percentage is unclear.

Researchers found that eighty-two people held for deportation from 2006 to 2008 at two immigration detention centers in Arizona were freed after immigration judges determined that they were American citizens after all. Some had been held for as long as a year.[2] In fiscal year 2011 ICE deported a record 396,000 immigrants.[3]

"Because of the scale of enforcement, the numbers of people who are interacting with Immigration and Customs Enforcement are just enormous right now," said Jacqueline Stevens, one of the researchers and a political science professor at Northwestern University.[4] She concluded that "a low but persistent" percentage of the nearly 400,000 people held for deportation each year are in fact citizens. Because an overwhelming number of these detainees, American or not, offer no physical threat to anyone, they're a perfect crop for prison corporations seeking to harvest custodial fees. For companies that lock people up for cash, the least troublesome inmates are the most profitable.

In December 2009 an Arizona legislator looking to crack down on nondocumented aliens took his idea not to the Arizona statehouse floor, but to an ALEC meeting at the Grand Hyatt in Washington, D.C. "I did a presentation," State Senator Russell Pearce told National Public Radio. "I went through the facts. I went through the impacts and they said, 'Yeah.'" The approximately fifty people in attendance, mostly businesspeople and legislators, included officials of CCA, according to two sources who were there. The group decided to turn the immigration idea into a model bill that could be introduced in state legislatures around the country. Members discussed and debated language. The final, approved policy was to boost private prison income by requiring local cops to lock up gardeners, housemaids, and field-workers. Although they did not explicitly say so, racial profiling would be the straw that stirred the drink.[5] (Pearce, who would become a key participant at Tea Party rallies, was voted out of office in November 2011 in a special recall election. He was defeated by the less-strident Republican Jerry Lewis.)

The next year CCA said that it expected to bring in "a significant portion of our revenues" from ICE, an agency it considered a barely tapped earnings source.[6] The ALEC draft was transformed into SB 1070, an Arizona bill that instructed local constables to round up suspects who might lack appropriate legal documents. Targets were deemed guilty (and held in custody) until proved innocent.

The state's Democratic governor, Janet Napolitano, had routinely vetoed right-wing legislation like SB 1070 since she had taken office in January 2003. In fact, in April 2008 she'd vetoed similar immigration legislation that would, she said, have been an unfunded mandate. Back in 2005, she set a single session record of fifty-eight vetoes, and in her six years as governor she had vetoed 180 pieces of legislation that, for example, curtailed the right to abortion, radically promoted the carrying of guns, and turned the state into a sort of quasichurch. But at the end of 2008 President-elect Obama, seemingly oblivious to the effect it might have on Arizona, named Napolitano his secretary of homeland security. Napolitano had backed Obama against Hillary Clinton in January 2008, a crucial point during the Democratic fight for the presidential nomination. To accept her new job in Washington, she resigned two years before the end of her second term. Arizona has no lieutenant governor, so an empty governor's chair is automatically filled by the secretary of state, in this case, Republican right-wing ideologue Jan Brewer. She would later gain notoriety as the seemingly crazed woman caught on camera pointing her finger in the president's face during a private argument on an airport tarmac. If you closed your eyes, you could almost hear the ghosts of Lyndon Johnson and Tip O'Neill wailing as Obama voluntarily surrendered a governor's mansion to the opposition party.

Brewer, the new governor, signed the immigration bill in April 2010. It was most unlikely that officials would ask Anglo-Saxons for their citizenship papers, whereas other U.S. citizens, particularly Hispanics, were clearly at risk under the new law. As the Arizona immigration law was being tested in the courts, the ACLU found that toward the end of 2010 approximately three thousand suspected illegal immigrants were detained in the state on any given day, a 58 percent increase over the previous six years.[7] The Arizona detainees accounted for 10 percent of the total U.S. detainee population.

A remarkably successful ad used to point out that you don't have to be Jewish to love Levy's Jewish rye bread. Neither do you have to be nondocumented to be arrested for having insufficient documentation of your residential status. In fact, you don't even have to be in Arizona. Ask college student Romy Campos, a Florida native who was jailed four days on an immigration detainer in November 2011 after she was arrested in Torrance, California, on a minor misdemeanor charge.[8] Denied bail, Campos was transferred to the Los Angeles County Jail. A public defender told her he was powerless to lift the federal detainer. Finally, an ACLU attorney provided her birth certificate. "I just felt violated by my own country," said Campos, who was deemed guilty until proved innocent.

ALEC's grab for a piece of the business of detaining immigration suspects devolved into a sloppy process that hurt right-wing legislators in the November 2012 election. Afterward, Republican leaders publicly declared their intention to mend fences with Hispanic voters. The abrasive policy embraced by ALEC and its Republican allies represents the sort of shortsighted thinking corporate executives employ when they exchange long-term profits and stability for short-term quick bucks and bonuses.

▪ ALABAMA TAKES IT FURTHER

In October 2011 the state of Alabama took the Arizona immigration initiative into coarser territory, implementing a law with "the most draconian and oppressive set of provisions that this country, which claims to be the bastion of liberties and rights, has seen since the era of segregation," according to the UK's *Guardian*. "Within hours," the *Guardian* reported, the new law "has claimed its first victims— from the detention of a man who later turned out to be residing legally, to the massive fleeing of migrant workers and school children, to even cutting off water services to families or individuals who can't prove their legal status. . . . It is not clear yet how many have been or will be arrested under this provision, but the number will surely make one sector happy: private detention facilities."[9]

The Alabama legislation included retribution against anyone doing business with undocumented residents. Providing them electricity or selling them a vehicle could be viewed as criminal acts. This meant that more inmates were headed to private detention centers inside the state, such as the one operated in Decatur by LCS Corrections Services. The law would "feed an already bloated national private prison system controlled by two major corporations, CCA (Corrections Corporation of America) and the GEO group, which have a combined profit of more than $5 billion a year," said the *Guardian*. CCA was running the largest private facility in the nation in neighboring Georgia and would probably take in many of the Alabama detainees. The *Guardian* article continued, "Charging $200 a night, this is an opportunity they'll jump at."[10]

As immigrant laborers began fleeing the state, John McMillan, its agriculture commissioner, proposed that the farm work they left behind be commissioned to inmate labor.[11] The result, which didn't seem to bother McMillan, was to transform paid workers into jailed workers, toiling at their previous occupations for a fraction of their old wages. In one sense the law and had opened a new gate to institutional slavery, or as the *Guardian* saw it, "another round of shame."[12] Old habits die hard, particularly when they're viewed as profitable.

14

The War against the Poor (and Middle Class)

PROMINENT BRITISH EPIDEMIOLOGISTS RICHARD WILKINSON AND KATE PICK-
ett mined a mountain of data showing that gross inequality of opportunity and income boosts rates of homicide, narcotics use, playground
bullying, mental illness, anxiety, teen pregnancies, academic failure,
physical ailments such as obesity and heart disease, and many other
disorders, many of them life threatening. In their book *The Spirit
Level: Why Greater Equality Makes Societies Stronger*, they wrote
that humans are acutely social animals, vividly conscious of the society around them. Consequently, suffering hardships in relation to
others can be far more injurious than individual suffering that's not
experienced within a societal context. Wilkinson and Pickett compared a list of countries with the greatest income inequality and a list
of countries with the greatest per capita drug use. They found that
the lists contained the same countries. Widespread drug use, a strong
indicator of societal ills, is more likely to occur in a disparate, harsh,
and more punitive culture.[1]

Paradoxically, countries that have relaxed narcotics laws, such as
the Netherlands, have lower rates of drug use. These places are less
vindictive and more egalitarian and forgiving. The same correlation
holds true among America's fifty states. Mississippi and Louisiana
have higher crime, disease, and disability rates than do Minnesota
and New Hampshire, which have a more forgiving legal structure
and a more equitable income distribution.[2]

147

This trend has been lost on tycoons such as David H. and Charles G. Koch, brothers who inherited vast riches and spend millions funding foundations and political campaigns to shape national politics and economics so that they can have even more wealth and privilege (and, correspondingly, so that everyone else can have less).[3]

In fact, genuine social justice benefits, not just those toward the bottom, but all society. A person who has amassed $10 billion can afford whatever he or she wants. A more grandiose estate in Tuscany or another billion or two in paper assets are unlikely to affect a billionaire's general happiness. But a billionaire's life can be enriched when other citizens are given equal opportunity to live up to their potential, to become symphony conductors or epidemiologists, not crack whores or auto thieves. Everyone benefits when a billionaire can exit his or her limo unaccompanied by armed guards.

Paul Pierson, a political scientist at the University of California–Berkeley, found that in Mexico a "small group of wealthy people are protected by guns mostly from the rest of the population and dart from one protected location to another protected location completely separate from the rest of society."[4] Economist Samuel Bowles of the Santa Fe Institute, a professor emeritus at the University of Massachusetts, has noted that as wealth increasingly flows to the top, the security sector takes on a bigger share of the economy. He concluded that for "every three workers in America that's producing something, there is one worker who's just keeping the lid on. These are the private security personnel. These are the police officers. These are the prison guards. These are the armed forces. These are the people whose job it is just basically to maintain the society's property rights and its social organization."[5]

Putting more people behind bars than is absolutely necessary promotes a basic unfairness. Demoting small-time offenders to the status of ex-convict stamps them as lesser beings, particularly in more retaliatory societies. Consequently, sending more and more people to prison generates even greater disparities and socioeconomic chasms.

Although laissez-faire hard-liners argue that it's natural for big fish to eat smaller fish, Senator Elizabeth Warren (D-MA) argued that these self-described rugged individualists see the world through a distorted lens. While speaking with supporters during her 2012 campaign, she said:

There is nobody in this country who got rich on his own. Nobody. You built a factory out there, good for you. But, I want to be clear: you moved your goods to market on the roads the rest of us paid for. You hired workers the rest of us paid to educate. You were safe in your factory because of police forces and fire forces that the rest of us paid for. You didn't have to worry that marauding bands would come and seize everything at your factory and hire someone to protect against this because of the work the rest of us did. Now look, you built a factory and it turned into something terrific or a great idea. God bless. Keep a big hunk of it. But part of the underlying social contract is you take a hunk of that and pay forward for the next kid who comes along.[6]

▨ CONSPIRACY?

The widening gap between the richest 1 percent of Americans and everyone else is no longer disputable. Even *Forbes*, one of the great bastions of hard capitalism, doesn't deny it. The real estate–banking collapse of 2008 exacerbated the trend. The incomes of the bottom 99 percent grew by only 6.8 percent between 2002 and 2007, compared to a 20 percent gain between 1993 and 2000. In the early 1980s the top 1 percent received an 8 percent share of all earnings. By 2012 that share was up to 20 percent—and still accelerating.[7] University of California economist Emmanuel Saez found that "1 percent captured 93 percent of the income gains in the first year of recovery (2010)." This, he said, "can help explain the recent public demonstrations against inequality."[8] Pierson and his coauthor, Yale political scientist Jacob S. Hacker, in *Winner-Take-All Politics: How Washington Made the Rich Richer—and Turned Its Back on the Middle Class*, point out that when the surge of economic catastrophes enveloped much of the world beginning around 2008, other developed countries experienced nothing like the increase in inequality that occurred in the United States.[9]

Left-leaning lawyer and political scientist Joseph Dillon Davey said it's no coincidence that America's prison population exploded at the same time its distribution of wealth shifted sharply in favor of the richest Americans. Davey saw mass incarceration as the ruling class's principal method of insuring against resistance and insurrection.[10]

Epidemiologists Wilkinson and Pickett agreed that if you accept high inequality, "you will need more prisons and more police. You will have to deal with higher rates of mental illness, drug abuse and every other kind of problem."[11]

Davey cited a 1971 speech, barely noticed at the time, by family patriarch David Rockefeller in which he declared that "the social contract" was "up for revision." Davey and his disciples believe that Rockefeller's words predicted the establishment of a new globalized economy that would crush American workers and jail resistors.[12] Although they give Rockefeller more soothsaying credit than he deserves, America's union workforce was in fact cut in half, the prison population tripled, and the rich became much, much richer while everyone else treaded water or sank to the bottom. When Occupy Wall Street directed attention to this growing income disparity, the group was monitored, investigated, and suppressed by the FBI, the Department of Homeland Security, and various police departments around the country.[13]

When in November 2011 the Census Bureau released a new, more accurate measurement of poverty, it showed that 100 million people—one in three Americans—were either in poverty or very close to it. The bureau included 51 million people with incomes less than 50 percent above the poverty line. These are people living paycheck to paycheck, one illness or one set of tires from falling off the edge. The numbers, which most economists agreed constitute a measure of poverty more accurate than previously possible, came as a surprise to those who gathered them, said Trudi J. Renwick, the bureau's chief poverty statistician. "There are more people struggling than the official numbers show," she said.[14]

■ ZERO NET WORTH

By 2009, as the real estate–banking collapse widened the chasm, nearly half of American families had a debt load that exceeded their assets, leaving them with zero net worth. That same year Goldman Sachs, one of the principal malefactors in the collapse, realized profits of $13.4 billion after paying enormous sums for salaries, bonuses, and the creature-comfort expenses of its top-tier executives. Total compensation for an average employee in the firm neared $500,000.[15] Presumably none of them fell into foreclosure.

A November 2011 report by the Pew Charitable Trusts' Economic Mobility Project pointed out that most children who grow up along the top or bottom of the American income spectrum keep their respective places all their lives. The practice of "legacy" admissions in our elite universities, for example, is naked affirmative action in favor of the silver-spoon set. America once had the highest proportion of college grads in the world. Now, thanks to deteriorating educational systems and less accessible systems of higher learning, we've fallen to twelfth.[16]

Much of this can be attributed to the waning political power of the nonrich as the rising impact of big money works its will. When the Great Recession struck, state and local governments laid off hundreds of thousands of middle-class teachers. It was a double whammy, devastating teacher families and, by weakening public education, making it harder for children of the nonelite to climb up from the economic basement. Although George Orwell's *1984* was seen by many as a harbinger of the future, totalitarian government never came to America. What we got instead was closer to Aldous Huxley's *Brave New World*, in which alphas and epsilons stay locked in place.

What's happening to America's class structure is well illustrated by passenger airliners. Year after year business and first-class grow more opulent and expensive, whereas passengers in the coach or economy sections are crowded together like lima beans in a can. They pay extra for pillows, blankets, legroom, or a better spot in the security line. Food, if available, costs extra and is a close approximation of prison fare that's been wrapped for transport.

Around the time Congress was passing the more regressive tax structure put forth by President George W. Bush, it dutifully enacted legislation to stiffen bankruptcy laws and make it much more difficult for citizens burdened by unmanageable debt to get out from under it. A key provision of the Bankruptcy Abuse Prevention and Consumer Protection Act of 2005 erected barriers to filing a Chapter 7 bankruptcy, under which most debts are forgiven. Instead the law required debt-ridden citizens to file under Chapter 13, which kept much of their debt on the books. Bankruptcy judges were still prevented by law from modifying mortgages, although there's no logic to this exemption. It exists only because the financial giants that buy and sell mortgages have the clout in Congress to make it exist.

■ $16 TRILLION TO THE RESCUE

Senator Bernie Sanders (I-VT), the only avowed socialist in Congress, managed to attach an amendment that established a periodic audit of the Federal Reserve to the scandalously tepid Wall Street Reform Act. "As a result of this audit, we now know that as the crisis raged the Federal Reserve provided more than $16 trillion" in secret loans to financial institutions and other well-placed corporations around the world, Sanders reported. "This is a clear case of socialism for the rich and rugged, you're-on-your-own individualism for everyone else."[17] President Obama, the election-year champion of "change," waited until the fourth year of his first term to propose a task force to investigate the now-cold trail of shady and downright illegal mortgage-lending practices that led to the housing crisis.

■ CITIZENS UNITED

Hard-right fanatics spent many thousands of work hours and millions of dollars to win the right to inject unlimited cash into political campaigns. When the Roberts court approved unlimited, untraceable corporate spending for campaign ads in its Citizens United ruling, those same fanatics quickly began to argue that the additional cash wouldn't make a difference. But long before the ruling, U.S. politics had moved decidedly to the right, a dynamic that had much to do with expanding the Gulag.

Over the last seventy-five years, the liberal stance on economic issues has drifted slowly to the right. Democratic president Bill Clinton, for example, signed the Financial Services Modernization Act, which repealed the Depression-era Glass-Steagall Act and removed barriers between banking, insurance, and Wall Street securities trading. Clinton also signed off on the Commodity Futures Modernization Act, which allowed all sorts of cowboy speculation in derivatives—including deadly credit default swaps—free of federal oversight. It's difficult to imagine Franklin D. Roosevelt, or for that matter, Republican trustbuster Teddy Roosevelt, working on behalf of such measures.

In the meantime, the Grand Old Party (GOP) rapidly became a party in which even conservatives like Alan Simpson, Bob Dole, and President George H. W. Bush were considered much too liberal. The party of Lincoln and Eisenhower is now the party of novelist Ayn Rand, whose pompous pulp fictional contempt for the nonrich is combined with relentless preaching that acute selfishness is a moral imperative. Still, as Republicans embrace the concept of downsizing budgets, there are signs that some of them may accept reforms in the criminal justice system. The conservative policy group Right on Crime declares that it's "possible to cut both crime rates and costly incarceration rates" and that prisons "are not the solution for every type of offender. And in some instances, they have the unintended consequence of hardening nonviolent, low-risk offenders—making them a greater risk to the public than when they entered." Among signatories to the group's statement of principles are conservative chieftains Jeb Bush, Newt Gingrich, and Grover Norquist.[18]

Still, in stratified twenty-first-century America, society continues kicking people after they're knocked to the ground. In May 2011 Florida governor Rick Scott signed a bill that forces welfare recipients to submit urine, blood, or hair samples for drug testing. Positive results carry an immediate six-month removal from the revamped welfare program established by Clinton and then–House Speaker Gingrich. The program in 2009 paid average annual cash assistance of $5,100 to a family of three. The Florida drug penalty is a collective punishment for the entire family. A second positive test results in an additional three-year ban on state assistance.

Backers of measures like these assume the poor are a sociological other, a group that's roughly approximate to the incarcerated. In 2012 congressional Republicans led by Senator John Barrasso (R-WY) sought to require that the unemployed submit to drug testing in order to receive jobless benefits. The status of unemployment made them, in Barrasso's mind, criminal suspects. The senator never thought to include among these suspects the financial insiders who plunged the economy into crisis by playing fast and loose with the law. Even as the $16 trillion in federal assistance rained down on them, not one had to pee in a cup.

15

Crazy Consequences

ON APRIL 15, 2010, MICHELLE LYN TAYLOR, AT THE AGE OF THIRTY-FOUR, WAS
sentenced to life in prison after being convicted of lewdness with a minor under fourteen. Her crime was to force a thirteen-year-old boy to touch her breast through her clothing and ask if he'd like to have sex with her. Although she accepted responsibility for her actions, she said she had no memory of the offense, which took place two years before she was sentenced.[1]

The boy involved in the crime, the son of a friend, was playing video games at her apartment. He could certainly be considered a victim. But Taylor, who, court records showed, had herself been molested as a child, was also a victim. She was intoxicated when she approached the boy and at trial appeared immensely concerned and embarrassed about what had transpired. Unfortunately, Nevada lawmakers had stiffened the statute a year before her offense, changing the mandatory minimum penalty to life, with no possibility of parole for at least ten years. If she'd killed the boy, she might have done less time. Taylor had no prior history of sexual misconduct, and the examining psychologist said she was unlikely to commit another offense.

Most U.S. state and local governments operate under a system of checks and balances, like that built into the federal constitution. State legislators can be restrained by a savvy governor; governors can be restrained by impartial judges. And prosecutors can skirt certain statutes by charging defendants with lesser offenses. In Taylor's case, Elko County district attorney Gary Woodbury contended that the defendant refused to consider a plea bargain that would force her to register as a sex offender. However, it's not entirely clear that she was offered any sort of deal at all. Plus, the jury on the case wasn't informed that the offense carried a mandatory life sentence. If the court hides the minimum penalty from the jury, the statute is likely unfair.

■ "I THINK IT'S DUMB"

After FAMM heard about the Taylor case and news media started sniffing around, Woodbury decided to place the blame on the Nevada legislature, noting that in 2007 it had amended the state's lewdness statute by imposing a blanket mandatory life sentence for all offenders. "I don't agree that the Nevada . . . Legislature should have made this a mandatory sentence," he told KOLOTV. "I think it's dumb. But they didn't ask me about that." Since Taylor was found guilty of precisely what she'd done, he said, his office had no other choice and had steered a correct course.[2]

Then, the judge openly questioned why Taylor hadn't been offered a plea bargain, which blew a hole in the district attorney's story. The legislation had basically demoted the judge to the rank of clerk. At sentencing time, he couldn't consider the report from the psychologist or Taylor's extensive personal history as a victim of sexual and physical abuse. Nor did he have an opportunity to determine what punishment might actually be fair.

Taylor's public defender, Alina Kilpatrick, researched the law and found only two other women sentenced in Nevada for lewdness with a child under fourteen. Both received plea bargains.[3] The first defendant, who ultimately received two to five years in prison and probation, pled guilty to attempted incest for engaging in oral sex with her son. The second woman was given a plea bargain for two counts of attempted lewdness for participating in the sexual abuse of her daughter with her husband. She was sentenced to four to twenty years.[4]

Taylor appealed her case on the grounds that her punishment was unconstitutionally cruel and unusual. Her attorney said it was the harshest sentence ever dealt to a female sex offender in Nevada. The state of Nevada, rather than admit it made a mistake, was clinging to its guns and claiming Taylor's sentence was perfectly legitimate. The law remained on the books, and Taylor remained in prison.

Anyone who reads the news on a regular basis has, in recent years, come across stories about female teachers having sex with boys who were their students. For this book, I researched crimes involving victims around the age of thirteen, and I couldn't find any first-time offender who received a sentence as harsh as Taylor's—even though many of those cases involved repeated sexual encounters.

Anne Knopf, thirty-nine, a substitute teacher in Ellsworth, Wisconsin, confessed that she'd had sex with a thirteen-year-old pupil on several occasions. She was sentenced in July 2008 to nine months in jail (time she'd already served while waiting for the case to be resolved). The judge also ordered her to register as a sex offender and to stay away from boys under eighteen for the next five years.[5] If we agree that Taylor's sentence was appropriate, clearly Knopf should have gotten the electric chair. But she didn't, and it's unlikely the republic is any less safe because of it.

Another teacher, Pamela Rogers Turner, twenty-seven, of McMinniville, Tennessee, was convicted of having sex on several occasions with one of her thirteen-year-old male students, and she continued communicating with him over the Internet even after her original arrest.[6] Turner was ultimately charged with four counts of sexual battery and violation of probation. Her sentence was 270 days in prison plus an eight-year suspended sentence and seven years and three months of probation. She also had to register as a sex offender and surrender her teaching certificate for life.

The lawmakers who fashioned the ironclad statute that nailed Taylor seemed to have a picture in their mind of what sort of crime would fall under its umbrella, but that picture didn't come close to dealing with the range of possibilities. The legal storm that struck Taylor was the logical result of a system that can make profoundly far-reaching decisions without having to put much thought into them. She became just one of many casualties who wind up forgotten, sitting in an iron capsule, where they're cut off from everything but the slow passage of time.

Every day judges see defendants like Taylor who are astonished to discover how harsh penalties can be and how years and years of imprisonment trip off the tongues of functionaries as though they hold no importance. "I think that a lot of people do not understand what is going on until all of a sudden they are caught up in the system," said David Doty, who was appointed U.S. district court judge in Minnesota by President Reagan in 1987. "And they find out that people have been mouthing all kinds of slogans, and when the slogans all come down to rest, they sometimes come to rest very hard on the shoulders of the individual."[7]

■ DEBTORS' PRISONS

Meanwhile, absurd laws roll on, expedited by less-than-thoughtful lawmakers working within a structure that seems powerless to curb their excesses. In January 2012 Republican Ralph Shortey, a freshman in the Oklahoma Senate, introduced a bill to prevent using fetuses for food.[8] Not surprisingly, while this sworn official concerned himself with an extremely unlikely crime, Oklahoma was one of many states reviving the centuries-old tradition of debtors' prison. Reinstitution of this tradition has helped make a growth industry out of buying up debt for pennies on the dollar and then wrenching a profit out of it.

Although civil judgments aren't supposed to trigger criminal penalties, judges might grant arrest warrants if debtors fail to show up for court dates or make court-ordered payments. In many cases, the court order for payment didn't reach the person. Still, more than one-third of states allow people to be arrested for these debts. The *Wall Street Journal*, attempting to determine how pervasive the practice was, couldn't come up with a broad estimate. Too many courts don't keep track. It was also impossible to determine how many such warrants result in arrests, but many do. Often motorists pulled over on a traffic charge learn they're wanted on debt warrants and are carted off to jail.[9]

In 2010 officials in McKintosh County, Oklahoma, near Tulsa, issued about fifteen hundred debt-related arrest warrants, up from eight hundred a year before. The *Journal* talked to many judges and consumer attorneys who said the number of such warrants had surged with the financial crisis. Maricopa County, Arizona, issued 260; Salt Lake City, Utah, 950. The *Journal* found a debtor in Carbondale, Illinois, who spent five days in jail in March 2010 after failing to pay a $275 debt to a payday lender. These payday creditors have in some states managed to hike their annual rates to 360 percent (not a misprint) without running afoul of usury laws. In January 2011 a judge sentenced a Kenney, Illinois, man to "indefinite incarceration" until he paid $300 on a debt to a lumberyard.[10]

In Minnesota, many debtors spend up to forty-eight hours in cells, often sharing them with actual criminal suspects. In extreme cases, people stay in jail until they satisfy the judge with a minimum payment. The median debt cited in Minnesota warrants was $3,512 in 2009, but one was as low as $85.[11]

■ EIGHT MONTHS OR $705

In seventh-century-BCE Athens, a dictator named Draco created a legal code, the first the city had ever known. Its underlying philosophy bears his name today—*Draconian*. The code permitted enslavement for debt, and almost all criminal offenses, great and small, carried the death penalty. The theory was that crime and unpaid debts would disappear in the face of these harsh punishments, and life would be beautiful for everyone. But Draco's code created hell on earth. The threat of enslavement or execution for some random trivial incident paralyzed ordinary life. To everyone's relief, Draco's successor, Solon, a poet king, humanized the code. Yet, as George Santayana noted, those who don't learn from history are doomed to repeat it, and the lessons of Draco's code have been forgotten and relearned across centuries and continents down to this day.

In keeping with Draco's model, many of America's jailed debtors fall into their predicament because they can't pay fees imposed by an earlier conviction. Edwina Nowlin, an utterly impoverished Michigan resident, was ordered to reimburse a juvenile detention center $104 for incarcerating her sixteen-year-old son. When she explained to the judge that she couldn't possibly pay, she was sent to prison. She spent twenty-eight days behind bars before the local ACLU managed to get her out.[12] ACLU attorneys said they were seeing a surge in such cases, as is the Brennan Center for Justice at New York University School of Law. There are legal precedents in place that ought to prevent these medieval practices, but the law can be a long way off from a courtroom whose judge sees things differently.

In 2006 the Southern Center for Human Rights sued on behalf of a woman locked up in Atlanta for eight months past her original sentence because she couldn't raise $705 to pay her fine.[13] In 2010 the Brennan Center for Justice issued a report based on its study of the fifteen states with the highest prison populations and their use of "user fees"—financial obligations imposed "not for any traditional criminal justice purpose such as punishment, deterrence, or rehabilitation but rather to fund tight state budgets." The study found that states across the board have introduced these new fees and are using drastic measures to ensure their collection. Debtors' prison is illegal in all states, yet "re-incarcerating individuals for failure to pay debt is, in fact, common in some" and building "new paths back to prison" for "individuals seeking to rebuild their lives after a criminal conviction." Eight of the fifteen states suspended driving privileges for missed payments, making it impossible for some people to get to work and leading to new convictions for driving with a suspended license. The report also found that when probation and parole officers have to devote time to fee collection instead of public safety and rehabilitation, they aren't as effective. The lust for money thus undermines community safety and becomes another cause of what the report termed "over-incarceration."[14]

In December 2011 Riverside County, California, began billing criminals in county lockups up to $142 a day for food, clothing, health care, and other jail expenses. The practice had been written into a bill by Supervisor Jeff Stone, a rhyming pharmacist, who said, "In these very challenging economic times, every dollar counts for counties, especially when you're $80 million in the hole. If you do the crime, then you're going to do the time and you're going to pay the dime."[15]

The county's policy stemmed from the state's efforts, after the Supreme Court ordered that the state thin its inmate herd, to keep many convicted felons in county jail rather than send them to a state lockup. Stone fashioned the county's new practice so that it was easy to garnish wages and slap liens on inmates who failed to pay the fees. "If somebody is out of jail and trying to make a living and feed their family, and then they get their wages garnished," said local defense attorney Steve Harmon, "they're going to be way behind the eight ball." Tallying the figures, he found that convicted criminals who spend six months in jail—a common sentence—could be on the hook for more than $25,000. Parents of convicted juveniles could also be subject to the fees. These fees proliferate around the country, said Riverside County public defender Gary Windom, in part because they are politically popular and meet basically no countervailing pressure. "The people who commit crimes," he said, "have very little ability to go to their legislators and argue their case."[16]

Sheriff Donny Youngblood pointed out that holding hearings to determine a defendant's ability to pay would further burden already crowded court dockets. Thanks to the county's unusually severe unemployment (approximately 14 percent when the policy was adopted) and the dire financial situations of most inmates, he predicted little money would end up being collected.

16

Crime Academies, Rape, Sex Slaves, Infection, Death

The convict slowly wastes away from afflictions that include the rare and untreatable spider endocarditis. No choir boy, he's left a trail of victims beaten, abused, double-crossed. Drifting to sleep, he dreams. Demons and shadows chase him in a malign darkness. Off in the corner, he spots a hole in the ceiling. A bit of light peaks through, but the demons almost have him. Frantic, he scrambles up into the opening as his pursuers pull at his legs. Intense pain. A nightmare of pain. He makes it through and finds an identical dark room. Demons still behind him, he races to another hole in another ceiling, jumps, scrambles. They have him by the legs. He sees now that it will be room after room, hole after hole without rest. An endless, ghastly eternity of pointlessness and terror.

"I know it was real," he tells his cellmate. "I'm going to hell." Maybe you can change, the cellmate says. "Too late," he responds. "Too late."

—A California cellmate's tale

When it starts, it starts fast and keeps moving fast. Just like on the street. Yet the horror might not end so quickly. To those on the receiving end, it's like being trapped in a corner with flames licking your flesh. Flames don't care. No sense pleading. There might be a reason, but an excuse will do. This time it was about paperwork. The new fish didn't have any. When the door slammed behind him, his hands were empty. A calamity he failed to understand. New cons always have paperwork. At least one sheet that lists your crime and how much time you have to do. Murderers, thieves, dopers, even rapists pass muster. But obvious snitches or, even worse, child molesters can't live among stand-up cons. Such detritus must dwell in a separate circle of hell. Everyone's information is inspected upon entry.

The first con to spot him saw he wasn't carrying any paperwork.[1]

"I don't have it," the new fish explained.

"Why not?"

"I got rid of it." The fish was upset and disgusted but, because of his ignorance, not as frightened as he should have been. His questioner, a younger man but schooled, guessed that this guy might be OK, that he just didn't understand. "Turn around and run," the young con told him. "Run! Back to that last door, and shout for the guard to let you in, understand?"

"What?"

"Listen to what I'm saying. Run! Now. Do it now!"

He seemed to think he'd have time to figure things out, like it was a crossword puzzle or something. But it was already too late. The word was out. *No paperwork.* The escape route was blocked, and a small mob converged, instantly worked to a boil. The younger con shook his head, stepped aside, and the horror began. When it was over the fish made it to the infirmary alive, but the attack left him a paraplegic.

As it turned out, the young man who'd tried to warn him had guessed correctly. The new guy was neither a child molester nor a snitch, just some fool still angry at himself and the universe around him, about to do time for a vehicular homicide he didn't want to be reminded of. He was driving, and someone in his family was killed. When he saw it spelled out on the document, it all came back to him, and he tore it up. But he was in the wrong place to look for patience or understanding. Even if they couldn't articulate it, those who crippled him were hungry for a release from the deadness and waste all around them, the lost years, missed opportunities, stupid coincidences, everything that led them to such a gray, sorrowful place. Jumping a pervert or a suspected pervert felt good, at least for a little while, like uncoiling a spring. And they were absolved because they did only what was expected of them. After all, he had broken the rule.

The young con never saw the unlucky man again. It often works that way inside the walls. You see or experience something searing, and yet, when it's over, it's almost as if you never saw it because now you have to stay alert for the next thing. Whatever that next thing is, you don't want it to be about you. You endure. You find religion or make jailhouse hooch, joke with your buddies, smoke five-dollar cigarettes (no-smoking rules ran up the price astronomically), and sometimes even dream sweet dreams.

■ PING-PONG IN HELL

Before Jesus Chavez won the International Boxing Federation (IBF) lightweight championship, he was a convict.[2] His Chicago homeys had drafted him as a lookout for an armed robbery that went wrong. A very tough yet scared eighteen-year-old, he was eventually transferred into Stateville Correctional Center in Joliet, Illinois, one of those impossibly crowded joints. Too many bodies inhabiting too small a space generate a relentless noise that's grating and cruel to the senses. It reaches inside people, not just into their ears. It hammers at nerves. But the worst time of all is when the noise stops because it means something awful is on the way, most likely a gang about to pounce and scatter. Other gangs might decide to move first. In Stateville, just the perception of trouble meant there would be trouble, even if the original perception had been incorrect. Those not part of a gang were prey for everyone. Those in a gang were drafted as warriors in battles they knew nothing about. And wars were only part of the violence, which was often expressed through a kind of methodical two-man combat, a violent ballet that was a Stateville tradition.

Chavez quickly learned that the lifers all around him avoided beefs with each other because making an enemy of another lifer would start an interminable back-and-forth vendetta. Thus, short-timers like Chavez were targets for a never-ending series of challenges and raging physical attacks from lifers who didn't really care if they lived or died. They fought because it felt good. Some prisons are more violent than others, and Stateville was a gladiator camp. Living in such close proximity, everyone was in everyone else's face. All it took to provoke a challenge was a wrong step, a wrong word in the chow line, or a too-narrow corridor. Two men would settle a challenge by entering an empty cell, closing the door behind them, and exploding. Sometimes one man would be twice the size of the other, but no one could duck a challenge.

Each warrior, usually from rival gangs, had his own representative outside the door. Inside the cell the two men fought until someone lost consciousness or the sentries spotted a guard approaching. The cells were tiny, and in the course of combat, heads smashed into walls, porcelain sinks and toilets, steel bars, and bunks. Convicts called these battles ping-pong. Chavez was a Golden Gloves champ back in Chicago, but sometimes he'd wake up from ping-pong in his own cell with his cellie trying to revive him.

▪ GANGED-UP DEPUTIES

In Los Angeles County's Men's Central Jail, the gang culture is so pervasive that it infects even the deputies' ranks. Although it's supposedly forbidden, these deputies have been known to form their own gangs. Jailer members sport gang tattoos, flash gang signs, and mimic the behavior of street gangs. Deputy gangs that have been discovered and documented include the Vikings, the Regulators, the Cavemen, and the 3000. Usually their ire is aimed at inmates, but at an off-premises Christmas party in 2010, six guards in the 3000 jumped two other guards who had "disrespected" them. The two suffered serious injuries.

By this time, the FBI was already investigating the over-the-top violence that deputies inflicted on inmates in Los Angeles County jails. Sheriff Lee Baca's reaction was to condemn the federal investigators. The department, he said, could handle its own problems.[3] Later he toned down his criticism and agreed to cooperate. At least that's what he told the news media. The FBI had become involved only after it concluded that the Baca administration had little interest in policing its own jail deputies. Jail chaplain Paulino Juarez had filed a formal complaint after witnessing a beating in February 2009. He said he was ministering to an inmate when he heard thumps and gasps. He walked toward the sounds and saw three deputies pounding an inmate pressed against the wall. Juarez believed the victim was handcuffed because he never raised his hands to protect his face from the deputies' fists, as he pleaded for them to stop. Finally, the inmate,

Juarez said, collapsed face first. The chaplain's statement recounted that the "body lay limp and merely absorbed their blows." The deputies continued kicking him for a full minute, he said. It might have gone on longer, but one of the assailants spotted Juarez. Juarez said the assault left a large pool of blood on the floor.[4]

In the weeks after he filed his complaint, he said, deputies would insult him and call him a "rat," among other things, as they passed him in the corridors. Eventually, having heard no response to his complaint for two years, Juarez asked to meet with Baca. During the meeting, Juarez recalled, Baca claimed no one had informed him about the complaint. He sent for the report, which said the beaten inmate was schizophrenic. "Punches are allowed, but kicks are not allowed in my department," Juarez recalled Baca saying.[5]

Scott Budnick, a producer for *The Hangover* movies and a former writing tutor at Men's Central Jail, gave a sworn declaration that in 2009 he witnessed three deputies kicking and punching an inmate in an empty chow hall. The inmate fell to the floor. The deputies, he said, repeatedly yelled, "Stop resisting!" even though the inmate put up no resistance. Presumably, their shouts were intended to foil any possible audio recording. On another occasion, in 2008, Budnick said he was standing outside his class when he saw a deputy stop an inmate for a search. "I then saw the . . . deputy grab the inmate's head and smash his head into the wall, hard. It was so hard that I could hear an audible crack," he said.[6]

Los Angeles County jails are so dangerous that deputies, to control the enemy, have become the enemy. Like any other gang members, they try to inspire fear and strike first. Joshua Sather, a rookie who graduated at the top of his class in the Sheriff's Academy, was assigned to the section of Los Angeles's Twin Towers Correctional Facility reserved for the mentally ill. Housing fourteen hundred inmates on any given day, it's now the largest mental institution in America, except it's not a mental institution. It's a storage facility. According to Sather, in March 2011 his supervisor ordered him to beat up an inmate. It's not clear whether he obeyed, but the next day Sather quit. He left town and found a job at an oil field in Colorado. Sather is one of the few deputies to come forward about gratuitous staff violence, but the department investigation of the March 2011 incident concluded that nothing incorrect had occurred. After the media learned about the case and similar cases that ended without any findings of deputy guilt, Baca reopened them.[7]

■ A FACE REARRANGED

In 2010 I sat through a series of hearings in superior court in Torrance, California. In one such hearing, deputies brought in a young inmate from Baca's jail who'd been charged with possession of heroin with intent to sell. His head was terribly swollen and disfigured, bruises everywhere. He looked as though he'd fallen off a scaffold and landed on his face. Only a week earlier, I'd seen this same man looking unscathed. The prosecutor and Judge Mark S. Arnold had also been present for both hearings, and in the second one, the inmate sat in full view of everyone for a full ten minutes. But Arnold, the prosecutor, the bailiff, the court secretary, and the judge's assistant all seemed quite determined not to notice the glaring rearrangement of his face. They performed business as usual without mention of the startling change.

After the hearing, I mailed Arnold a note and commended him on his ability to ignore what he clearly didn't want to see. Judge Arnold, like so many criminal court judges, was a former prosecutor. He had also served thirteen years as a deputy in the Sheriff's Department. No doubt he worked part of that time as a county jail guard, as do all rookie deputies. After receiving the note, the judge, I would learn later, did in fact contact the jail to ensure that the man received medical attention. Among his injuries was a cracked orbital bone surrounding one eye. The inmate was informed that eventually he'd need surgery. He would later try to interest civil attorneys in helping him file a lawsuit against the county, but they uniformly said they had learned of many similar instances within the jail and had grown selective. They would take only cases involving disabling injuries, the kind that would never heal.

Later I found out what had happened to the inmate. In the jail, a cauldron of racism, gangs form around ethnicities. The principal groups are Hispanic, white, and African American, although there are subsets, such as Salvadoran Hispanics and skinheads. When racial tension in the jail is high, which is most of the time, the guards can prevent confrontations by keeping the groups separated. If a man uses the wrong toilet, walks in the wrong location, stops in front of the wrong TV, he's asking for punishment. Inmates even shower in ethnic groups, and therein lies the tale.

One day the inmate, who was white, was sent into the shower room, beyond the vision of the deputies, with another white man and six Hispanics. After the shower, back in the changing room—also outside the deputies' view—the six Hispanics jumped the other two. They fought back but sustained a number of bad injuries. Later, when questioned by an investigating deputy, all eight inmates, as the investigator knew they would, said they didn't see or know anything about the incident, and the investigation ended.

The two battered inmates didn't even consider the six Hispanics as being responsible for the beating they meted out. "They only did what they were supposed to do," the white inmate told me. He and the other inmate had been set up by the deputies in charge, possibly because of a personal grudge or possibly because they were bored. Officially, the jail administration doesn't sort inmates by race because the practice is illegal. Unofficially, if they didn't, there would be homicides and mayhem every day. Because they'd followed official race-blind protocol instead of the rules of the jail's parallel universe, the deputies knew they would never be disciplined.

■ TEACHING VIOLENCE

Most incarcerated people, whether in Los Angeles, Chicago, or any other U.S. town, were accused of crimes that involved no violence. Yet, if they remain behind bars for any length of time, they will be taught both to expect violence at any moment and to solve problems through violence. It's not that American criminals are more vicious than criminals elsewhere. Rather, American penal institutions are more likely to allow violence to rule. The guards are more likely to let the strong prey on the weak and forget about what they've seen when they go home to their families.

The millions of ex-cons now walking the streets were conditioned to stand up for themselves to avoid ending up at the bottom of the food chain, with the raped, the beaten, and the lost. This lesson was provided by the justice system, and it's yet another reason—along with poor literacy, widespread drug addiction, and other social ills—that successful convicts don't generally turn into successful citizens. They're likely suffering from posttraumatic stress disorder, the same psychological condition that afflicts so many war veterans.

Although the prison-industrial complex is economically tiny compared to the military-industrial complex, prisons and jails have a far more profound effect on the nation than ledgers might show. More people are in prisoners' uniforms than military uniforms. In fact, the number of people locked up or on parole or probation—more than 7 million—is larger than the number of residents in Pennsylvania and Massachusetts combined. In the most recent available figures from the Department of Justice, 713,473 prisoners were released from incarceration in 2006.[8] The fashions and attitudes of prison—drooping trousers, for example—are so prevalent among the population at large that it's not always easy to know the source. Did street gang violence invade prisons, or did prison violence take over the streets? Because America made the choice to incarcerate so many people, their convict ethos is all around us.

▪ GAMING THE NUMBERS

A corporation, according to the Citizens United ruling by the Roberts court, is a person, but the 2.3 million people behind bars are, in many ways, not even equal to the three-fifths of a person that was the sum of a preemancipation slave. Although they've sunk to the bottom of the U.S. socioeconomic structure, they aren't counted when statisticians put together the numbers on unemployment, housing, or income. Before their arrests, many were jobless and some homeless as well, but on landing in the Gulag, they were miraculously cured of socioeconomic ailments, which makes the nation's maldistribution of income and assets look less odious than it really is. These nonexistent people can, however, be counted when numbers are run to determine representation in Congress, the Electoral College, and the state legislature. Although they probably hail from an urban area, they are often counted as residents of the rural town where the prison is located, boosting that district's population.

The New York Times estimated in 2008 that 5.3 million felons and ex-felons would be barred from voting that November.[9] Although they boost the voting power of prison districts, they, like slaves under the Constitution, get no share of this power. It's a remarkable contortion for a democracy.

■ ALL ALONE

Many prison systems, aided by obliging judicial interpretations of statutes, have unilaterally altered court sentences by placing so-called troublesome inmates in solitary confinement, often for years and possibly even for life. In 2005 the Bureau of Justice counted 81,622 prisoners in "restricted housing" (solitary confinement).[10] Their ailments are so predictable that psychiatrists have given them a name—security housing unit (SHU) syndrome. Symptoms include a variety of anxieties such as severe depression, hallucinations, and paranoia.

Many of these convicts who spend twenty-two to twenty-three hours a day in a windowless cell are suspected of being gang members. They remain cordoned off until they renounce the gang and provide intelligence to prison authorities. If they do so, they are placed in protective custody (PC), which is more confining than standard prison but less debilitating than staying in "the hole." Once a convict has gone into PC, it becomes his everlasting shadow. Should he ever go into a standard lockup anywhere in the country again, he will likely be marked for retaliation.

John McCain, who was physically tortured on a regular basis by his North Vietnamese captors, singled out solitary confinement as the cruelest punishment. "It crushes your spirit and weakens your resistance more effectively than any other form of mistreatment," he said.[11]

Thousands of isolated convicts in California staged a hunger strike in 2011 that ended after three weeks of on-and-off negotiations. The prisoners ultimately settled for the promise of warm hats, wall calendars, and a loose pledge by prison officials to reconsider the isolation regulations.[12] When inmates have to go on a hunger strike to win protection from cold, civilization has made a wrong turn.

Colin Dayan, a Vanderbilt professor who visited a solitary confinement unit at the Arizona State Prison in Florence, described inmates who were allowed no human contact except when handcuffed or chained to leave their cells. Even the "dog pen," or exercise yard, was surrounded by cement so high that when they were outside, the inmates could see nothing but the sky. After his visit, an inmate wrote to Dayan, "Now I can't see my face in the mirror. I've lost my skin. I can't feel my mind."[13]

Long ago progressive zoos moved their mammals from cages into more natural environments because the animals clearly were stir-crazy. When isolation drive inmates stir-crazy it can create a dystopian hell where the bizarre becomes commonplace. Some inmates look for opportunities to throw feces and urine at passing guards. The standard guard response is to send a specially equipped and armored unit of peacekeepers into the cell with the mission of mercilessly clubbing the offender into submission.

■ SEX SLAVES AND RAPE

It's difficult to think of a prison movie made in the last few decades that doesn't incorporate the subject of prison rape. Stand-up comedians joke about it. Cops-and-robbers films commonly depict detectives threatening suspects with the prospect of prison rape. All this attention is based on how much fact? In August 2010 the Bureau of Justice Statistics reported that 4.4 percent of prison inmates and 2.1 percent of jail inmates said they had been sexually victimized in the previous twelve months.[14] These statistics were based on a survey, and it's unlikely that all victims reported their experiences. It's common for rape victims—in or out of a penal institution—to bottle up the memory.

In 2001 Human Rights Watch released a book-length study that documented case after case of sexual intimidation and rape inside U.S. prisons. It was startling how similar were so many independently recalled stories from all across the country. The genesis of the study was a small announcement posted by the nonprofit group in *Prison Legal News* and *Prison Life Magazine*, two publications with a wide audience in U.S. prisons. Activists had been claiming that prison rape was a monumental problem, so Human Rights Watch decided to investigate. The result was a deluge of painful letters from victims.[15]

■ HORRIFYING TALES

As the organization's staff proceeded to gather information in thirty-four states, many prison administrations denied the existence of rape in their facilities. At the same time, convicts were telling opposite, horrifying tales, and victims said prison staffs were very much aware of their plight.

Human Rights Watch concluded that "rape and other sexual abuses occur in prison because correctional officials, to a surprising extent, do little to stop them from occurring. While some inmates with whom Human Rights Watch is in contact have described relatively secure institutions—where inmates are closely monitored, where steps are taken to prevent inmate-on-inmate abuses, and where such abuses are punished if they occur—many others report a decidedly laissez faire approach to the problem."[16]

One of the worst systems surveyed was that of the state of Texas, where victims, after being "turned out," were routinely auctioned, sold, and rented by their assailants. These activities were discovered in other states too. One Texas inmate complained to a chaplain after a series of brutal rapes and beatings by another inmate. He was put in touch with an investigator who interviewed the victim and his attacker together in the same room. Although frightened, the victim told the truth. The assailant claimed the sex was consensual. The investigator announced that the institution had no interest in "lovers' quarrels." The men were sent back to their cells, and the attacker immediately raped the victim again in a particularly savage assault. This story brings to mind Aleksandr Solzhenitsyn's conclusion about the selection process for camp guards in his *Gulag Archipelago*: "Every man with the slightest speck of spiritual training, with a minimally circumspect conscience, or capacity to distinguish good from evil is instinctively going to back out and use every available means to avoid joining this dark legion."[17]

A Florida inmate, in a letter to Human Rights Watch, chronicled his unsuccessful efforts to induce prison authorities to protect him from abuse. He'd been knifed and raped and had attempted to slash his own wrists. But prison authorities continued denying him protection. Summing up these experiences, he wrote, "The opposite of compassion is not hatred, it's indifference."

Among the many dangers of prison rape is the risk of infection with HIV. Evan Wood, a leading HIV/AIDS researcher at the University of British Columbia, has noted that "the mass incarceration of drug users [in the United States] is particularly alarming, given the spread of HIV in prisons." HIV and hepatitis C tend to travel to the same places, and as much of 30 percent of the prison population carries these diseases. According to one inmate,

> I had no choice but to submit to being Inmate B—'s prison wife. Out of fear for my life, I submitted to sucking his dick, being fucked in my ass, and performing other duties as a woman, such as making his bed. In all reality, I was his slave. I determined I'd be better off to willingly have sex with one person, than it would be to face violence and rape by multiple people. The most tragic part to this is that the person I chose to be with has AIDS.

Another inmate wrote,

> I've been sentenced for a D.U.I. offense. My 3rd one: When I first came to prison, I had no idea what to expect. Certainly none of this. I'm a tall white male, who unfortunately has a small amount of feminine characteristics. And very shy. These characteristics have got me raped so many times I have no more feelings physically. I have been raped by up to 5 black men and two white men at a time. I've had knifes at my head and throat. I had fought and been beat so hard that I didn't ever think I'd see straight again. One time when I refused to enter a cell, I was brutally attacked by staff and taken to segragation [sic] though I had only wanted to prevent the same and worse by not locking up with my cell mate. There is no supervision after lockdown. I was given a conduct report. I explained to the hearing officer what the issue was. He told me that off the record, he suggests I find a man I would/could willingly have sex with to prevent these things from happening. I've requested protective custody only to be denied. It is not available here. He also said there was no where to run to, and it would be best for me to accept things. . . . I probably have AIDS now. I have great difficulty raising food to my mouth from shaking after nightmares or thinking to hard on all this. . . . I've laid down without physical fight to be sodomized. To prevent so much damage in struggles, ripping and tearing. Though in not fighting, it caused my heart and spirit to be raped as well. Something I don't know if I'll ever forgive myself for.

The Human Rights Watch report prompted Congress to initiate hearings and a study of its own, which confirmed the report's findings. Congressional staff conservatively estimated that at least 13 percent of inmates then incarcerated had been sexually assaulted in prison and therefore concluded that nearly 200,000 inmates then behind bars had been or would be victims of prison rape. The total number of inmates sexually assaulted in the previous twenty years likely exceeded 1 million, and many of them, as the first-person testimonies showed, were single victims raped repeatedly. Some were murdered as well. The investigation resulted in the Prison Rape Elimination Act, which Congress passed and President George W. Bush signed in 2003. But despite the aggressiveness and determination denoted in its title, the new law resulted mostly in the gathering of more statistics, not in the establishment of measures to end the horror.

■ THE RACIAL COMPONENT

Human Rights Watch concluded that there's a definite racial component to prison rape. Blacks in particular considered this kind of aggression to be normal in a prison setting, and many seemed to look upon raping whites as a form of reparations. But researchers also found that blacks raped blacks, Hispanics raped Hispanics, and both groups, along with aggressive whites, raped white prisoners. Hispanics didn't rape blacks, and blacks didn't rape Hispanics because neither group would stand for it. In contrast, whites, often outnumbered and not as proficient at forming gangs, were less likely to establish group resistance. In fact, two inmate categories stood out as most likely to be victimized—whites and the weak.

According to the report,

A few of the victims who provided information to us were convicted of serious, violent crimes such as murder, but a striking proportion of them were nonviolent felons, many of them convicted of crimes such as burglary, drug offenses, passing bad checks, car theft, etc. Of the minority of victims who were aware of the criminal history of the perpetrator of abuse, many reported serious and violent crimes. This general pattern is consistent, of course, with the idea that perpetrators of rape tend to be more violent people than victims, both inside and outside of prison.

Unfortunately, the extensive documentation of this ghastly, pervasive problem has not inspired America to reconsider its policies, particularly its policy regarding imprisoning minor offenders, who are so often the victims of prison rape. Society should take action on this issue, even if it's only for selfish reasons. Neither the damaged victims nor their assailants will likely become model citizens upon their release. But the problem persists, and in fact rape is built into the criminal justice system, an essential part of the sentence, a de facto element that keeps violent offenders from turning on the guards. The ruling credo is "Give the animals what they want," as long as the victims are other inmates.

17

The Insanity of
Mental Health Practices

BACK IN 1955 THERE WAS ONE PSYCHIATRIC BED FOR EVERY THREE HUNDRED Americans. But by 2010 most of those beds had disappeared, and the ratio was one for every three thousand.[1] Some of this immense decline in residential treatment can be attributed to advances in psychiatric care, particularly the formulation of a whole new galaxy of medications. But wholesale deinstitutionalization of mental patients had little to do with good medical practice. The patients weren't cured. We just stopped looking after them. The most acute cases remained in institutions, but the rest, if they had no families to care for them, were left out on the curb like abandoned furniture. Many spent the rest of their lives bouncing from homelessness on the street to homelessness in jail. At least two generations of mentally ill people have lived this way.

Two groups with different perspectives converged to make this happen. Human-rights reformers believed it was unethical to keep noncriminals confined against their will. Most of these patients, they said, could be cared for in their communities as outpatients. Meanwhile, conservatives looking to cut government spending decided they didn't want to pay for any more patient care than they had to. These two perspectives met in the Community Mental Health Act of 1963.[2] Among its many provisions, the act mandated that state hospitals liberalize release criteria. Released patients were supposed to be placed in single-room occupancy (SRO) hotels and enrolled in community mental health centers for treatment and follow-up. But, for the most part, new local clinics never came into being, and those that did exist didn't receive nearly enough funding. Patients, many of them schizophrenic, wandered off onto the streets without medication.

Meanwhile, available SRO spaces dwindled as property owners found more profitable uses for their real estate. The relatively limited population of homeless people at the time was suddenly joined by hundreds of thousands of mental patients, substance abusers, and unemployed people who'd run out of options. They all competed for sidewalk space and soup-kitchen meals. Skid row populations seemed to double every year or so. Entire families were now out on the street. More and more people lived in vehicles. Aging motels took in those who couldn't pass credit checks or scare up enough cash for a security deposit for an apartment. These beaten-down rooms were often a last stop before the sidewalk. The National Coalition for the Homeless estimates that 20–25 percent of the single adult homeless population suffers from some form of severe and persistent mental illness.[3]

"Too often, a person with a severe mental illness is not treated until an encounter with law enforcement or the criminal justice system," says the Treatment Advocacy Center, a national nonprofit that promotes effective treatment for severe mental illness. Police officers can grow weary of dealing with the mentally ill. In July 2011, for example, six officers at a bus station in Fullerton, California, beat and tased Kelly Thomas, a homeless schizophrenic, into a coma as witnesses looked on in horror. Moments before the assault, Officer Manuel Ramos had sat Thomas on a curb and ordered him to stick his legs straight out and place his hands on his knees. Thomas, confused, had trouble complying. Ramos put on latex gloves and told Thomas, "Now see my fists? They are getting ready to fuck you up." The beating went on for ten minutes, a blue orgy of violence against a victim who, witnesses said, didn't fight back.[4]

Why did five other officers follow Ramos's lead? Because cops on the street have an unwritten rule: once it starts, you join in. An officer who hangs back invites suspicion and acrimony from his coworkers. One day when that officer needs help, he might not get it. Former LAPD detective Mike Rothmiller described how joining in the fight became a kind of Pavlovian response. And the decision to attack or not to attack was always in the hands of the most vicious cop on the scene.[5]

A photo taken of Thomas at the hospital shows his face grotesquely swollen and covered with bruises and cuts. He couldn't breathe without a machine; his brain flatlined. Five days after the incident, his parents consented to take him off life support, and he died.

In a video taken by a bystander, Thomas, thirty-seven, can be heard screaming for his father to help him over the clicking sounds of the Taser. But his father wasn't there, and witnesses were frightened by the raging cops. "The world," said Albert Einstein, "is a dangerous place, not because of those who do evil, but because of those who look on and do nothing."

Ramos was charged with second-degree murder and involuntary manslaughter. Another officer was charged with involuntary manslaughter and the use of excessive force. They both posted bail and proceeded to craft a defense with their respective attorneys. History shows it's an uphill climb to get assault convictions against police officers on the job. The case was still moving through the courts as we went to press.

■ THE LIBRARY SOLUTION

Ironically, our society's solutions for mental illness may be as irrational as the patients. Anyone who frequents a big-city public library knows that librarians are often the de facto day-care attendants for discarded schizophrenics and other mentally ill homeless people. But jailers are their principal attendants. The International Association for Forensic and Correctional Psychology found that New York's Riker's Island, Chicago's Cook County Jail, and the Los Angeles County Jails are the largest mental health institutions in the United States. Estimates vary, but probably about 10 percent of the inmates in these facilities are mentally ill.[6] Human Rights Watch estimates that across the United States, approximately 300,000 mentally ill prisoners are in jails and penitentiaries on any given day.[7]

"Asking prisons to treat people with serious mental illness is pushing round pegs into square holes," said Jamie Fellner, senior adviser of Human Rights Watch's U.S. program and co-author of a 2003 report on mental illness and prisons. "People who suffer from mental illness need mental health interventions, not punishment for behavior that may be motivated by delusions and hallucinations."[8]

Even when arresting police act with patience, the situation can turn ugly later. "I saw different people picking on this one guy," a former inmate at Los Angeles County's Twin Towers Correctional Facility told me. "You could see there was something wrong with him. He just didn't respond to things. You see enough of these people and you recognize it. There was no way he could handle himself in there. He was like this big target to any asshole who liked pushing people around." The former inmate knew this man would fare better in the less dangerous "ding" section for the mentally ill, but transferring prisoners into this section isn't easy. "I took him aside and told him to tell the deputies he was going to kill himself," he said. If deputies don't react to a suicide threat, they're in clear violation of jail rules. The inmate followed the advice and was transferred. "But not everybody like this guy gets somebody to tell him what to do," said the good Samaritan. "The guards, they should have taken care of it as soon as he showed up. Anybody could see what he was, but they just don't care."[9]

Mississippi's Atiba Parker, who in his adolescence began hearing voices and seeing faces that no one else could hear or see, was diagnosed at age twenty-four with schizoaffective disorder, an illness characterized by hallucinations, extreme paranoia, mania, and depression. After he began self-medicating with street drugs, he was arrested and fined twice for marijuana possession. When he left his mother's home and went out on his own, Parker began selling small amounts of crack cocaine. On two occasions, he sold small amounts to a woman working as a police informant. The informant was trying to avoid prison time for several felonies. Around this time, Parker was charged with possessing 2.41 grams of crack and 1.5 grams of marijuana. Police had found the drugs in his mother's car, which they confiscated thanks to a statute that allowed them to keep vehicles used to transport drugs. After this incident, Parker's mother helped him get into rehab, he began taking prescribed medications, and he landed a full-time job, which he worked for nine months.[10]

Although Parker's therapeutic outcome was positive, prosecutors charged him with two counts of selling cocaine for selling those small amounts to the informant. Parker was offered a plea deal of sixteen years, but he opted for trial. In 2006, at age twenty-nine, he was sentenced as a habitual offender to forty-two years. His projected release date was November 6, 2048. Said his mother, Ann Parker, "I have always taught my children that if they do something wrong there are consequences. . . . Nevertheless, the amount of drugs my son was prosecuted for did not justify his life being taken away."[11]

In Neolithic times, medicine men, in an effort to release the evil spirits thought to cause derangement, chipped a hole in the skull to provide an exit. It's not clear how many survived the procedure, but at least it was performed in hopes of helping the afflicted. The same can't be said about the methods used to deal with Parker.

■ BETWEEN THE CRACKS

If authorities didn't have more than 7 million prisoners, parolees, and probationers to keep track of, they might have paid more attention to the danger posed by John Albert Gardner III, an ex-convict who served five years for molesting his thirteen-year-old neighbor. California authorities released Gardner from parole in 2008, even though he'd violated its terms on several occasions. He then, on separate occasions, murdered two teenage girls near his mother's home in the San Diego suburbs. In both cases, he killed his victim while attempting to rape her. In 2010 he was finally put away for good, sentenced to two life terms without possibility of parole.[12] It's reasonable to suspect that Gardner's parole agent let his case slip between the cracks because the agent was buried in other cases, including those involving mentally ill offenders who should have been shifted out of the criminal justice system into a therapeutic setting,

■ NO INTERVENTION

From February to September 2010, while a student at Pima Community College, high school dropout Jared Lee Loughner had five encounters with college police for classroom and library disruptions. A teacher and a classmate both said at the time that they thought he might commit a school shooting. The college made no attempt to provide the student with assistance or treatment and ultimately suspended him. On January 8, 2011, at the age of twenty-two, he showed up at a political event sponsored by U.S. Representative Gabrielle Giffords and shot six people to death, including Chief U.S. District Court Judge John Roll. The shooting left fourteen others injured, including Giffords, who sustained a critical head wound. Facing years of physical and cognitive intense therapy, she resigned her office a year later. In May a judge ruled that Loughner was incompetent to stand trial. Yet in preparing for the attack, this severely disturbed young man easily purchased a Glock 19, the Rolls Royce of handguns, for about five hundred dollars at a Sportsman's Warehouse. He also purchased a jumbo clip that held thirty-one nine-millimeter rounds. One Walmart store actually refused to sell him ammunition because he exhibited "strange behavior," but he was able to pick up what he wanted at another Walmart store.

■ "WOULD BE LESS ILL"

Although schizophrenia rarely leads to violent behavior, Loughner showed a host of schizophrenia-like symptoms before the shooting that should have prompted professional intervention. In fact, "a growing body of evidence [suggests] that there are some special things we can do for people in the early stage" of schizophrenic illness, said Max Marshall, professor of community psychiatry at the University of Manchester in the UK.[13]

Oliver Freudenreich, director of the First Episode and Early Psychosis Program at Massachusetts General Hospital, said, "If we could get people at an earlier stage, they would be less ill, and the disease would not yet have wreaked the damage to social, vocational and family life that often accumulates. . . . The illness strikes in the developmental years."[14] Loughner was a classic case of a severely mentally ill person who had no substantive contact with institutional therapy until he ended up as a ward of the criminal justice system.

Loughner went on his shooting spree while states were drastically downsizing their mental health programs in response to the Great Recession. The National Association of State Mental Health Program Directors estimated that in 2008–11 states cut $3.4 billion in mental health services, while an additional 400,000 people sought help at public mental health facilities. "These are people without a previous psychiatric history who are coming in and telling us they've lost their jobs, they've lost sometimes their homes, they can't provide for their families, and they are becoming severely depressed," said Dr. Felicia Smith, director of the acute psychiatric service at Massachusetts General Hospital in Boston.[15]

Said Linda Rosenberg, president of the National Council for Community Behavioral Healthcare, "It's been horrible. Those that need it the most—the unemployed, those with tremendous family stress—have no insurance."[16] More than 70 percent of emergency department administrators said they have kept patients waiting for twenty-four hours, according to a 2010 survey of six hundred hospital emergency department administrators by the Schumacher Group, which manages emergency departments across the country.[17] Ten percent said they had "boarded" patients for a week or more because the only alternative was to put them on the street. Social workers who deal with these unfortunates know that in many cases they'll end up running afoul of the criminal justice system. That's when they're finally given a bed.

PART 5
Failed Vision

18

Legacy Inmates

Authority and obedience are not enough to hold social orders together.

—Edmund Burke

Brenda Valencia, who served nearly a dozen years in federal penitentiaries after she gave a ride to a drug dealer, noticed that she kept meeting inmates whose parents were doing time in other prisons, often on drug charges.

These girls would be put in foster care and end up pregnant at thirteen. They'd meet an older guy who promises to take care of them and these boyfriends basically worked them into the system and they'd end up behind bars themselves, usually for drugs. But they just wanted to be loved. It happens over and over. I heard so many stories like that. It's just crazy. Drugs are still easy to get. They're still in the schools. What they're doing hasn't worked. It hasn't helped. It's just made more kids grow up without parents, and now to top it off they're getting abused by older guys. How much better can that be? What it can do to you is just make you bitter and hate everybody. So I made a promise to myself. I wouldn't allow the system to change who I was. Unfortunately, a lot of women did. It got the best of them. There's a lot of resentment. They just didn't understand that any wrong move can take ten years from their life.[1]

Valencia, working for a privately funded group, saw variations of the same story over and over in her job counseling girls in juvenile detention. "If these girls don't want to be where they're placed by the foster system," she said, "they just go out there on the street." And the next time the system encounters them, she said, it defines them not as victims but criminals.

■ "HOW BAD IT WAS"

In 1996 St. Louis cop Kevin Cunningham, who'd boxed in the army, created a makeshift boxing gym in the basement of an abandoned police station in a neighborhood that reeked of poverty, drugs, and gangs. The newly dubbed Hyde Park Boxing Club was his bid to get kids off street and "teach them self-respect," a practically unknown commodity on his beat. He told Kevin Iole of Yahoo Sports,

> We were responding to so much gang violence and so many shootings and robberies and drive-bys and homicides. What really threw me for a loop was most of the time when we were responding, most of the time, the victims were 14-, 15-, 16-year-old young black males. . . . . You can't even imagine how bad it was. . . . Of all the kids that have come through my program, I think I've met what, three, four of the fathers. It ain't many. Most of these kids are from single-parent homes and, even with that, nobody paid them any attention. Nobody cared where they were, at any time of the day or night.[2]

Cunningham started the program with thirty kids. Not many years later he tallied names on the list, and at least twenty of the original thirty "were dead or in prison."[3] And those were youths that somebody (Cunningham) cared about and tried to help, as opposed to their neighborhood peers. One boy who beat the odds was Devon Alexander, who, with Cunningham still working his corner, would grow up to hold the IBF and World Boxing Council (WBC) light welterweight titles. His older brother, Vaughn, however, lost to the street. An equally gifted boxer, he was sentenced to eighteen years for robbery.

■ WRONG ZIP CODE, WRONG LIFE

Just as members of elite families are reserved a special place within the most prestigious universities one generation after another, the children of the poorest Americans are practically guaranteed a ticket to poverty and incarceration. Benjamin Todd Jealous, president of the NAACP, and Rod Paige, secretary of education during the George W. Bush administration, studied one zip code in the rough Bedford Stuyvesant neighborhood of Brooklyn—11216—and found that $16.6 million was being spent each year to incarcerate its residents.[4] Among the neighborhood's alumni was heavyweight champion and ex-con Mike Tyson. "Residents of 11216 suffer from a 53 percent unemployment rate," they wrote, "and the local high school has a 50 percent graduation rate. A reformed criminal justice system, along with a renewed focus on education, would benefit this neighborhood immensely and produce immediate savings for New York." But the political will to transform research findings into policy is minimal at best.

In January 2004 the Sentencing Project estimated that a black man had a one-in-three chance of serving time in prison at some point in his life.[5] This makes it more difficult for African American men to find jobs, more difficult for black women to find suitable husbands, and less common for black children to grow up in stable families with black male role models. Drugs have certainly devastated black communities—but the remedy of wholesale criminal sentencing has made the situation worse.

Police tend to arrest people who look to them like people who get arrested. Blacks are arrested for minor drug possession at seven times the rate of whites, even though national surveys consistently show that whites smoke marijuana more than blacks or Hispanics.[6] *New York Times* columnist Charles M. Blow concluded that one reason blacks have started to leave New York City en masse is "hyper-aggressive police tactics that have resulted in a concerted and directed campaign of harassment against the black citizens of this city." He found that in 2009 there were a record 580,000 stop-and-frisks in New York. Most of those stopped (55 percent) were black, and many of the rest were Hispanic.[7]

The stop-and-frisk tactics that Blow and other civil libertarians condemn were championed by William J. Bratton, an innovative but controversial supercop whom Mayor Rudolph Giuliani appointed New York Police Department (NYPD) commissioner in 1994. Bratton became best known for his policy of zero-tolerance, "broken-windows" policing, which operates on the theory that when minor offenses are not dealt with, neighborhood crime will grow. Through this lens a man holding a brown paper bag that might contain an open alcoholic beverage looks like a possible challenge to the social order and should be stopped and frisked. Or an officer can interpret a "furtive" look by a person on the street as possibly relating to a crime; the person could be a lookout. The practice of stop-and-frisk rests on a 1968 Supreme Court decision that established the benchmark of "reasonable suspicion"—a standard lower than the "probable cause" benchmark used previously.

During the two years Bratton ran the NYPD, the record shows, homicides fell 44 percent and serious crime overall dropped 25 percent, and these numbers continued to fall after he left. But everywhere he's been in charge, Bratton has been criticized by experts who contend that he has a gift for manipulating numbers. Sometimes crime statistics can be used to distract the public from actual problems, the way standardized test scores sometimes stand in the way of substantive education.

To young black and Hispanic males, stop-and-frisk and broken-windows policing can turn them into targets rather than ordinary citizens. In Harlem, George Lucas changed his route home from work to avoid a stretch of Seventh Avenue because of frequent brushes with police. "The inconvenience of walking out of my way still saves me the worry and frustration about being stopped," said Lucas, twenty-eight.[8]

Another major Bratton innovation was to use computers and statistics to discover where and when crimes were most likely to occur and to saturate those places with police patrols at the right time. This technique was probably more effective at lowering the crime rate. After leaving the NYPD in 1997, Bratton, who had been competing for media attention with Giuliani, took the helm of the LAPD before entering the private sector. Stop-and-frisk, which has been used in other cities as well, remains a New York City mainstay and has left a coast-to-coast trail of civil justice controversies.

■ 3 MILLION PAT DOWNS

Jeffrey Fagan, a professor of law and public health at Columbia University, has noted that rates of gun and contraband seizures resulting from stop-and-frisks in New York "are no greater than would be produced simply by chance." This finding turns the concept of reasonable suspicion on its head. *New York Times* columnist Bob Herbert provided some perspective: "From 2004 through 2009, city police officers stopped people on the street and checked them out three million times. Many were patted down, frisked, made to sprawl face down on the ground, or spread-eagle themselves against a wall or over the hood of a car. Nearly 90 percent of the people stopped were completely innocent of any wrongdoing." While crime has been going down, he pointed out, "the number of people getting stopped has been going up." Of 575,000 stops made in 2009, 504,594 were people who had "committed no crime, were issued no summonses, and were carrying no weapons or illegal substances."[9]

"No one," Herbert argued, "wants to stop the police from going after the bad guys." But he also noted, "Blacks and Latinos are more likely to be stopped than whites, even in areas where there are low crime rates and where residential populations are racially or predominantly white."[10] Given the evidence, it's difficult to contest the assumption that stop-and-frisk tactics can constitute an around-the-clock roundup of usual suspects, most of them black or brown.

Lieutenant Neal Griffin of the San Diego County, California, Police Department described how some of these procedures work on a real-life street. One of his pet peeves is what he refers to as the phony weapons charge. The way he explains it, an officer pulls over a young man and inside the car finds a toy bat—the kind often handed out on bat day at baseball stadiums around the country. If the driver fits a "certain demographic" and admits that he keeps the bat for self-defense, which is a common response, he's in a world of trouble. "But don't worry," Griffin said. "Neither of us would be arrested for it because we're 50-plus-year-old white guys. . . . But if you are 17–20, brown or black, stopped by the police and the above scenario plays out . . . the cuffs are going on and you're getting booked. Bail is between five and twenty grand. If it's Thursday, you'll sit in jail until Tuesday." And that's if you can post bond. Typically, Griffin said, the prosecutor visits the arrested youth and points out that what he's done is defined as a felony. "But I'll tell you what I'll do," said Griffin, acting out a role he knows so well. "My one-time offer. . . . You plead out today to a misdemeanor conviction . . . and I'll let you walk out of here with time served and three years' probation." Or does the arrestee prefer to "sit in jail for the next 90 days or so and wait for a trial date?"[11]

If the young man takes the deal, Griffin noted, he's surrendered his civil rights for three years. During that time, police can stop and search him solely because of his probationary status. Police can search his home too. And even if he finishes the three years with no new charges, he'll be permanently stained by a criminal weapons conviction that will follow him the rest of his life, an indelible mark of Cain that will torpedo job applications and other efforts he might make to improve his situation. Prospective employers won't see the specifics. They'll just see a weapons conviction and conclude this is a bad-news gang kid who was caught carrying a gun.

■ QUOTA ARREST SCANDAL

In New York, the dark side of stop-and-frisk can be heard in the digital recordings of roll call secretly made by Officer Adrian Schoolcraft at the Eighty-First Precinct in Brooklyn.[12] The recordings were damning evidence that commanders had threatened to fire officers who didn't write their share of summonses and conduct their share of stop-and-frisks. Schoolcraft's evidence made it clear that the NYPD, while officially denying the existence of quotas, was punishing cops for not meeting quotas. At the same time, to boost their statistics, commanders refused to follow up on more serious criminal complaints and even went so far as to downgrade felonies such as rape to misdemeanors.[13] If crime was down, then the cops in charge could climb the promotion ladder based on subterfuge. Meanwhile, cops on the street had an inaccurate picture of what was going on in their precinct because twisting the numbers took precedence over reporting reality. The aim was to aggressively harass residents for minor violations or no violations at all and to ignore serious offenses that would make the commanders look bad, thus steering officers into behavior that was precisely the opposite of their mission.

Schoolcraft, who was uniformly respected on the street, was targeted by his commanders. Eventually, he played the recordings, made in 2008 and 2009, for the *Village Voice* and also reported his findings to Internal Affairs. His superiors responded by ordering officers to burst into his home, handcuff him, and place him in a psychiatric ward, where he was held against his will for six days.[14] The action was eerily reminiscent of the Soviet regime's response to dissidents. When the hospital finally let Schoolcraft go, he was handed a bill for $7,000.

Placed on suspension without pay, he filed a $50 million lawsuit against the NYPD. There was no feasible way to deny what he'd recorded, and eventually, the department was forced to file internal charges against a commander, two sergeants, and two officers, based on his report. "This is a citywide problem. It is not limited to the 81st Precinct," said Schoolcraft's attorney, Jon Norinsberg.[15]

The NYPD scandal graphically illustrated a policy that saw young minority males as forgotten souls with a hopeless future who could be abused by scheming officials without fear of legal action. Statistics backed up the authorities' cynical assessment. By 2004, 50 percent of black men in their twenties who lacked a college education were jobless.[16] In addition to all the usual causes, such as poverty, the lack of strong male role models, substandard schools, gang rule, drugs, and bullying, union jobs in manufacturing were rapidly diminishing. Those jobs used to be a lifesaver for countless Americans lacking higher education. Among those young black men who were high school dropouts, the jobless figure was a jaw-dropping 72 percent, wrote Bruce Western, a Princeton sociologist who compiled the data.[17] These were more than double the rates for white men without high school diplomas.

And a 2010 study by Jill Doerner at the University of Rhode Island and Stephen Demuth at Bowling Green State University found that all other things being equal, federal courts doled out harsher sentences to Hispanics and blacks than to whites convicted of identical offenses. Young Hispanic males had the greatest likelihood of incarceration, and young black males received the longest sentences.[18]

Steven Raphael of the University of California–Berkeley analyzed 2000 Census data and determined that on any given day more black male dropouts in their twenties were in prison—34 percent—than were working—30 percent.[19] And after the 2000 Census rates of incarceration and unemployment went up.

19

"The Future"

And now the wheels of heaven stop
you feel the devil's riding crop
Get ready for the future:
it is murder.
            —Leonard Cohen, "The Future"

Tolstoy's heartfelt novel *Resurrection* follows the life of Katusha, a penniless servant girl who is raped, impregnated, thrown into the street by the family that had employed her, and driven to prostitution. Although innocent of the charge, she's convicted as an accessory to murder largely because jurors and court officials were eager to break for lunch. Prince Nekhlyudov, a juror, is also the blackguard who deflowered her years earlier and moved on. Now reformed, he is both startled and revolted by the court's action. He hires an attorney to appeal Katusha's case and takes her on as an all-consuming personal project. When all appeals are denied, the determined prince follows her from jail to jail. By the time she lands in Siberia, he's met other convicts who, like Katusha, were clearly innocent but thrown into the bowels of the czar's vast prison complex by a sloppy, horrifically untroubled criminal justice apparatus. The majority of convicts he encounters, although apparently guilty of their offenses, are lost souls who, since birth, were "neglected and twisted like uncared-for plants."

After seeing Russian criminal justice up close, the prince despairs at the power of well-entrenched functionaries whose livelihoods depend on the vast network of police, courts, and prisons. How can reform take place when such powerful forces stand in its way? Perhaps, he speculates, it is possible to dislodge the functionaries by continuing to pay their salaries or "even to pay them a premium, to leave off doing all that they are doing now."[1]

Were Tolstoy around to focus his acute observational powers on the U.S. criminal justice system, it would be very unlikely to earn a passing grade either. Al Martinez, a Korean War veteran who's been a metro columnist for the *Los Angeles Times* and more recently the *Los Angeles Daily News*, has seen many inmates and crazy sentences over the course of his career. "Once they get you in the system," he told me, "they have a way of hanging on to you." Groups such as FAMM and the Innocence Project have found thousands of convicts whose sentences were ridiculously harsh or unmerited, but few of them receive mercy, even after volunteers work on their behalf for years. Attorney Marcia G. Shein has resigned herself to the fact that she will never get Alabama's Wilmer Breckenridge out of federal prison. Earlier legal mistakes, cruel decisions, and inflexible rules ruined his chances of reversing either his narcotics conviction or his life-without-parole sentence. Anthony Fletcher still sits on death row in Pennsylvania, not for any crime, but because he refused to accept a plea bargain in 1992. Atiba Parker is serving his forty-two years in Mississippi for selling cocaine that weighed less than a half of a sugar packet. It's impossible to know how many crushed souls like these languish within the impossible vastness of the U.S. Gulag. As a rule its functionaries don't advertise their atrocities. But the more you dig, the more you find.

Supreme Court Justice Stephen Breyer, while still a judge on the U.S. Court of Appeals in Boston, asked, "What happens if we keep increasing mandatory prison terms through the legislature? We will have tens of thousands of men 20 years from now in their 50s, 60, and 70s, and the expense of warehousing these old men will be enormous. It will be hundreds of billions of dollars."[2] That was in 1992. Since then Human Rights Watch has found that between 2007 and 2010 the number of sentenced state and federal prisoners age sixty-five or older grew at ninety-four times the rate of the overall prison population. In January 2012, the nonprofit group reported that the number of prisoners age fifty-five or older grew at six times the rate of the overall prison population between 1995 and 2010.[3]

In one state, Michigan, the average annual health-care cost for a prison inmate was $5,801; that cost increases with age, from $11,000 for those age 55–59 to $40,000 for those age 80 or older. "Prisons were never designed to be geriatric facilities," said Jamie Fellner. "Yet U.S. corrections officials now operate old age homes behind bars."[4]

Government can shrug off the health problems of poor citizens when they're out on the street, but when elderly convicts are wards of the state, totally at its mercy for all sustenance, the moral imperative to care for them is harder to dodge. Human Rights Watch visited nine states and twenty prisons as part of its study, and everywhere it found officials scrambling to respond to the needs and vulnerabilities of older prisoners.

Even as crime grows less severe, the criminal justice system keeps churning out more prisoners and keeping them into their senior years.[5] The Pew Center on the States released a report in 2009 that found penitentiary systems have been the fastest-growing spending area for states after Medicaid, with spending on criminal justice increasing more than 300 percent in the previous twenty years.[6]

As state legislatures wrestled with their battered budgets, some members began to recognize the savings that could accrue from a more reasonable approach to criminal justice. In 2007 Texas began placing more low-risk, nonviolent offenders on probation or freeing them on parole. It also started providing treatment to inmates suffering from drug and alcohol addiction or mental health problems. "This [group] is the ones you're mad at, you're angry at," said State Representative Jerry Madden, who helped lead the overhaul. "They've done something that's really dumb, stupid against the law, but you're not terribly afraid of them." Texas also began making extensive use of electronic monitoring to track probationers and parolees, and it reduced penalties for those guilty of technical violations instead of sending them back to prison to serve their full sentences. In January 2011 Madden figured the state avoided about $2 billion in prison costs by following these practices. The state's prison population of 155,000 grew only slightly in that span rather than increasing by more than 17,000 inmates as predicted.[7]

In Florida, Republican state senator Paula Dockery said that lawmakers had been discussing similar proposals for three years without effecting any change. "It's politically difficult to do," she observed.[8]

Florida, in an orgy of punishment, had in 1983 abolished parole and now required inmates to serve at least 85 percent of their sentences.[9] But that still wasn't good enough for Republican state senator Mike Fasano, who wanted everyone to serve 100 percent of every sentence.[10]

In California, where one out of six prisoners is serving a life sentence, a survey conducted by the *Los Angeles Times* and the University of Southern California's Dornsife College of Letters, Arts, and Sciences showed a clear shift in attitudes toward less harsh sentencing. The poll, conducted in July 2011, found that the ailing economy easily outweighed crime as the respondents' top concern.[11] Nearly 70 percent approved the idea of early release of low-level offenders whose crimes didn't involve violence. Only 12 percent of respondents said they'd be willing to accept less state spending on health care or education to pay for more prisons. Less than two years after the poll was taken, state voters approved Proposition 36, which at last began reforming the harshest three-strikes law in the nation.

The same week the California poll on criminal justice came out, a study was released showing that the state's higher education system ranked last among states in state funding per student and that fewer state students were able to afford the spiraling costs being tacked on to their bills. The analysis by the Institute for Higher Education Leadership and Policy at California State University–Sacramento also found that California, once celebrated nationally for its three-tiered system of public colleges, ranked forty-first in the number of bachelor's degrees awarded for every hundred high school graduates six years after graduation. The report was titled "Consequences of Neglect."[12]

▪ FAILURE'S CONTAGIOUS

The teetering criminal justice system appears to stand apart from society because so much of it is hidden behind walls. But, in fact, the system affects all of us, and its failures are contagious. It is yet another segment of the nation's crumbling infrastructure that is being passed from one generation to the next in the hope that someone down the line will plunge in and try to fix it. But a bridge in need of reinforcement won't do real harm until it collapses. The broken justice system inflicts harm around the clock, ruining lives and even ending them as sure as waves breaking on the shore.

We know that certain strategies work, and imposing excessive prison sentences isn't one of them. "Prisons should not be used with the expectation of reducing criminal behaviour," concluded academicians at the University of New Brunswick and University of Cincinnati who conducted an exhaustive recidivism inquiry. The study of inmates and ex-inmates also examined the effect of prison versus "community-domain" supervision and rehabilitation. It found higher recidivism rates for the incarcerated group. Based on their findings, the authors declared, "The primary justification of prison should be to incapacitate offenders (particularly those of a chronic, higher risk nature) for reasonable periods and to exact retribution."[13]

■ DRUG SOLUTIONS

An appreciable reduction in drug use would deal a terrific blow to crime in general. In the early seventies, an amazingly effective program was implemented after U.S. Representatives Robert Steele (R-CT) and Morgan Murphy (D-IL) returned from a fact-finding trip to Vietnam in May 1971 and reported that approximately 15 percent of U.S. servicemen there were addicted to heroin. The next month President Nixon created the Special Action Office of Drug Abuse Prevention, which laid out a program of prevention and rehabilitation. Nixon ensured that whatever the results of the program, they would be scrupulously documented. Jerome Jaffe, the director of the new office, hired psychiatric researcher Lee Robins to help with the project, promising her unprecedented access to service members.[14]

As part of the program, every enlisted man was tested for heroin addiction before he was allowed to return home to the United States. Robins discovered the problem was even worse than feared. About 20 percent of the soldiers identified themselves as addicts. They were kept in Vietnam until they dried out, and their rehabilitation was remarkably successful, so much so that for years experts thought the reported results must have been phony. In the first year only 5 percent of returning soldiers returned to heroin. How could this be when addicts who'd become hooked in the United States were relapsing at rates that hovered around 90 percent?[15]

Robins "spent months, if not years, trying to defend the integrity of the study," Jaffe recalled. But forty years later, its findings are widely accepted as real, not fudged. Many behavioral scientists believe that the plan worked because the soldiers, after being treated for their physical addiction in Vietnam, returned to a place radically different from the environment in which their addiction took hold. "People, when they perform a behavior a lot—especially in the same environment, same sort of physical setting—outsource the control of the behavior to the environment," explained Duke University psychologist David Neal.[16] In a new environment without the habitual triggers, addicts have a much better chance of interrupting their past behavior. Smokers who always light a cigarette after finishing a meal in the kitchen may, if they want to quit, have to stop eating in that particular kitchen. Jaffe's team concluded that addicts in programs that let them remain in the environment where they were chasing after and using drugs have a much lower chance of kicking their habit. Yet we still rely excessively on nonresidential regimens because they appear less costly on the surface.

■ WHAT ABOUT EVIDENCE?

When the Job Corps, an antipoverty program that was part of Lyndon Johnson's Great Society, was on the ropes and facing deep budget cuts in the mid-1990s, popular two-time heavyweight champion George Foreman came to its defense. "Job Corps," he said, "took me from the mean [Houston] streets and out of a nightmare lifestyle into a mode where the most incredible of dreams came true." There's plenty of evidence to back up Foreman's tribute. Studies find that the Job Corps measurably improves the education and job prospects of disadvantaged youth. Its sixty thousand annual graduates, all of them at-risk youths, make more money than control groups and are 20 percent less likely to be arrested, charged with, or convicted of a crime.[17] If convicted, they served less jail time. Mathematica Policy Research, an objective referee of social policy research, examined the data and concluded that the Job Corps is "the only large-scale education and training program shown to increase the earnings of disadvantaged youth."[18]

It costs about $26,000 to put a youth through the eight months of Job Corps training. That's comparable to the price of incarceration for approximately a year. But the Job Corps produces productive citizens, whereas pragmatic experience backed up by studies such as the one conducted by the University of New Brunswick and University of Cincinnati (see above) show that prison does not. In 2011, however, the Republican-controlled House tried yet again to gut the Job Corps. This time it wanted to close 85 of its 124 centers. Enemies of the program scoffed that for approximately the same amount, taxpayers could send someone to Harvard. But Harvard's true costs are of course much greater than the $36,000-plus tuition, and Harvard isn't charged with undoing a lifetime of deprivation. In January 2013 the Labor Department discontinued accepting new Job Corps recruits as a cost-saving measure. It wasn't clear if or when the freeze would be lifted.[19]

■ EFFECTIVE MODELS

Convicts who maintain contact with family and friends in the outside world are less likely to be convicted of additional crimes and usually have an easier reintegration back into society, yet the clumsy federal system still incarcerates inmates far from home. Brenda Valencia, for example, was convicted in Florida but imprisoned in California.

Narcotics Anonymous meetings are often heavily populated with addicts ordered there by judges, and the meeting places are often prime locations for drug buys, an unintended negative consequence that's also seen around many methadone dispensaries. If judges took the time to check out some of these gatherings in person, they might draw up a different strategy. In the meantime, they repeat their mistakes and pretend they're accomplishing something.

Specialized women's and veterans courts, which hear cases involving particular types of defendants and focus on turning their lives around, show promise. Also, we don't always have to reinvent the wheel. Over the last decade, Portugal, for example, has tested a method that could easily be applied in the United States. As of 2001, people caught with small amounts of any drug can no longer be charged with a criminal offense, but they may be placed before a panel that includes a psychologist, social worker, and legal adviser. The panel suggests an appropriate treatment for the user, but the user reserves the right to refuse help. Drug trafficking is still a crime. Before 2001 Portugal had one of the worst drug problems in Europe. In the years since the law was changed, however, the libertarian Cato Institute, the World Health Organization, and *BMJ* (formerly the *British Medical Journal*) have documented a turnaround.[20]

But even though several more effective models are out there, we have to recognize that some U.S. and state policies are so damaging that they've made solutions more elusive. When we revoked the Volstead Act in 1933, the criminal gangs that had taken over distribution and sales of alcoholic beverages didn't all disappear. Many of the groups pursued other criminal ventures. Like the gangster network of the Prohibition era, narcotics syndicates that reach around the globe are dug in and staffed by nasty, organized characters. It's unlikely that any legalization could suddenly crush the traffickers, whose power along much of the U.S. border rivals and often exceeds that of the Mexican government. They'd use their elaborate criminal networks to commit other crimes, such as kidnapping and shaking down legitimate businesses, practices they've already adopted. Frankenstein's monster walks among us, but we can at least choose to stop feeding it its meal of choice.

Up to 60 percent of ex-convicts in New York State are still unemployed one year after release, according to a study from the Independent Committee on Reentry and Employment.[21] Glenn Martin, vice president of the Fortune Society in Queens, a nonprofit group that trains former inmates in job-hunting skills, says that ex-cons are "always at the back of the line, and the line . . . got a lot longer" after the economic tremor of 2008. When ex-cons are laid off and forced to return to job searching, they face the stigma of criminal conviction" all over again.

Not nearly enough resources have been brought to bear on the crisis of hyperincarceration. The problem has been heating up like the frog that sits undisturbed in a pan of water while it's brought slowly to a boil. A long-term solution is to educate the public, primarily in schools but also with accurate and substantial news coverage—the kind that's a rarity in today's degraded twenty-four-hour news cycle. Democracy works best when the electorate understands the issues.

But even if we adequately educated the public, we couldn't wipe out crime and addiction. We're dealing with human beings, after all. Financiers and corporate chieftains take mad chances and commit reprehensible acts to expand their already enormous fortunes, while cabdrivers barely earning minimum wage turn in jewelry and wallets left on the rear seat. Some corners of the heart can't be fully understood.

Still, we can and should recognize the overwhelming evidence that incarceration is not always the best answer to crime and that in many cases it makes the problem worse. Then we must incorporate this understanding into actual practice. The key to this overdue reassessment is redefining the meaning of "crime" because when no victim exists, as is true in so many substance abuse cases, for example, that's a pretty solid clue that no criminal offense was committed. Making the penal system our automatic response to drug addiction and mental illness is an outmoded course of action that so far continues to prevail over reason. Additionally, we need to find and act upon buried injustices—the legions of wrongly confined prisoners like Anthony Fletcher in Pennsylvania, Atiba Parker in Mississippi, and former Alabama deputy sheriff Wilmer Breckenride, who's locked up somewhere in the federal system.

Good, well-intentioned people work in the criminal justice system, but they're repeatedly undermined by the sloppy, malevolent practices of their colleagues. As a consequence, our bloated penal structure probably holds two or three times the number of prisoners it should. A model for remedial action can be found in the Truth and Reconciliation Commission that investigated human rights violations after South Africa abolished apartheid. That's how tragic and askew our situation has become.

And although the U.S. Supreme Court protects outlaw prosecutors from civil suits, it hasn't made them immune from criminal prosecution when they hide or manufacture evidence, conspiring to convict defendants who are clearly innocent. Yet in case after case their fellow prosecutors have looked the other way and filed no charges despite strong clues of criminality by authorities. (See, for example, the John Thompson case in chapter 8.)

A free country should protect its prisoners from inhumane treatment, but as I write this, convicts in Texas still auction off convict-victims to convict-rapists while authorities look the other way. Our knowledge of right and wrong seems to have little or no effect on such facts on the ground, where broad sections of our penal system are out of control. Finally the profit motive must be removed from the criminal justice equation. We have to stop locking up more people and extending sentences in order to satisfy the financial cravings of California prison guards or Gulag corporations such as Corrections Corporation of America. Justice Kennedy accurately defined that kind of revenue-based policy as "sick"—sick justice.

Tolstoy speculated that if nothing else worked, perhaps the czarist government should continue to pay prison profiteers in exchange for their stepping aside to allow reforms. Our republic, based on the inalienable principle of liberty and justice for all, surely has the courage and know-how to find better answers and achieve a better result.

NOTES

1. THE MOSTLY INVISIBLE CATASTROPHE

1. All quotations by Brenda Valencia are from the author's several interviews with her during August and September 2011.
2. David B. Kopel, *Prison Blues: How America's Foolish Sentencing Policies Endanger Public Safety*, Cato Policy Analysis No. 20 (Washington, DC: Cato Institute, May 17, 1994).
3. Human Rights Watch (http://www.hrw.org/sites/default/files/reports/usprisons0112webwcover_0.pdf), the Sentencing Project, and the U.S. Justice Department (http://bjs.gov/index.cfm?ty=tp&tid=11) websites all concur on the number of U.S. prisoners.
4. Lauren E. Glaze and Erika Parks, *Correctional Population in the United States, 2011* (Washington, DC: Bureau of Justice Statistics, November 2012).
5. Etienne Benson, "Rehabilitate or Punish?" *Psychiatric News*, October 20, 2006.
6. Carol J. Williams, "Justice Kennedy Laments the State of Prisons in California, U.S," *Los Angeles Times*, February 4, 2010.
7. Laura Sullivan, "Prison Economics Help Drive Ariz. Immigration Law," *Morning Edition*, NPR, October 28, 2010, http://www.npr.org/2010/10/28/130833741/prison-economics-help-drive-ariz-immigration-law.
8. "Inmate Count in U.S. Dwarfs Other Nations," *New York Times*, April 23, 2008.
9. Ibid.
10. Jack Leonard, "'Pizza Thief' Walks the Line," *Los Angeles Times*, February 10, 2010.
11. "Third Defendant Is Convicted In Dragging Death in Texas," *New York Times*, November 19, 1999.
12. Karl Menninger, *The Crime of Punishment* (New York: Viking Press, 1969).

13. *"The Nation's Toughest Drug Law: Evaluating the New York Experience,"* Final Report of the Joint Committee on New York Drug Law Evaluation, March 1978, https://www.ncjrs.gov/pdffiles1/Digitization/47795NCJRS.pdf.

14. Human Rights Watch, *Incarcerated America* (New York, April 2003); United States Crime Rates 1960–2009. Source: FBI, Uniform Crime Reports, http://www.disastercenter.com/crime/uscrime.htm

15. Written statement of Mary Price, Vice President and General Counsel Families Against Mandatory Minimum (FAMM), before the United States Sentencing Commission public hearing on proposed amendments 2011 regarding drugs, March 17, 2011, http://www.famm.org/Repository/Files/Written%20Statement%20of%20Mary%20Price%203-17-11%5B1%5D.pdf.

16. Paul Cassell, quoted in Erica Goode, "Life Sentence for Possession of Child Pornography Spurs Debate over Severity," *New York Times*, November 4, 2011.

17. "Cost of Locking up Americans Too High: Pew Study," Reuters, March 2, 2009.

18. Wendy Fry, "The Cost of Life In Prison," KPBS, January 20, 2010.

19. "Cost of Locking up Americans."

20. Ofra Bikel, "The Plea," *Frontline*, PBS, June 17, 2004; and Jason Cato, "Beating a Federal Rap Not Easy," *Tribune-Review*, July 31, 2006.

21. Innocence Project Website, http://www.innocenceproject.org/Content/Facts_on_PostConviction_DNA_Exonerations.php; and Jeffrey Rosen, "The Wrongful Conviction as Way of Life," *New York Times*, May 26, 2011.

22. "Jury Trial Rate at All-Time Low in Va.," *Richmond Times-Dispatch*, October 18, 2009.

23. Details of Haskell's story are from the author's interviews with him, November 20 and 21, 2010.

24. Eric Schlosser, "The Prison-Industrial Complex," *The Atlantic*, December 1998.

25. Author interview with Mike Tyson.

26. Sentencing Project, *Incarcerated Children and Their Parents: Trends, 1991–2007* (Washington, DC, February 2009).

2. FEAR, LOATHING, AND GUNS

1. The Pew Charitable Trusts, "One in 31 U.S. Adults are Behind Bars, on Parole or Probation," press release, March 2, 2003, http://www.pewtrusts.org/news_room_detail.aspx?id=49696.

2. Lauren E. Glaze, "Correctional Populations in the United States, 2009," *Bureau of Justice Statistics*, December 2010, http://bjs.gov/content/pub/pdf/cpus09.pdf.

3. Adam Liptak, "Justices, 5-4, Tell California to Cut Prisoner Population," *New York Times*, May 23, 2011.

4. Brevard's papers are in the Wilson Special Collections Library at the Chapel Hill campus of the University of North Carolina.

5. Casey Mullenaux, letter to the author, July 1, 2011.

6. Economic Mobility Project and Public Safety Performance Project, *Collateral Costs: Incarceration's Effect on Economic Mobility* (Washington, DC: Pew Charitable Trusts, 2010).

7. Alan Greenblatt, "How Much Can Potential Employers Ask About You?" NPR, May 22, 2012, http://www.npr.org/2012/05/21/153201730/how-much-can-potential-employers-ask-about-you.

8. The Pew Cheritable Trusts, "Collateral Costs: Incarceration's Effect on Economic Mobility," Washington, DC: The Pew Charitable Trusts, 2010, http://www.pewstates.org/uploadedFiles/PCS_Assets/2010/Collateral_Costs(1).pdf.

9. Persis S. Yu and Sharon M. Dietrich, *Broken Records: How Errors by Criminal Background Checking Companies Harm Workers and Businesses* (Boston: National Consumer Law Center, April 2012). Reported in several articles in 2010, including one in the *New York Times*.

10. Liliana Segura, "Michelle Alexander on California's 'Cruel and Unusual' Prisons," *The Nation*, May 26, 2011.

11. Neal Griffin, conversations and e-mail exchanges with the author from November 2011 through February 2012.

12. Casey Mullenaux, interview by the author, December 13, 2012.

13. Interview, December 14, 2012.

14. Justice Policy Institute, "FBI: Crime Fell in 2010," fact sheet, May 2011.

15. Mark Kleiman, quoted in Mandalit Del Barco, "L.A.'s Homicide Rate Lowest in Four Decades," *Morning Edition*, NPR, January 6, 2011, http://www.npr.org/2011/01/06/132677265/las-homicide-rate-lowest-in-four-decades.

16. Ibid.

17. Jessica Wolpaw Reyes, "Lead Exposure and Behavior: Effects on Antisocial and Risky Behavior among Children and Adolescents," Draft Feb. 2012, http://www3.amherst.edu/~jwreyes/papers/LeadBehavior.pdf.

18. See Robert Perkinson, *Texas Tough: The Rise of America's Prison Empire* (New York: Metropolitan Books, 2010).

19. Kent Scheidegger and Michael Rushford, "The Social Benefits of Confining Habitual Criminals," *Stanford Law and Policy Review* 11 (Winter 1999): 59.

20. See Bert Useem and Anne Morrison Piehl, *Prison State: The Challenge of Mass Incarceration* (Cambridge: Cambridge University Press, 2008); and John Donohue, "Assessing the Relative Benefits of Incarceration: The Overall Change over the Previous Decades and the Benefits on the Margin," *Selected Works of Jon Donohue*, 2009, http://works.bepress.com/john_donohue/65/.

21. Adam Liptak, "U.S. Prison Population Dwarfs that of Other Nations, *New York Times*, April 23, 2008. Michael Tonry, professor at the University of Minnesota Law School, has authored many books on criminal justice, including *Punishing Race: A Continuing American Dilemma* (New York: Oxford University Press, 2011).

22. Adam Liptak, "Inmate Count in U.S. Dwarfs Other Nations'," *New York Times*, April 23, 2008.

23. Glenn Reynolds, "A Rifle in Every Pot," *New York Times*, January 16, 2007.

24. Mayors Against Illegal Guns, "Tiahrt Amendment Facts," *Protectpolice.org*, 2009, http://protectpolice.org/facts.

25. See Mayors Against Illegal Guns, "Statement by Mayors against Illegal Guns Co-Chairs on Obama Administration's Reform of the Tiahrt Amendments," May 7, 2009, http://www.mayorsagainstillegalguns.org/html/media-center/pr003-09.shtml.

3. INFORMANTS

1. The author interviewed Fletcher many times by mail and telephone and read hundreds of pages of documents from his original trial and subsequent appeals. See also the Free Anthony Fletcher website, http://freeanthonyfletcher.com/index.html.

2. Ken Armstrong and Steve Mills, "Ryan: 'Until I Can Be Sure,'" *Chicago Tribune*, February 1, 2000.

3. Tina Rosenberg, "The Deadliest D.A.," *New York Times*, July 16, 1995.

4. Lindsey Devers, *Plea and Charge Bargaining: Research Summary* (Washington, DC: Bureau of Justice Assistance, January 24, 2011), https://www.bja.gov/Publications/PleaBargainingResearchSummary.pdf.

5. "Declaration of Hydow Park, M.D. in the Court of Common Pleas of Philadelphia County, Pennsylvania," Nos. 6001, 6003, and 6004, June 7, 2001, http://freeanthonyfletcher.com/drpark.html.

6. Rothmiller was coauthor of my first book, *L.A. Secret Police: Inside the LAPD Elite Spy Network* (New York: Pocket Books, 1992).

7. Ibid.

8. Barbara Dougan, quoted in "Rough Justice in America: Too Many Laws, Too Many Prisoners," *Economist*, January 22, 2010.

9. The facts of Ealy's case are extensively documented in a FAMM document that can be found at http://www.famm.org/Repository/Files/FG fall09FINAL.pdf

10. Jack Dolan, "Judge Overturns Murder Conviction in 1994 Slaying," *Los Angeles Times*, October 1, 2011. Also see Beth Schwartzapfel, "No Country for Innocent Men," *Mother Jones*, January–February 2012, http://www.motherjones.com/politics/2011/12/tim-cole-rick-perry.

11. Innocence Project, "Informants," *Understand the Causes*, accessed February 15, 2012, http://www.innocenceproject.org/understand/Snitches -Informants.php. Also see Raymond Bonner, "When Innocence Isn't Enough," *New York Times*, March 2, 2012.

12. Covered in scores of articles in the *Boston Herald*, the *New York Times*, and, after Bulger was captured, the *Los Angeles Times*. Also see Robert Fitzpatrick, *Betrayal: Whitey Bulger and the FBI Agent Who Fought to Bring Him Down*, with Jon Land (New York: Forge Books, 2012).

4. THE WAR ON DRUGS (AND REASON)

1. All quotations in this chapter by Ms. Reavey are from the author's interviews with her.

2. The author attended federal hearings for James Allen and interviewed him on multiple occasions over a period of many years, beginning in 1998. We remain friends.

3. The repeated practice of snaring and punishing small fry, not kingpins, is documented in Global Commission on Drug Policy, *War on Drugs: Report of the Global Commission on Drug Policy* (Rio de Janeiro, June 2011), http://www.globalcommissionondrugs.org/wp-content/themes/gcdp_v1/pdf/Global_Commission_Report_English.pdf; and Jacob G. Hornberger, "Drug War Sentencing Injustice," *Hornberger's Blog*, May 31, 2012, http://fff.org/2012/05/31/28468/.

4. Valencia interview, August and September 2011.

5. Global Commission on Drug Policy, *War on Drugs*.

6. "'Global War on Drugs Has Failed,' Key Panel Says," NBC News, June 2, 2011, http://www.nbcnews.com/id/43248071/ns/us_news-crime_and _courts/#.UUjN8BeG2So.

7. Jimmy Carter, "Call Off the Global Drug War," *New York Times*, June 16, 2011.

8. Ginnie Graham, "Mom of 4 Reflects on First Year in Prison for $31 Pot Sale," *Tulsa World*, December 26, 2011.

9. Cary Aspinwall, "Patricia Spottedcrow Paroled Early in 12-year Sentence for $31 Bag of Marijuana," *Tulsa World*, November 30, 2012.

10. FAMM, "Michelle Collette," *Faces of FAMM: Success Stories*, accessed February 24, 2011, http://www.famm.org/facesoffamm/Success Stories/MichelleCollette.aspx.

11. Carter, "Call Off the Global Drug War."

12. *Breaking the Taboo*, produced by Sam Branson (London: Sundog Pictures/Spray Filmes, 2011).

13. Inimai Chettiar, "Just What Is So Wrong with the War on Drugs?" *Blog of Rights*, June 14, 2011, http://www.aclu.org/blog/criminal-law-reform/just-what-so-wrong-war-drugs.

14. Nathan Miller, telephone conversations and e-mail exchanges with the author during September 2011.

15. Keith Richards, *Life*, with James Fox (New York: Little, Brown, 2010).

16. See Ian Carr, *Miles Davis: The Definitive Biography* (Boston: De Capo Press, 2006).

17. See Steven J. Lee, *Overcoming Crystal Meth Addiction: An Essential Guide to Getting Clean* (Boston: De Capo Press, 2006); and Sterling Brasswell, *American Meth: A History of the Methamphetamine Epidemic in America* (Bloomington: iUniverse, 2006).

18. Jack Cole, "The War on Drugs," Law Enforcement Against Prohibition (LEAP), April 6, 2011, http://www.leap.cc/the-war-on-drugs/.

19. Jonathan P. Caulkins, Susan S. Everingham, James Chiesa, and Shawn Bushway, *The Benefits and Costs of Drug Use Prevention: Clarifying a Cloudy Issue* (Santa Monica, CA: RAND, 1999).

20. See Norm Stamper, *Breaking Rank: A Top Cop's Exposé of the Dark Side of American Policing* (New York: Nation Books, 2005).

21. LEAP, "On 40th Anniversary of 'War on Drugs,' Cops Release Report Showing Its Failure," news release, June 14, 2011, http://www.leap.cc/40years/.

22. Ryan Grim, "Watch: DOJ Official Blows Cover off Patriot Act," *Huffington Post*, November 23, 2009, http://www.huffingtonpost.com/2009/09/23/watch-doj-official-blows_n_296209.html.

23. *Reauthorizing the USA Patriot Act: Ensuring Liberty: Hearing Before the Subcommittee on Administrative Oversight and the Courts of the Committee on the Judiciary, U.S. Senate*, 111th Cong. (2009) (statement of Russell D. Feingold, U.S. Senator from Wisconsin), http://www.gpo.gov/fdsys/pkg/CHRG-111shrg55610/html/CHRG-111shrg55610.htm.

24. David Nutt, *Estimating Drug Harms: A Risky Business?* (London: Centre for Crime and Justice Studies, October 2009), http://www.crime andjustice.org.uk/estimatingdrugharms.html.
25. Ruxandra Guidi, "Hiring Boom Connected to Rise in Corruption at Border Agency," KPBS, July 14, 2011.
26. An excellent firsthand account of evidence planting is Justin Hopson, *Breaking the Blue Wall: One Man's War against Police Corruption* (Bloomington, IN: Westbow Press, 2011).
27. Shalia Dewan and Brenda Goodman, "Prosecutors Say Corruption in Atlanta Police Dept. Is Widespread," *New York Times*, April 27, 2007.
28. Ibid.
29. Jim Dwyer, "Those Drugs? They Came From the Police," *New York Times*, October 13, 2011.
30. Ibid.
31. Omer Gillham, "Inmate Asks for Review of Life Sentence," *Tulsa World*, October 31, 2010.
32. Kim Brown, "Recently Released Prisoner Gets New Look, Outlook on Life," *Tulsa World*, September 27, 2011.
33. Gillham, "Inmate Asks for Review of Life Sentence."
34. Ibid.
35. Singh's story is retold based on letters from and telephone conversations with Singh; his wife, Linda Singh; and convicts incarcerated with him throughout 2011 and ending in early 2012.
36. Ayala's story is based on letters from and telephone conversations with Ayala and convicts incarcerated with him, but most of the material is from a letter he wrote to me dated August 3, 2011.
37. ACLU–New Mexico, "ACLU Sues Border Patrol for Retaliating against Agent for Political Beliefs," news release, January 20, 2011, http://www.aclu-nm.org/tag/free-speech/page/2/. Also see Jordan Smith, "The War on Talking about the Drug War," *Austin Chronicle*, February 4, 2011.
38. ACLU–New Mexico, "ACLU Sues Border Patrol."
39. Ibid.
40. Lucia Graves, "Border Patrol Agent Fired for Views on Drug Legalization Files Lawsuit," *Huffington Post*, May 25, 2011, http://www .huffingtonpost.com/2011/01/26/border-patrol-fired-drug-legalization _n_813999.html.
41. Patricia Allard, "Life Sentences: Denying Welfare Benefits to Women Convicted Of Drug Offenses," The Sentencing Project, February 2002, http://www.sentencingproject.org/doc/publications/women_life sentences.pdf.

42. Rutgers University is one of many schools of higher learning that quotes the statute as it explains student aid to prospective students. See Rutgers Office of Financial Aid, "Loss of Student Eligibility for Federal Aid Due to Drug Conviction," accessed May 15, 2011, http://studentaid.rutgers.edu/drug.aspxhttp://studentaid.rutgers.edu/drug.aspx.

43. See Craig Reinarman and Harry G. Levine, eds., *Crack in America: Demon Drugs and Social Justice* (Berkeley: University of California Press, 1997).

44. Gary Fields, "New Terms in Crack Debate," *Wall Street Journal*, June 2, 2011, http://online.wsj.com/article/SB10001424052702303745304576359151139005180.html.

45. See ibid. for a good summation of these responses.

46. Richard A. Serrano, David G. Savage, and Carol J. Williams, "Early Release Proposed for Crack Cocaine Offenders," *Los Angeles Times*, June 1, 2001.

47. FAMM, "DeJarion Echols," *Faces of FAMM: Federal Profiles*, accessed December 24, 2001, http://www.famm.org/facesofFAMM/FederalProfiles/DeJarionEchols.aspx.

48. Ibid.

49. Stephannie Behrens, "How Many People Are Incarcerated for Drug Related Offenses?" *Open Salon*, May 17, 2010, http://open.salon.com/blog/stephannie/2010/05/16/how_many_people_are_incarcerated_for_drug_related_offenses.

50. Wilson's case has been reported extensively by a long list of news media outlets, particularly the *Times of Trenton*, which refuses to let it die.

51. "18 Legal Medical Marijuana States and DC: Laws, Fees, and Possession Limits," *ProCon.org*, February 22, 2013, http://medicalmarijuana.procon.org/view.resource.php?resourceID=000881.

52. All quotations by Ms. Shein are from interviews with the author during November and December 2011.

5. THE DEATH OF RACHEL HOFFMAN

1. Attorney Nathan Miller, a friend of the Hoffman family, alerted me to Rachel Hoffman's case before it was well-known, and he knew many details. Eventually, it received coverage in a variety of news media. For a detailed look at the case, see Sarah Stillman, "The Throwaways," *New Yorker*, September 3, 2012.

2. John Frank, "Man Found Guilty in Rachel Hoffman's Murder," *Tampa Bay Times*, December 17, 2009, http://www.tampabay.com/

news/courts/criminal/man-found-guilty-in-rachel-hoffmans-murder/ 1059484.

3. John Poltilove, "Rachel's Law on Confidential Informants Takes Effect Wednesday," *Tampa Tribune*, June 30, 2009.

4. In 2012 Tallahassee commissioners approved a $2.6 million settlement with Rachel's parents for her wrongful death. "Tallahassee Settles Rachel Hoffman Death Suit for $2.6 Million," *Orlando Post*, January 7, 2012.

6. THREE STRIKES AND YOU'RE OUT

1. Jack Leonard, "L.A. Judge Begins Reducing Sentences of Three-Strikes Inmates," *Los Angeles Times*, February 11, 2013.

2. Ibid.

3. Many articles on Gregory Taylor can be found in the *Los Angeles Times*, and his case is thoroughly explored in Joe Domanick, *Cruel Justice: Three Strikes and the Politics of Crime in America's Golden State* (Berkeley: University of California Press, 2005).

4. Victoria Kim, "Three-Ttrikes Inmate Welcomes His Freedom," *Los Angeles Times*, August 20, 2010.

5. Ibid.

6. Bruce Golding, "NY 3-Time Loser Law Upheld by Fed Court," *New York Post*, October 19, 2010.

7. "Editorial: Time to Reform State's 'Three Strikes' Law," *Seattle Times*, January 23, 2013. An excellent history of the origins and development of three-strikes legislation can be found in Domanick, *Cruel Justice*.

8. Bureau of Justice Statistics, "Profile of Nonviolent Offenders Exiting State Prisons," fact sheet, October 2004.

9. Interviews with experienced criminal court attorney Kevin Donahue of Torrance, California, were vitally important to my understanding of the twists and turns of the state's three-strikes law.

10. Chris Martinez's story is based on multiple conversations and letter exchanges between him and the author over fifteen years, beginning in 1998.

11. Greg Krikorian, "Three-Strikes Law Has Little Effect, Study Says," *Los Angeles Times*, March 5, 2004.

12. Domanick, *Cruel Justice*.

13. Michael Greenbergerg, "Introduction: Our Collective Responsibility for 'Unjust' Laws," *Human Rights Magazine*, American Bar Association 31, No. 1 (Winter 2004).

14. Domanick, *Cruel Justice*.

15. Ibid.

16. FAMM, "James Belt," *Faces of FAMM: State Profiles*, accessed March 18, 2013, http://www.famm.org/profilesofinjustice/StateProfiles/James Belt.aspx.

7. DIVINE RIGHT PROSECUTORS

1. The information was on the official website, http://www.da-tulareco .org/, prior to Philip Cline's resignation.

2. Mark Curriden, "Harmless Error? New Study Claims Prosecutorial Misconduct Is Rampant in California," *ABA Journal*, December 1, 2010; and "Study: Prosecutorial Misconduct Ignored," *North County Gazette*, October 5, 2010.

3. Innocence Project, "Report: Prosecutorial Misconduct Often Unpunished in California," *Innocence Blog*, October 5, 2010, http://www .innocenceproject.org/Content/Report_Prosecutorial_Misconduct _Often_Unpunished_in_California.php.

4. Innocence Project, "Government Misconduct," *Understand the Causes*, accessed March 18, 2013, http://www.innocenceproject.org/understand/ Government-Misconduct.php.

5. Brady v. Maryland, 373 U.S. 83 (1963), U.S. Supreme Court Center, *Justia.com*, http://supreme.justia.com/cases/federal/us/373/83/case.html.

6. Ibid.

7. See Ronald F. Wright, "How Prosecutor Elections Fail Us," *Ohio State Journal of Criminal Law* 6 (2009): 581–610.

8. All quotations from Kevin Donahue are from the author's interviews with him. This particular conversation was in April 2011.

9. This phone interview with the author took place in March 2011.

10. August 3, 2011, letter from Ayala to author. Public defenders and private court-appointed attorneys do tend to be overwhelmed, but I've personally seen instances of their doing fine work anyway.

11. Miller interviews and e-mail correspondence.

12. Rosalind Alexis Sargent, "The Federal Sentencing Guidelines: An Infectious Antidote," *Court Review*, Winter 2003, 24–34.

13. Ibid.

14. Jed Stone and Nina Morrison were quoted in Andrew Martin, "The Prosecution's Case against DNA," *New York Times*, November 25, 2011.

8. THE INNOCENT AND THE DEAD

1. Unless otherwise cited, the details of Tim Cole's story and related quotations are from Schwartzapfel, "No Country for Innocent Men." See

also Innocence Project, "Timothy Cole," *Know the Cases*, http://www
.innocenceproject.org/Content/Timothy_Cole.php; and Wade Goodwyn, "Judge Posthumously Clears Man Convicted of Rape," NPR,
February 7, 2009, http://www.npr.org/templates/story/story.php?story
Id=100383293.

2. Jonah Goldberg, "The Tyranny of Clichés," *National Review*, July 10,
2002.

3. Alexander Volokh, "Guilty Men," *University of Pennsylvania Law Review*, 1997.

4. Goldberg, "Tyranny of Clichés."

5. Adam Liptak, "Study Suspects Thousands of False Convictions," *New
York Times*, April 19, 2004.

6. Ibid.

7. "N.Y.C. DA Vance Announces Conviction Integrity Program," *Bloomberg News*, March 4, 2010.

8. Liptak, "Study Suspects Thousands of False Convictions."

9. Ibid.

10. Brandon Garrett, quoted in Beth Schwartzapfel and Hannah Levintova,
"How Many Innocent People Are in Prison?" *Mother Jones*, December
12, 2011.

11. Ibid.

12. Nicholas Confessore, "After 21 Years, DNA Testing Sets Man Free in
Rape Case," *New York Times*, November 7, 2006; and Innocence Project, "Scott Fappiano," *Know the Cases*, http://www.innocenceproject
.org/Content/Scott_Fappiano.php.

13. Jack Leonard, "Murder Conviction Voided after 20 Years," *Los Angeles Times*, March 16, 2011.

14. Liptak, "Study Suspects Thousands of False Convictions."

15. Arlette Saenz, "Death Penalty: Applause for Rick Perry's 'Ultimate
Justice' at Republican Debate," ABC News, September 8, 2011.

16. John Rudolf, "Humberto Leal Garcia Executed in Texas after Obama
Administration Argued for Stay," *Huffington Post*, December 1, 2011,
http://www.huffingtonpost.com/2011/07/07/humberto-leal-garcia
-executed_n_892762.html.

17. David Grann, "Trial by Fire: Did Texas Execute an Innocent Man?"
New Yorker, September 7, 2009.

18. Ibid.

19. Ed Lavandera, "DNA Cleared Them, but They'll Never Feel Free,"
CNN, May 19, 2008, http://articles.cnn.com/2008-05-19/justice/dna
.cleared_1_dna-evidence-innocence-project-jeff-blackburn; and Innocence Project, "Wiley Fountain," *Know the Cases*, http://www.innocence
project.org/Content/Wiley_Fountain.php.

20. Innocence Project, "Wiley Fountain."
21. Lavandera, "DNA Cleared Them."
22. Ibid.
23. Ibid.
24. "Georgia Executes Troy Davis after His Last Pleas Fail," NBC News, September 22, 2011, http://www.nbcnews.com/id/44592285/ns/us _news-crime_and_courts/.
25. "Troy Davis Executed; Supporters Cry Injustice," *USA Today*, September 22, 2011.
26. Unless otherwise cited, details of the Bozella case are from Peter Applebome, "Exonerated of Murder, a Boxer Makes a Debut at 52," *New York Times*, October 10, 2011.
27. "Dewey Bozella," BoxRec, http://boxrec.com/list_bouts.php?human _id=583595&cat=boxer.
28. Kevin Drum, "The Right Not to Be Framed," *Mother Jones*, November 4, 2009.
29. Ibid.
30. David G. Savage, "Supreme Court Shields Prosecutors in Wrongful Convictions," *Los Angeles Times*, April 3, 2011.
31. Claire Suddath, "When Is It Legal to Frame a Man for Murder?" *Time*, November 5, 2009.
32. David G. Savage, "Supreme Court Rejects Damages for Innocent Man Who Spent 14 Years on Death Row," *Los Angeles Times*, March 30, 2011.
33. John Thompson, "The Prosecution Rests, but I Can't," *New York Times*, April 9, 2011.
34. Ibid.
35. Ibid.
36. Ibid.
37. Savage, "Supreme Court Rejects Damages for Innocent Man."
38. Thompson, "Prosecution Rests."
39. Ibid.
40. Jack Leonard, "Supreme Court Takes Dim View of Suing Prosecutors," *Los Angeles Times*, January 9, 2011.
41. David G. Savage, "U.S. Supreme Court Says District Attorneys Are Immune from Wrongful-Conviction Suits," *Los Angeles Times*, January 27, 2011.
42. Leonard, "Supreme Court Takes Dim View of Suing Prosecutors."
43. Gerald Burge v. State of Louisiana, No. 10-C-2229, Supreme Court of Louisiana (2011); Innocence Project New Orleans, "Gerald Burge," 2011, http://www.ip-no.org/exonoree-profile/gerald-burge.

44. Miller interview.
45. Innocence Project, "Juan Rivera," *Know the Cases*, http://www .innocenceproject.org/Content/Juan_Rivera.php; and Martin, "Prosecution's Case against DNA."
46. Martin, "Prosecution's Case against DNA."
47. Lisa Black, "Under Fire, Lake County Prosecutor Retiring," *Chicago Tribune*, December 8, 2011.
48. Martin, "Prosecution's Case against DNA."
49. Ibid.
50. Ibid.
51. Dan Hinkel, "Suspect in Zion Killings Denied Change of Venue in Federal Murder Trial," *Chicago Tribune*, September 24, 2012.
52. Martin, "Prosecution's Case against DNA."
53. Campbell Robertson, "Deal Frees West Memphis Three in Arkansas," *New York Times*, August 19, 2011. A particularly thorough treatment of this compelling case is Mara Leveritt, *Devil's Knot: The True Story of the West Memphis Three* (New York: Atria Books, 2003).
54. *Paradise Lost*, directed by Joe Berlinger and Bruce Sinofsky, was released by HBO in 1996.
55. The study is Richard A. Leo and Steven A. Drizin, "The Problem of False Confessions in the Post DNA World," *North Carolina Law Review* 82 (2004): 891–1007. See also Liptak, "Study Suspects Thousands of False Convictions."
56. Liptak, "Study Suspects Thousands of False Convictions."

9. WALKING THE "TOUGHEST BEAT" IN GUCCIS

1. Margaret Carlson and Charles Keating, "Interview with Charles Keating Money Talks," *Time*, April 9, 1990.
2. Prerna Anand, "Winners and Losers: Corrections and Higher Education in California," *California Common Sense*, September 5, 2012; Aaron Sankin, "California Spending More on Prisons than Colleges, Report Says," *Huffington Post*, September 6, 2012, http://www.huffingtonpost .com/2012/09/06/california-prisons-colleges_n_1863101.html.
3. Mark Martin and Pamela J. Podger, "Prison Guards' Clout Difficult to Challenge," *San Francisco Chronicle*, February 2, 2004.
4. Allysia Finley, "California Prison Academy: Better than a Harvard Degree," *Wall Street Journal*, April 30, 2011.
5. Ibid.
6. Jenifer Warren, "Gov. Names Interim Prison System Chief," *Los Angeles Times*, February 27, 2006.

7. Joe Mathews, "How Prospects for Prop. 66 Fell So Far, So Fast," *Los Angeles Times*, November 7, 2004.

8. Arianna Huffington, "The Battle over CA Prop 5: Special Interests Overwhelming the Public Interest," *Huffington Post*, October 30, 2008, http://www.huffingtonpost.com/arianna-huffington/the-battle-over -ca-prop-5_b_139474.html.

9. Steve Lopez, "Video by Prison Guards Union Links Campaign Donations to New Contract," *Los Angeles Times*, May 22, 2011.

10. Finley, "California Prison Academy."

11. Ibid.; Jack Dolan, "New Contract for California Prison Guards Lifts Cap on Saved Vacation," *Los Angeles Times*, April 19, 2011.

12. Laura Sullivan, "San Quentin's Gym Becomes One Massive Cell," *All Things Considered*, NPR, July 7, 2008.

13. Marisa Lagos, "Cuts in Programs to Help Inmates Questioned," *San Francisco Chronicle*, February 16, 2010.

14. Don Thompson, "US Supreme Court to Consider California Prison Overcrowding," *Huffington Post*, November 29, 2010.

15. David G. Savage and Patrick McGreevy, "U.S. Supreme Court Orders Massive Inmate Release to Relieve California's Crowded Prisons," *Los Angeles Times*, May 24, 2011.

16. Ibid.

17. Ibid.

18. Ibid.

19. Don Thompson, "California Inmate Release: Schwarzenegger Prison Reform Policies Were Mixed," *Huffington Post*, May 24, 2011, http:// www.huffingtonpost.com/2011/05/24/california-inmate-release_n _866189.html.

20. Ibid.

21. Lois Davis, "California's Prisoner Shuffle," *Los Angeles Times*, August 19, 2011.

22. Ibid.

23. Associated Press, "Calif. Expands New Parole Program Based on Hawaii Model," *Star Advertiser*, September 18, 2011.

24. Ibid.

25. Davis, "California's Prisoner Shuffle."

26. James Sterngold, "Illiteracy Reinforces Prisoners' Captivity," *San Francisco Chronicle*, December 27, 2006.

27. Ibid.

28. "From Cellblocks to Classrooms: Reforming Inmate Education To Improve Public Safety," Legislative Analysts Office, February 2008.

29. Lagos, "Cuts in Programs to Help Inmates Questioned."

30. Jack Dolan and Carol J. Williams, "No Easy Fix for California's Prison Crisis," *Los Angeles Times*, May 25, 2011.

31. David G. Savage and Patrick McGreevy, "U.S. Supreme Court Orders Massive Inmate Release to Relieve California's Crowded Prisons," *Los Angeles Times*, May 24, 2011.

32. Dolan and Williams, "No Easy Fix for California's Prison Crisis."

33. "12 Million Verdict Hits Calif. Prison Guards Union," *Ventura County Star*, October 23, 2010.

34. Dan Strumpf, "With Fewer to Lock Up, Prisons Shut Doors," *Wall Street Journal*, February 10, 2013.

10. MONGO AND SQUEAKY

1. See GEO Group home page, http://www.geogroup.com, accessed June 2012.

2. "The Stanford Prison Experiment: A Simulation Study of the Psychology of Imprisonment Conducted at Stanford University," August 20, 1971, http://www.prisonexp.org.

3. Natalie Martinez, "Chicago to Have Most Expensive Parking Meters in North America," NBC Chicago, December 27, 2012, http://www.nbcchicago.com/traffic/transit/chicago-parking-meters-2013-rates-184874621.html.

4. Federal Contractor Misconduct Database, Project on Governmental Oversight, http://www.contractormisconduct.org/index.cfm/1,73,223,html?criteria=Geo+wackenhut&submit=search; Deborah Dupre, "Wachenhut/ GEO Private Prison Abuse Spotlight," *Examiner.com*, January 10, 2012, http://www.examiner.com/article/wackenhut-geo-private-prison-abuse-spotlight.

11. PRISON PRIVATEERS AND JAILING FOR CASH

1. Alan Greenspan, *The Age of Turbulence: Adventures in a New World* (New York: Penguin, 2008).

2. See Frances Fox Piven, *Who's Afraid of Frances Fox Piven? The Essential Writings of the Professor Glenn Beck Loves to Hate* (New York: New Press, 2011).

3. Patrick Russell, interview with the author, October 6, 2011.

4. More than half of the many people I've spoken to who've taken collect calls from inmates via Global Tel Link, including lawyers,

complained of technical problems or prices. I've also experienced problems myself.

5. "Corrections Corporation of America (CXW)," *Yahoo! Finance*, http://finance.yahoo.com/q?s=cxw&ql=1.

6. Corrections Corporation of America, "About CCA," 2008, http://www.cca.com/about/.

7. Andy Obermueller, "Strapped States Are Bullish for Private Prisons," *Forbes*, March 18, 2010.

8. Ibid.

9. Chris Kirkham, "Private Prison Corporation Offers Cash in Exchange for State Prisons," *Huffington Post*, February 14, 2012, http://www.huffingtonpost.com/2012/02/14/private-prisons-buying-state-prisons_n_1272143.html.

10. Office of Governor Frank Keating, "Governor Declares Prison Emergency," news release, undated, http://www.ok.gov/osfdocs/nr6-13a.html.

11. Tom Lindley, "Oklahoma Lawmakers Seek to Strike Budget Balance for Prisons," *Oklahoma Watch*, December 9, 2010.

12. Tom Lindley, "Packed Oklahoma Prisons, Rising Costs," *Oklahoma Watch*, December 4, 2010.

13. See ALEC's own detailed website, http://www.alec.org.

14. See ibid.; and ALEC Exposed home page, http://www.alecexposed.org/wiki/ALEC_Exposed.

15. "A Plan to Reduce Prison overcrowding and Violent Crime'Conditional Post-Conviction Release Bond Act,'" undated ALEC report, http://www.americanbailcoalition.com/documents/ALEC_State_Factor_Prison_Overcrowding.pdf.

16. Steve Yoder, "The Prisoner's Dilemma," *American Prospect*, March 14, 2011.

17. "A Plan to Reduce Prison Overcrowding."

18. Kirkham, "Private Prison Corporation Offers Cash."

19. James Austin and Garry Coventry, *Emerging Issues on Private Prisons* (Washington, DC: U.S. Justice Department, February 2001).

20. Ibid.

21. K. C. Carceral, *Prison, Inc.: A Convict Exposes Life Inside a Private Prison*, ed. Thomas J. Bernard (New York: New York University Press, 2005) cites Bernard's study.

22. Kirkham, "Private Prison Corporation Offers Cash."

23. American Civil Liberties Union, *Banking on Bondage: Private Prisons and Mass Incarceration* (New York, November 2011), www.aclu.org/files/assets/bankingonbondage_20111102.pdf.

24. Mark Niquette, "Ohio Selling Its Lake Erie Prison to CCA, Hiring Company to Run Two Others," *Bloomberg News*, September 1, 2011.

25. William Bales et al., *Recidivism: An Analysis of Public and Private State Prison Releases in Florida* (Tallahassee: Florida State University, Florida Department of Corrections, Correctional Privatization Commission, December 2003).

26. 2008 study cited in Private Corrections Institute Inc., "Quick Facts about Prison Privatization," fact sheet, 2009, http://www.privateci.org/private_pics/Private%20prison%20fact%20sheet%202009.pdf.

27. Paul Wright et al., "Deconstructing Gus: A Former CCA Prisoner Takes On, and Takes Down, CCA's Top Lawyer," *Prison Legal News*, March 2009.

28. Richard P. Seiter, *Private Corrections: A Review of the Issues* (Nashville, TN: Corrections Corporation of America, March 2008), http://www.cca.com/static/assets/Private_Corr_Review_of_Issues.pdf.

29. Richard A. Oppel Jr., "Private Prison Prisons Found to Offer Little in Savings," *New York Times*, March 18, 2011; and Davis Shapiro, "For-Profit Prisons: A Barrier to Serious Criminal Justice Reform," CNBC, October 12, 2011, http://www.cnbc.com/id/44874053/ForProfit_Prisons_A_Barrier_to_Serious_Criminal_Justice_Reform.

30. Oppel, "Private Prison Prisons Found to Offer Little in Savings."

31. Russ Van Vleet and Steve Owen, quoted in Oppel, "Private Prison Prisons Found to Offer Little in Savings."

32. Leonard C. Gilroy et al., *Public-Private Partnerships for Corrections in California: Bridging the Gap between Crisis and Reform* (Los Angeles: Reason Foundation, April 2010), http://reason.org/news/show/private-prisons-california-budget.

33. Miller interviews.

34. U.S. Department of Justice Federal Prison System FY 2012 Performance Budget, http://www.justice.gov/jmd/2012justification/pdf/fy12-bop-se-justification.pdf.

12. CAPTIVE EMPLOYEES

1. Elaine Woo, "Sofia Cosma Dies at 96; Concert Pianist and Prison Camp Survivor," *Los Angeles Times*, February 22, 2011.

2. Center for Interdisciplinary Studies in Philosophy, Interpretation, and Culture, "Resisting the Prison Industrial Complex," State University of New York–Binghamton, http://cpic.binghamton.edu/resisting.html.

3. Unicor, "Call Centers," http://www.unicor.gov/services/contact_help desk/.

4. Caroline Winter, "What Do Prisoners Make for Victoria's Secret?" *Mother Jones*, July–August 2008.
5. For a comprehensive history of post–Civil War convict labor, see Douglas A. Blackmon, *Slavery by Another Name: The Re-Enslavement of Black Americans from the Civil War to World War II* (New York: Anchor Books, 2008). Also see David M. Oshinsky, *Worse than Slavery: Parchman Farm and the Ordeal of Jim Crow Justice* (New York: Free Press, 1996).
6. Details of the Tabert tragedy are from Roy J. Harris Jr., *Pulitzer's Gold: Behind the Prize for Public Service Journalism* (Columbia: University of Missouri Press, 2010).
7. Gordon Lafer, "Captive Labor," *American Prospect*, December 19, 2001, http://prospect.org/article/captive-labor.
8. Robbie Brown and Kim Severson, "Enlisting Prison Labor to Close Budget Gaps," *New York Times*, February 24, 2011.
9. Vicky Pelaez, *The Prison Industry in the United States: Big Business or a New Form of Slavery?* (Montreal: Centre for Research on Globalization, March 2008), http://www.globalresearch.ca/the-prison-industry-in-the-united-states-big-business-or-a-new-form-of-slavery/8289.
10. Ibid.

13. DEPORTING FOR CASH

1. Suevon Lee, "By the Numbers: The U.S.'s Growing For-Profit Detention Industry," *ProPublica*, June 20, 2012.
2. Ted Robbins, "In the Rush to Deport, Expelling U.S. Citizens," *All Things Considered*, NPR, October 24, 2011, http://www.npr.org/2011/10/24/141500145/in-the-rush-to-deport-expelling-u-s-citizens.
3. Ibid.
4. Julia Preston, "Immigration Crackdown Also Snares Americans," *New York Times*, December 13, 2011.
5. Sullivan, "Prison Economics Help Drive Ariz. Immigration Law."
6. Ibid.
7. Renee Feltz, "5 Things You Need to Know about Arizona's Immigration Law," PBS, July 29, 2010, http://www.pbs.org/wnet/need-to-know/five-things/arizonas-immigration-law/2531/.
8. Preston, "Immigration Crackdown Also Snares Americans."
9. Axel Caballero, "Alabama Brings Back Slavery for Latinos," *Guardian*, October 12, 2011.
10. Ibid.

11. Dan Rivoli, "Alabama Immigration Law: Worker-Strapped Farm Groups Doubt Prisoner Remedy," *International Business Times*, October 7, 2011.

12. Caballero, "Alabama Brings Back Slavery."

14. THE WAR AGAINST THE POOR (AND MIDDLE CLASS)

1. Richard Wilkinson and Kate Pickett, *The Spirit Level: Why Greater Equality Makes Societies Stronger* (London: Bloomsbury, 2011).

2. Ibid.

3. Peter Fenn, "Tea Party Funding Koch Brothers Emerge from Anonymity," *U.S. News & World Report*, February 2, 2011. All four Koch brothers, who inherited their fortunes from their father, industrialist Fred C. Koch, spent twenty years in court squabbling over the precise distribution of assets. They settled in 2001. See "Billionaire Family Feuds: The High Stakes of Dysfunction and Dissent," *Forbes*, June 1, 2012.

4. Paul Pierson and Jacob Hacker, interview with Bill Moyers, *Moyers and Company*, PBS, January 15, 2012.

5. See Paul Solman, "Many Americans Feel 'Stuck in a Rut' as Economy Improves, but Inequality Grows," *NewsHour*, PBS, March 24, 2011, http://www.pbs.org/newshour/bb/business/jan-june11/inequality_03-24.html.

6. See "Elizabeth Warren on Fair Taxation," YouTube video, 1:17, posted by "ahmnatheist," September 21, 2011, http://www.youtube.com/watch?v=hOyDR2b71ag.

7. Robert Lenzner, "Income Inequality from Generation to Generation," *Forbes*, March 26, 2012.

8. Emmanuel Saez, *Striking It Richer: The Evolution of Top Incomes in the United States*, March 2, 2012, http://elsa.berkeley.edu/~saez/saez-UStopincomes-2010.pdf.

9. Paul Pierson and Jacob S. Hacker, *Winner-Take-All Politics: How Washington Made the Rich Richer—and Turned Its Back on the Middle Class* (New York: Simon & Schuster, 2011).

10. Joseph Dillon Davey, *The New Social Contract: America's Journey from Welfare State to Police State* (Westport, CT: Praeger, 1995).

11. Wilkinson and Pickett, *Spirit Level*.

12. Dillon, *New Social Contract*.

13. See Partnership for Civil Justice Fund, "FBI Documents Reveal Secret Nationwide Occupy Monitoring," *JusticeOnline.org*, December

22, 2012, http://www.justiceonline.org/commentary/fbi-files-ows.html. This report extracted the information on the government campaign against Occupy Wall Street by demanding answers through the Freedom of Information Act.

14. Jason DeParle, Robert Gebeloff, and Sabrina Tavernise, "Older, Suburban and Struggling, 'Near Poor' Startle the Census," *New York Times*, November 18, 2011.

15. "Goldman Sachs 2009 Pay Up as Profit Soars," MSNBC.com, January 21, 2010, http://www.nbcnews.com/id/34972351/ns/business-earnings/#.UUDXsFdT0ww.

16. Pew Charitable Trusts, Economic Mobility Project, http://www.pew states.org/projects/economic-mobility-project-328061.

17. See Sanders's official Senate website.

18. Right on Crime, "Statement of Principles," 2010, http://www.righton crime.com/the-conservative-case-for-reform/statement-of-principles/.

15. CRAZY CONSEQUENCES

1. Taylor's case has received only sporadic coverage by larger media but is detailed in FAMM, "Michelle Taylor—Nevada," *Faces of FAMM: State Profiles*, accessed March 22, 2013, http://www.famm.org/profiles ofinjustice/StateProfiles/MichelleTaylorNevada.aspx.

2. "Does the Punishment Fit the Crime?" KOLO8 News, April 15, 2010, http://www.kolotv.com/home/headlines/90976314.html; and FAMM, "Michelle Taylor."

3. Howard Copelan, "Life Sentence for Molester Was Cruel and Unusual? Taylor's Sentencing Video Reposted," Coyote TV, February 1, 2013, http://www.coyote-tv.com/2013/02/01/life-sentence-for-molester-was-cruel-and-unusual/.

4. "Does the Punishment Fit the Crime?"

5. "Wisconsin Sex Offender Archive Record for Anne M. Knopf," Sex Offender Archives, accessed March 22, 2013, http://www.sorarchives. com/citydirectory/WI/Ellsworth/Anne_M_Knopf_627379.

6. Jake, "*The 50 Most Infamous Female Teacher Sex Scandals*: #4 Pamela Rogers Turner," Zimbio, May 26, 2009, http://www.zimbio.com/ The+50+Most+Infamous+Female+Teacher+Sex+Scandals/articles/ zTQENnMYVVc/4+Pamela+Rogers+Turner.

7. FAMM, "What the Experts Say," *About Sentencing*, accessed March 22, 2013, http://www.famm.org/aboutsentencing/WhattheExpertsSay.aspx.

8. "No Fetuses in Food: Oklahoma Lawmaker Explains Intent behind Bill," *Los Angeles Times*, January 26, 2012.

9. Jessica Silver-Greenberg, "Welcome to Debtors' Prison, 2011 Edition," *Wall Street Journal*, March 17, 2011.
10. Ibid.
11. Chris Serres and Glenn Howatt, "In Jail for Being in Debt," *Minneapolis Star Tribune*, March 17, 2011.
12. "The New Debtors' Prisons," *New York Times*, April 5, 2009.
13. ACLU, *In for a Penny: The Rise of America's New Debtors' Prisons* (New York, October 2010), http://www.aclu.org/files/assets/InForA Penny_web.pdf.
14. Rebekah Diller, Alicia Bannon, and Mitali Nagrecha, *Criminal Justice Debt: A Barrier to Reentry* (New York: Brennan Center for Justice, 2010), http://www.brennancenter.org/publication/criminal-justice -debt-barrier-reentry.
15. Phil Willon, "Riverside County to Make Inmates Pay Jail Costs," *Los Angeles Times*, November 20, 2011.
16. Ibid.

16. CRIME ACADEMIES, RAPE, SEX SLAVES, INFECTION, DEATH

1. The ex-convict who told me this story preferred to remain anonymous. So did the ex-convict who related his cellmate's nightmare.
2. Jesus Chavez, interviews with the author, 2000. Chavez's life story was told in Adam Pitluk, *Standing Eight: The Inspiring Story of Jesus "El Matador" Chavez, Who Became Lightweight Champion of the World* (Cambridge, MA: Da Capo Press, 2006).
3. The *Los Angeles Times* has written many stories about the horrors of Baca's jails that describe many of these incidents. Some were described to me by people on the scene. A good place to start is Robert Faturechi and Jack Leonard, "L.A. County Sheriff's Deputy Alleges Colleague Pointed Gun at Him," *Los Angeles Times*, February 15, 2012.
4. See Sarah Liebowitz, Peter Eliasberg, Margaret Winter, and Esther Lim, *Cruel and Unusual Punishment: How a Savage Gang of Deputies Controls L.A. County Jails* (New York: ACLU National Prison Project, ACLU of Southern California, September 2011), http://www.nlg-npap .org/reports/cruel-and-usual-punishment-how-savage-gang-deputies-controls-la-county-jails.
5. Ibid.
6. Ibid.
7. "Sheriff Baca Reopens Cases of Alleged Inmate Abuse by Deputies," *Los Angeles Times*, October 9, 2011.

8. Heather C. West, William J. Sabol, and Sarah J. Greenman, "Prisoners in 2009," *Bureau of Justice Statistics Bulletin*, December 2010, http://bjs.ojp.usdoj.gov/content/pub/pdf/p09.pdf.

9. Editorial, *New York Times*, October 1, 2008.

10. Lisa Guenther, "The Living Death of Solitary Confinement," *New York Times*, August 26, 2012.

11. Ruth Marcus, "The Cruelest Punishment," *Washington Post*, October 16, 2012.

12. "Solitary-Confinement Inmates Threaten New Hunger Strike," *Los Angeles Times*, December 21, 2012.

13. Colin Dayan has written extensively on this topic. See his "Barbarous Confinement," *New York Times*, July 17, 2011; and *The Law Is a White Dog: How Legal Rituals Make and Unmake Persons* (Princeton, NJ: Princeton University Press, 2011).

14. Allen J. Beck, Paige M. Harrison, Marcus Berzofsky, Rachel Caspar, and Christopher Krebs, *Sexual Victimization in Prisons and Jails Reported by Inmates, 2008–09* (Washington, DC: Bureau of Justice Statistics, August 2010), http://bjs.ojp.usdoj.gov/content/pub/pdf/svp jri0809.pdf.

15. Human Rights Watch, "Rape Crisis in U.S. Prisons," April 19, 2001, http://www.hrw.org/en/news/2001/04/18/rape-crisis-us-prisons.

16. Unless otherwise cited, quotations and stories in the following sections are from Human Rights Watch, *No Escape: Male Rape in U.S. Prisons* (New York, 2001).

17. Aleksandr I. Solzhenitsyn, *The Gulag Archipelago* (New York: Harper & Row, 1974).

17. THE INSANITY OF MENTAL HEALTH PRACTICES

1. See E. Fuller Torrey et al., *More Mentally Ill Persons Are in Jails and Prisons than Hospitals: A Survey of the States* (Arlington, VA: Treatment Advocacy Center, May 2010), http://www.treatmentadvocacy-center.org/storage/documents/final_jails_v_hospitals_study.pdf.

2. See Debbie Dawn Ramsey, "Evolution of Mental Health Organizations in the United States," *Journal of Global Health Care Systems* 1, no. 3 (2011).

3. National Coalition for the Homeless, "Mental Illness and Homelessness," Fact Sheet No. 5, June 2006.

4. The death and its aftermath were covered in detail in a series of articles in the *Orange County Register* and *Los Angeles Times*. See "Grand

Jury: Third Fullerton Officer Beat Kelly Thomas," *Los Angeles Times*, October 11, 2012.

5. Rothmiller interviews.

6. Treatment Advocacy Center, "Criminalization of Individuals with Severe Psychiatric Disorders," briefing paper, April 2007, http://www.treatmentadvocacycenter.org/storage/documents/criminalization_of_individuals_with_severe_psychiatric_disorders.pdf.

7. Jamie Fellner and Sasha Abramsky, "Prisons No Place for the Mentally Ill," Human Rights Watch, February 13, 2004, http://www.hrw.org/news/2004/02/12/prisons-no-place-mentally-ill.

8. "United States: Mentally Ill Mistreated in Prison," Human Rights Watch, October 22, 2003, http://www.hrw.org/news/2003/10/21/united-states-mentally-ill-mistreated-prison.

9. Anonymous inmate, interview with the author.

10. FAMM, "Atiba Parker—Mississippi," *Faces of FAMM: State Profiles*, accessed March 22, 2013, http://www.famm.org/facesofFAMM/StateProfiles/AtibaParker.aspx.

11. Ibid.

12. Tony Perry, "Sex Offender John Albert Gardner III Sentenced to Life in Prison," *Los Angeles Times*, May 15, 2010.

13. "Early Interventions for Schizophrenia Look Promising, but Evidence Is Inconclusive," *Health Behavior News Service*, June 14, 2011. Also see Til Wykes and Max Marshall, "Reshaping Mental Health Practice with Evidence: The Mental Health Research Network," *Psychiatric Bulletin* 28 (2004), http://pb.rcpsych.org/content/28/5/153.full.

14. Ibid.

15. Ibid.

16. Ibid.

17. Jessica Grogan, "ACEP Poll Pulls Back the Curtain on ED Overcrowding," *MDNews.com*, May 11, 2011, http://www.mdnews.com/news/2011_05/acep-poll-pulls-back-the-curtain-on-ed-overcrowding.aspx.

18. LEGACY INMATES

1. Valencia interviews.

2. Kevin Iole, "Cunningham Offers Alternative to Violence," *Yahoo! Sports*, January 25, 2011, http://sports.yahoo.com/box/news?slug=ki-cunningham012511.

3. Ibid.

4. Benjamin Todd Jealous and Rod Paige, "Prison Spending Bleeds Education System," CNN, April 7, 2011, http://articles.cnn.com/2011-04-07/opinion/jealous.prison.reform_1_prison-populations-prison-spending-offenders-from-state-prisons.

5. Marc Mauer and Ryan Scott King, *Schools and Prisons: Fifty Years after Brown v. Board of Education* (Washington, DC: Sentencing Project, January 2004), http://www.sentencingproject.org/doc/publications/rd_brownvboard.pdf.

6. Harry G. Levine and Deborah Peterson Small, *Marijuana Arrest Crusade: Racial Bias and Police Policy in New York City, 1997–2007* (New York: New York Civil Liberties Union, April 2008), http://www.nyclu.org/files/MARIJUANA-ARREST-CRUSADE_Final.pdf.

7. Charles M. Blow, "Escape from New York," *New York Times*, March 18, 2011.

8. Colleen Long, "Stop and Frisk: Police Stop More than 1 Million People on Street," *Huffington Post*, October 8, 2009, http://www.huffington-post.com/2009/10/08/stop-and-frisk-police-sto_n_314509.html.

9. Bob Herbert, "The Shame of New York," *New York Times*, October 29, 2010.

10. Ibid.

11. Griffin interview. Griffin volunteered this information shortly after seeing yet another instance of the standard episode he described.

12. Stories about Schoolcraft first appeared in the *Village Voice*; later the New York dailies published many stories of their own. See Jim Dwyer, "An Officer Had Backup: Secret Tapes," *New York Times*, March 13, 2012.

13. Graham Rayman, "New Evidence Emerges about Police Downgrading of Crimes," *Village Voice*, September 18, 2012.

14. Graham Rayman, "For Detained Whistle-Blower, a Hospital Bill, Not an Apology," *New York Times*, March 15, 2012.

15. Al Baker and Ray Rivera, "5 Officers Face Charges in Fudging of Statistics," *New York Times*, October 15, 2012.

16. Michael Gerson, "The Overlooked Plight of Black Males," *Washington Post*, December 13, 2012.

17. Bruce Western, *Punishment and Inequality in America* (New York: Russell Sage Foundation, 2007).

18. Jill K. Doerner and Stephen Demuth, "The Independent and Joint Effects of Race/Ethnicity, Gender, and Age on Sentencing Outcomes in U.S. Federal Courts," *Justice Quarterly*, January 2010, 1–27.

19. Erik Eckholm, "Plight Deepens for Black Men, Studies Warn," *New York Times*, March 20, 2006.

19. "THE FUTURE"

1. Leo Tolstoy, *Resurrection* (Oxford, UK: Oxford University Press, 2009), 529.
2. FAMM, "What the Experts Say."
3. Human Rights Watch, *Old Behind Bars: The Aging Prison Population in the United States* (New York, January 28, 2012), http://www.hrw.org/reports/2012/01/27/old-behind-bars.
4. Ibid.
5. See Del Barco, "L.A.'s Homicide Rate Lowest in Four Decades."
6. Lisa Lambert, "Cost of Locking up Americans Too High: Pew Study," Reuters, March 2, 2009, http://uk.reuters.com/article/2009/03/02/usa-prisons-idUKN0240756920090302.
7. "State Lawmakers Look to Texas for Prison Advice," Associated Press, January 24, 2011.
8. Travis Pillow, "Prison Reform Proposals Prompt Political Fears," *Florida Independent*, January 26, 2011.
9. See Florida Parole Commission statement on parole and post release at https://fpc.state.fl.us/Parole.htm.
10. Ibid.
11. Jack Dolan, "No New Taxes for Prisons, Residents Say," *Los Angeles Times*, July 21, 2011.
12. Carla Rivera, "State College System Said to Be on Decline," *Los Angeles Times*, July 21, 2011.
13. Paula Smith, Claire Goggin, and Paul Gendreau, *The Effects of Prison Sentences and Intermediate Sanctions on Recidivism: General Effects and Individual Differences* (Gatineau, QC: Public Works and Government Services Canada, 2002), http://www.ccoso.org/library%20articles/200201_Gendreau_e.pdf.
14. Alix Spiegel, "What Vietnam Taught Us about Breaking Bad Habits," *Morning Edition*, NPR, January 2, 2012.
15. Ibid.
16. Ibid.
17. Alan B. Krueger, "Economic Scene: A Study Backs Up What George Foreman Already Said: The Job Corps Works," *New York Times*, March 30, 2000.
18. Mathematica Policy Research, "Does Job Corps Work? An Update," March, 24, 2013, http://www.mathematica-mpr.com/labor/jobcorps.asp.
19. Nick McCrea, "Maine Job Corps Centers Stop Taking New Students after Enrollment Freeze," *Bangor Daily News*, February 20, 2013.

20. See Glenn Greenwald, *Drug Decriminalization in Portugal: Lessons for Creating Fair and Successful Drug Policies* (Washington, DC: Cato Institute, 2009).

21. "Independent Committee on Reentry and Employment Report and Recommendations to New York State on Enhancing Employment Opportunities for Formerly Incarcerated People," November 2006, http://sentencing.nj.gov/downloads/pdf/articles/2006/Nov2006/document03 .pdf.

SELECTED BIBLIOGRAPHY

ACLU. *In for a Penny: The Rise of America's New Debtors' Prisons*. New York, October 2010, http://www.aclu.org/files/assets/InForAPenny_web .pdf.

American Civil Liberties Union. *Banking on Bondage: Private Prisons and Mass Incarceration*. New York, November 2011, www.aclu.org/files/ assets/bankingonbondage_20111102.pdf.

Anderson, David C. *Sensible Justice: Alternatives to Prison*. New York: New Press, 1998.

Bales, William, et al. *Recidivism: An Analysis of Public and Private State Prison Releases in Florida*. Tallahassee: Florida State University, Florida Department of Corrections, Correctional Privatization Commission, December 2003.

Blackmon, Douglas A. *Slavery by Another Name: The Re-Enslavement of Black Americans from the Civil War to World War II*. New York: Anchor Books, 2008.

Boothe, Demico. *Why Are So Many Black Men in Prison? A Comprehensive Account of How and Why the Prison Industry Has Become a Predatory Entity in the Lives of African-American Men*. Memphis: Full Surface Publishing, 2007.

Burton-Rose, Daniel, and Paul Wright. *The Celling of America: An Inside Look at the US Prison Industry*. Monroe, ME: Common Courage Press, 2002.

Carceral, K. C. *Prison, Inc.: A Convict Exposes Life Inside a Private Prison*. Edited by Thomas J. Bernard. New York: New York University Press, 2005.

Chekhov, Anton. *Sakhalin Island*. Translated by Brian Reeve. Richmond, Surrey, UK: Alma Books, 2013.

231

Christie, Nils. *Crime Control as Industry*. New York: Routledge, 2000.

Currie, Elliott. *Crime and Punishment in America*. New York: Picador, 1998.

Davey, Joseph Dillon. *The New Social Contract: America's Journey from Welfare State to Police State*. Westport, CT: Praeger, 1995.

Dayan, Colin. *The Law Is a White Dog: How Legal Rituals Make and Unmake Persons*. Princeton, NJ: Princeton University Press, 2011.

Diller, Rebekah, Alicia Bannon, and Mitali Nagrecha. *Criminal Justice Debt: A Barrier to Reentry*. New York: Brennan Center for Justice, 2010, http://www.brennancenter.org/publication/criminal-justice-debt-barrier -reentry.

Domanick, Joe. *Cruel Justice: Three Strikes and the Politics of Crime in America's Golden State*. Berkeley: University of California Press, 2005.

Fitzpatrick, Robert. *Betrayal: Whitey Bulger and the FBI Agent Who Fought to Bring Him Down*. With Jon Land. New York: Forge Books, 2012.

Hopson, Justin. *Breaking the Blue Wall: One Man's War against Police Corruption*. Bloomington, IN: Westbow Press, 2011.

Human Rights Watch. *Incarcerated America*. New York: Human Rights Watch, April 2003.

———. *Old Behind Bars: The Aging Prison Population in the United States*. New York: Human Rights Watch, January 28, 2012, http://www.hrw. org/reports/2012/01/27/old-behind-bars.

Koppel, David B. *Prison Blues: How America's Foolish Sentencing Policies Endanger Public Safety*. Cato Policy Analysis No. 20. Washington, DC: Cato Institute, May 17, 1994.

Leveritt, Mara. *Devil's Knot: The True Story of the West Memphis Three*. New York: Atria Books, 2003.

Levine, Harry G., and Deborah Peterson Small. *Marijuana Arrest Crusade: Racial Bias and Police Policy in New York City, 1997–2007*. New York: New York Civil Liberties Union, April 2008, http://www.nyclu .org/files/MARIJUANA-ARREST-CRUSADE_Final.pdf.

Liebowitz Sarah, Peter Eliasberg, Margaret Winter, and Esther Lim. *Cruel and Unusual Punishment: How a Savage Gang of Deputies Controls L.A. County Jails*. New York: ACLU National Prison Project, ACLU of Southern California, September 2011, http://www.nlg-npap .org/reports/cruel-and-usual-punishment-how-savage-gang-deputies -controls-la-county-jails.

Mauer, Marc, and Ryan Scott King. *Schools and Prisons: Fifty Years after Brown v. Board of Education*. Washington, DC: Sentencing Project, January 2004, http://www.sentencingproject.org/doc/publications/ rd_brownvboard.pdf.

Menninger, Karl. *The Crime of Punishment*. New York: Viking Press, 1969.

Nutt, David. *Estimating Drug Harms: A Risky Business?* London: Centre for Crime and Justice Studies, October 2009, http://www.crimeandjustice .org.uk/estimatingdrugharms.html.

Oshinsky, David M. *Worse than Slavery: Parchman Farm and the Ordeal of Jim Crow Justice*. New York: Free Press, 1996.

Page, Joshua. *The Toughest Beat: Politics, Punishment, and the Prison Officers Union in California* (Studies in Crime and Public Policy). Oxford, UK: Oxford University Press, 2011.

Pelaez, Vicky. *The Prison Industry in the United States: Big Business or a New Form of Slavery?* Montreal: Centre for Research on Globalization, March 2008, http://www.globalresearch.ca/the-prison-industry-in-the-united-states-big-business-or-a-new-form-of-slavery/8289.

Perkinson, Robert. *Texas Tough: The Rise of America's Prison Empire*. New York: Metropolitan Books, 2010.

Pitluk, Adam. *Standing Eight: The Inspiring Story of Jesus "El Matador" Chavez, Who Became Lightweight Champion of the World*. Cambridge, MA: Da Capo Press, 2006.

Piven, Frances Fox. *Who's Afraid of Frances Fox Piven? The Essential Writings of the Professor Glenn Beck Loves to Hate*. New York: New Press, 2011.

Reinarman, Craig, and Harry G. Levine, eds. *Crack in America: Demon Drugs and Social Justice*. Berkeley: University of California Press, 1997.

Sentencing Project. *Incarcerated Children and Their Parents: Trends, 1991–2007*. Washington, DC: February 2009.

Simon, Jonathan. *Governing through Crime: How the War on Crime Transformed American Democracy and Created a Culture of Fear*. Oxford, UK: Oxford University Press, 2009.

Solzhenitsyn, Aleksandr I. *The Gulag Archipelago*. New York: Harper & Row, 1974.

Stamper, Norm. *Breaking Rank: A Top Cop's Exposé of the Dark Side of American Policing*. New York: Nation Books, 2005.

Tolstoy, Leo. *Resurrection*. Oxford, UK: Oxford University Press, 2009.

Tonry, Michael H. *Punishing Race: A Continuing American Dilemma*. New York: Oxford University Press, 2011.

Torrey, E. Fuller, et al. *More Mentally Ill Persons Are in Jails and Prisons than Hospitals: A Survey of the States*. Arlington, VA: Treatment Advocacy Center, May 2010, http://www.treatmentadvocacycenter.org/ storage/documents/final_jails_v_hospitals_study.pdf.

Useem, Bert, and Anne Morrison Piehl. *Prison State: The Challenge of Mass Incarceration*. Cambridge: Cambridge University Press, 2008.

Western, Bruce. *Punishment and Inequality in America*. New York: Russell Sage Foundation, 2007.

Wilkinson, Richard, and Kate Pickett. *The Spirit Level: Why Greater Equality Makes Societies Stronger*. London: Bloomsbury, 2011.

Wright, Paul, and Tara Herivel, eds. *Prison Profiteers*. New York: New Press, 2007.

Zimring, Franklin E. *The City That Became Safe: New York's Lessons for Urban Crime and Its Control*. Oxford, UK: Oxford University Press, 2011.

INDEX

235

ABOUT THE AUTHOR

IVAN G. GOLDMAN COVERED CONGRESS FOR THE *WASHINGTON POST*, WORKED the National Desk of the *Los Angeles Times*, and was an editorial writer and op-ed columnist for the *Seattle Post-Intelligencer*. A longtime boxing columnist, he has written for *Columbia Journalism Review*, *Utne Reader*, *The Nation*, *National Review*, *Rolling Stone*, the *New York Times*, and other publications. He has done dozens of commentaries for *Marketplace*, a show heard throughout the NPR network. His previous nonfiction work, *L.A. Secret Police: Inside the LAPD Elite Spy Network*, coauthored with ex-detective Mike Rothmiller, was a *New York Times* bestseller. He has also written four novels: *Where the Money Is: A Novel of Las Vegas*; *The Barfighter*, which was nominated as a 2009 Notable Book by the American Library Association; and most recently, *Isaac: A Modern Fable*, which received a starred review in *BookList*. Goldman, who holds an MA from the University of Kansas, was a Fulbright Scholar in Malaysia. Born and raised in Chicago, he now lives with his wife in Southern California. He can be reached at ivangoldman@yahoo.com.